ENGLAND'S WEALTHIEST SON

By the same author
LIFE AT FONTHILL
JOURNAL IN PORTUGAL

BECKFORD AS A BOY probably by William Hoare

ENGLAND'S WEALTHIEST SON

A STUDY OF

William Beckford

BY

Boyd Alexander

There thou too, Vathek! England's wealthiest son,
Once form'd thy Paradise, ...
But now, as if a thing unblest by Man,
Thy fairy dwelling is as lone as thou!

Byron

We know what swarms of flatterers a grand reputation for riches has always engendered, and, as at this period I had the honour of passing for 'England's wealthiest son', the exaggerated praise I received may be easily accounted for.

Beckford

Centaur Press Ltd.
1962

© BOYD ALEXANDER 1962

*First published 1962 by the Centaur Press Ltd.,
11-14 Stanhope Mews West, London, S.W.7,
and printed in Great Britain by
The West Yorkshire Printing Co. Ltd., Wakefield
in 11 on 12 Baskerville*

TO HIS GRACE
THE DUKE OF HAMILTON AND BRANDON
without whose trust and help my studies
could never have been undertaken,
this book is gratefully dedicated.

CONTENTS

LIST OF ILLUSTRATIONS	ix
PREFACE	1
ACKNOWLEDGMENTS	7
INTRODUCTION	9
CHAPTER I: BACKGROUND	29
II: EARLY YOUTH, 1760-1777	39
III: FAMILY QUARRELS	51
IV: SWITZERLAND AND SAVOY, 1777-1778	60
V: ENGLAND AND ITALY, 1779-1781	70
VI: THE ORIGINS OF VATHEK, 1780-1781	79
VII: VATHEK AND ITS EPISODES	91
VIII: 1784: WAS BECKFORD GUILTY?	103
IX: FLIGHT, 1785-1786	118
X: PORTUGAL	125
XI: FRANCE AND RADICALISM	139
XII: THE ORIGIN OF FONTHILL	152
XIII: THE SPLENDOUR OF FONTHILL	162
XIV: PERSECUTION	181
XV: THE SALE OF FONTHILL, 1822	189
XVI: THE BECKFORD FORTUNE	200
XVII: LAST YEARS, 1823-1844	226
XVIII: CHARACTER AND TASTES	240
APPENDIX: BECKFORD'S CURIOUS LETTER	263
ABBREVIATIONS	267
NOTES	268
NOTE ON ILLUSTRATIONS	299
INDEX	300

ILLUSTRATIONS

BECKFORD AS A BOY, probably by William Hoare *frontispiece*
By permission of Mrs. Lovette West of New York

ALDERMAN BECKFORD REBUILDING FONTHILL, 1755   *facing page* 4
By permission of Ministry of Works

CARICATURE OF BECKFORD, 1803   39
By permission of Hamilton & Kinneil Estates

LADY MARGARET BECKFORD, by Maria Cosway   54
By permission of the Earl of Harrowby

BECKFORD'S BOY FRIEND IN PARIS Self-portrait of the Chevalier Sequeira, 1826   103
By permission of Hamilton & Kinneil Estates

BECKFORD'S OWN PLAN of his Lisbon house, drawn by himself   118
By permission of Hamilton & Kinneil Estates

BECKFORD'S DWARF by the PRESIDENT OF THE ROYAL ACADEMY (Benjamin West)   150
By permission of Swarthmore College, U.S.A.

THE RUINS OF FONTHILL, 1825, by John Buckler   166
From Colt Hoare's 'History of S. Wilts-Dunworth', 1829

BECKFORD'S DEATHBED, by Willis Maddox   230
By permission of Scottish National Trust and the late Duchess of Montrose

BECKFORD IN MIDDLE-AGE, by Hoppner   246
By permission of Salford Art Gallery.

A note on the illustrations will be found on page 299

PREFACE

This is not a biography of Beckford, for which the general reader can consult Dr. J. W. Oliver, whose fair and sympathetic study has long been out of print, and Professor Guy Chapman, who gave the first great impetus to modern Beckford studies and has published so much. I do not wish to travel over the same ground. Their books remain indispensable for much Beckford material. But the wealth of his Papers and my other fresh sources is so great that it has been possible to use new material. I have also approached some of Beckford's writings from a different angle. Beckford touches so many spheres of human activity that it is impossible for one man or book to deal adequately with, or even include, them all.

My primary interest is in Beckford's baffling and contradictory character. He has too often been pictured as a trifling personage of no consequence, for whom it is difficult to feel any sympathy. I have therefore presented some of his positive sides—his feeling for the poor, his early sympathy for the French Revolution, his belief in vigorous young America (only just liberated from her colonial yoke), his gardening, and his virtue as a man of taste. At any given moment of his life I have asked myself how things looked to him. I have, in fact, tried to read his mind from his fascinating private notes and jottings, pursuing him like a private detective for a dozen years.

The greatest prejudice against Beckford arises from his homosexual nature. It is cynically assumed that he gave way to it without a struggle, like so many men today. If this were so, he would be a far less interesting character than in fact he is. I have therefore examined

ENGLAND'S WEALTHIEST SON

the evidence anew, making use of his vivid dreams, and have reconstructed the scandal of 1784 which blasted his career. On the strength of a suspicion which was never confirmed, he was boycotted for the rest of his life, which added further twists to his character, as I shall show. Contrasting with this period his former gaiety and extrovert activities in Switzerland as a youth, one asks: What happened to those spirits, that *élan*? They seem to peep out again only when he was a remarkable old man in Bath!

It has always been supposed that sheer extravagance forced England's wealthiest son to sell Fonthill in order to avoid bankruptcy. But it has never been asked how wealthy he really was and what his unavoidable commitments were. This has obliged me to unravel his Parliamentary activities and the machinations of his unbelievably crooked West India agents. A consideration of his wealth leads one to its effect upon him and to an examination of his family background, in which looms menacingly the compelling figure of his father, from whom he inherited his Radicalism. His youth is discovered to be wretchedly disturbed by the quarrels with his father's bastards, which throws new light on the development of his character.

But divided though that character was, certain threads run through his life, making of it an unexpected unity. He could not help, for example, playing up to the gallery and taking people in. This trait provides one of the first and one of the last incidents known to us in his life, and gives the key to his behaviour in despotic Portugal and revolutionary France! He was also one of the earliest Romantics; his life was spent in giving corporeal expression at Fonthill to a youthful Gothic dream, which made him an important patron of artists and craftsmen. But the Romantics, as explorers in psychology, plumbed the depths as well as the heights and were as interested in the devil as in God. Beckford was a pioneer in these shady realms, as his reading-notes

PREFACE

show, and his life was shaped by identification with strange Romantic heroes—figures who make us uneasy despite our unsqueamish epoch! His own writings, published and unpublished, are as self-revealing as his reading-notes and cannot therefore be ignored by anyone grappling with his character and tracing its development. I do not approach them as a literary critic or historian. There is a strangely prophetic note in them—he was able to foreshadow his own doom. Yet his earliest attempts at journal-making contain delightful, detached descriptions of scenery and every-day incidents, and some of these fragments are worth presenting.

I owe it to Beckford's memory, in the bicentenary year of his birth, to offer these studies as a corrective to his letters in *Life at Fonthill*, in which, with his usual frankness and "profligacy of tongue" he did, as he said, "my utmost to make myself appear worse than I am in reality". Many readers of those letters will have been put off by his coarseness and complaining, and not looked beneath the surface to perceive a lively and cultivated mind and a life at Fonthill neither empty nor useless. The same is to some extent true of his Portuguese Journal, in which the question of his presentation to the Queen of Portugal looms too large for any modern reader who does not understand what was at stake. It is therefore necessary to sketch his unparalleled position in Portugal, using for the first time letters to him in Portuguese.

Some episodes in my book can be told as a story without covering stale ground, since I present fresh and more detailed information; these are the scandal of 1784, the sale of Fonthill, and the quarrels with the bastards (here divulged for the first time). From all this it can be seen that my purpose is to discuss various aspects of Beckford's life and character, which either have not been developed before or which I can handle afresh. Since my book is based largely on the unpublished sections of Beckford's own Papers and other large manuscript collections hitherto unexamined, it is limited by their nature and scope. It was not possible to study printed sources, contemporary and modern, in so many fields, with the same thoroughness. But I am content to offer original material to more widely read scholars, who can make use of it in their period histories of Romanticism, Taste, Architecture and Economics. Mine is primarily the study of an individual caught in the toils of his background, his society and his own psychology.

I have already acknowledged our great permanent debt to the two principal biographers. Literary historians are now under obligation to a learned academic thesis of nearly six hundred pages by Dr. Parreaux, entitled *William Beckford, auteur de Vathek: étude de la création littéraire* (1960). This is chiefly concerned with Beckford's Arabian stories and translations and their literary origins; the new Beckford material in it consists of items from Beckford's Papers which I made available to him, together with my typed transcriptions of some of them. Unfortunately this massive work appeared after my own book had been written.

It is also pleasant to pay tribute to the work of Beckford's first biographer, Redding, after a century of denigration. His labours have been universally decried—justly so on the showing of his printed *Memoirs of William Beckford* (1859). But his own manuscript for this work, submitted to a publisher in 1846, is still amongst Beckford's Papers; it is quite different from the later printed book. Evidently Beckford's daughter, the Duchess of Hamilton, took strong exception to it for its revelation of her father's character. In many sections she made Redding substitute colourless slabs which are a mere hashing-up of Beckford's books, and she presumably bought the original manuscript off him to ensure its suppression. Although his style is bad and his arrangement poor, Redding had a journalist's ear: in these manuscript pages we can really hear Beckford talking. Redding also had one important source, now lost—the

ALDERMAN BECKFORD REBUILDING FONTHILL, 1755

PREFACE

manuscript diary of Beckford's tutor Lettice, which was kept up to 1786.[1]

To give the background to these studies, I outline Beckford's career and chronology in my Introduction. Where necessary for the sake of clarity and their appearance in print, I have repunctuated Beckford's texts, which are full of dots and dashes and often erratically punctuated. I have also ignored his eighteenth-century use of capital letters. Material quoted is unpublished unless indicated to the contrary in a footnote; and unless similarly indicated, it is taken from Beckford's Papers (but one or two short quotations from Melville's biography of Beckford come from other sources which he does not identify in his text, e.g. an article in *Temple Bar* for June 1900, which contains extracts of Beckford's letters to his bookseller George Clarke; it is easier for the general reader to be referred to Melville rather than an obscure periodical).

Some of my footnotes being very long, I have put them *all* at the back; this is in line with modern practice followed by an increasing number of our best historians and biographers, however irritating and inconvenient this may to be some readers and critics. In order to keep down the number of notes, I have normally not mentioned sources already given for the same fact by Dr. Oliver and Prof. Chapman. For the same reason I have as far as possible avoided biographical notes, where these can be found, for example, in Peerages or the *Dictionary of National Biography* (D.N.B.). A checklist of M.P.s is in Gerrit Judd *Members of Parliament, 1734-1832*, Yale, 1955. I have already given biographical notes about many relevant persons in *Life at Fonthill* and Beckford's *Journal in Portugal*. A bibliography is given in Prof. Chapman's *Beckford*, but many additional titles and sources will be found in my notes.

BOYD ALEXANDER.

(1) Redding's letter in *The Critic* (1861), xxiii. 70.

ACKNOWLEDGMENTS

My Dedication page shews to whom I am most indebted (together with the other Directors of Hamilton and Kinneil Estates, and their Curator of Manuscripts, Miss Bruce Johnston). Any scholar is under a special debt to Sir Owen Morshead who, when Royal Librarian at Windsor Castle, deposited in the Print Room of the British Museum a full typescript of the vast Farington Diaries (in Her Majesty's possession), of which the eight printed volumes edited by Mr. Greig are an abridgement. I have made extensive use of this typescript, thanks to the courtesy of the B.M. Print Room.

My special thanks are also due to Mr. Noel Blakiston of the Public Record Office, who extracted from their original sacks the Tax Collector's Returns from Fonthill Gifford for 1800 and 1803, and to his office for my extensive use of their Chancery and other records; to the Clerk of the Privy Council Office, where I studied their unique Appeal volumes; to the Librarian of the House of Lords, where I found the rare Memoranda concerning the Appeals of Alderman Beckford's bastards; to Mr. Black of the Record Office in Spanish Town, Jamaica; to Lord Harrowby, who gave me several important references and the text of a letter from his ancestress, Margaret Beckford; to the late Duchess of Montrose and the Scottish National Trust, for allowing me to quote from material I found at Brodick Castle; Mr. Trappes-Lomax, for showing me material in the Royal College of Arms; Mr. Ian Christie, for explaining the significance of the Saltash Parliamentary transactions; Mr. Anthony Hobson, Mr. John Hayward of the Victoria & Albert

Museum, Mr. Martin Davies of the National Gallery, and Prof. Waterhouse.

I am grateful to Prof. von Erffa of Rutgers University, U.S.A., for photographs of portraits of Beckford as a boy and his dwarf; to Mr. Richard Walker for telling me of Alderman Beckford's portrait; and to Mr. James Babb, Librarian of Yale, who with his usual kindness allowed me to quote from letters in his collection. Dr. Parreaux gave me the text of the official Report concerning Beckford and his bookseller Chardin; and Mr. John N. Phillips the extract from the unpublished Prangins Journal, with the permission of the late Mlle. N. Guiguer de Prangins. Mr. Butcher, Chief Librarian of Hampstead Public Libraries, pin-pointed for me the site of the old Beckford house at West-End. The Director of the Victoria & Albert Museum allowed me to quote from the typescript of Constable's correspondence (compiled by Mr. Beckett), and the Keeper of Manuscripts at the British Museum from an unpublished manuscript.

My thanks are due to those who helped me latterly with research—Mrs. William Phipps (then Miss H. Lamb) and Miss M. Flower; to Mr. Charles Wrinch, who read my typescript and made suggestions; to Sir John Summerson for my quotations from *Architecture in Britain: 1530-1830*; and to Messrs. Macmillan for permitting quotations from Mr. Steegman's *Rule of Taste from George I to George IV*, and from Miss Lucy Sutherland's essay in *Essays Presented to Sir Lewis Namier* (she was a great help in other matters).

INTRODUCTION

Since my book is a study and not a biography, it is necessary to give now an outline of Beckford's life, which is taken for granted later. I am also including much original material which does not fit into the main sections of my book.

William Beckford was born on 29th September 1760, the only child of a late marriage, and reputed to be England's wealthiest son. A good deal is said in my first three chapters about his background and early youth at Fonthill, near Salisbury. When he was very young he was "of a very tender and delicate constitution, and his health required a very strict attention";[1] there were "many nights of affliction and anxiety". This enabled his mother to give full rein to her possessiveness, particularly after her husband's death in 1770. Nevertheless, as I shall shew, his father was the greatest influence in his life, and his sudden death was decisive in the formation of the boy's character.

Like Gibbon, he was sent to Switzerland in 1777 to finish his education, and thus imbibed a cosmopolitan outlook, and wrote as easily in French as English. After little more than a year there, his autocratic mother removed him, disturbed by certain rumours about him and his company. She was methodistically inclined, and he had fallen in with the agnostic Huber family; also, he had already developed his innate homosexual inclinations. More important, he had already become a writer. In 1777 he wrote his clever *Biographical Memoirs of Extraordinary Painters* (not published until 1780) and began his unfinished "Long Story" (published in 1930 as *The Vision*). This Swiss stay is described in Chapter IV.

ENGLAND'S WEALTHIEST SON

He remained in England from November 1778 until June 1780. From August until October 1779 he went on an English tour with his former tutor Lettice, who accompanied him wherever he went, at home and abroad. He sporadically kept a diary on this trip, a habit he had first acquired in Switzerland in 1778 to record some of his excursions. When he arrived at Plymouth there was a Franco-Spanish fleet lying off the coast, ready to bombard or attack; the town and its environs were filled with troops. Its "inhabitants are all in confusion", he wrote in his diary, "filled with alarms and suspicions, staring about with rusty guns in one hand and telescopes in the other".[2] One evening he and Lettice took out their notebooks to compare accounts of these goings-on. They were at once surrounded by soldiers and a mob and marched off under arrest as spies[3]—an amusing start for the future diarist of Portugal!

Early in this tour he stayed at Powderham Castle, near Exeter, the home of Viscount Courtenay. He fell in love, in a sentimental way, with the only son of the house, William Courtenay, then aged eleven. The boy was to be the cause of his social ruin. But at the same time his head was full of that other nameless youth in Switzerland, "that blest vision".[4] Before he left for abroad again he also met for the first time another fatal personage—Louisa, the wife of his first cousin Peter Beckford, of *Thoughts upon Hare and Fox Hunting* fame. Young Beckford's long-drawn-out romance with her has been fully dealt with by his biographers Oliver and Chapman, and is not of great importance in his life (beyond giving us a series of letters); I will therefore say no more about it.

After witnessing the Gordon Riots, he left England in June 1780 to make the customary Grand Tour, with Italy as his main objective. By this time, except for building and collecting, his general penchant is already clear. He was easily influenced by friends who grossly flattered him and who disgraced themselves in society—

INTRODUCTION

Louisa, Lady Craven (later Margravine of Anspach), and in Venice the egregious Count Benincasa and shady Countess Rosenberg, friend of Casanova; Beckford's women friends were usually older than himself and experienced in Society. He developed heady passions for pretty youths, some of whom, like Courtenay, turned out to be worthless; this dissipated his energies and produced a sharp inner conflict.

But despite his ill-mannered and witty sallies into society, he had a deeply serious side. Rousseau-like (he was one of our earliest Romantics), he loved Nature and seclusion, whether at Fonthill or in the Alps. His reading from the earliest age was prodigious, and included travel-books about China, Japan and Africa, and literature about India. He claimed to be able to quote the Persian and Turkish poets Hafiz and Mesihi,[5] and had Arabic lessons with a Mussulman in order to translate (into French) manuscripts of the *Arabian Nights*. He was, in fact, always reading, "pencil in hand", and scribbling—sometimes imaginary Arabian Tales of his own in French, such as *Darianoc*. He threw himself into his activities with enthusiasm and indiscretion. Next to literature and writing, his greatest love at this time was Italian opera; he was the friend and patron of one of the greatest Italian *castrati* of all time, Pacchierotti. His imagination was most influenced by the Orient and was that of a literary man, although he looked at scenery and events like the Gordon Riots and the Fall of the Bastille "with the eye of an artist".

Whatever he wrote has a strongly autobiographical flavour. A satirical picture of himself and his future life at Fonthill is given in his earliest unpublished novel, *L'Esplendente* (written before 1780): "The pride of Ancestry and a haughty consciousness of his descent (which he strove in vain to dissemble) rendered him obnoxious to the World in general. And finding himself disliked and dreaded, he had retired from Court to the solitude of an ancient castle in the midst of his Duchy, where he employed himself in literary pursuits and forgot his ennuis and ill-humours in the cultivation of the arts and the sciences. He was surrounded by poets, musicians, sculptors and designers, who lost and gained by turns the empire of his mind. Sometimes he was enchanted by chimical researches; another moment, Architecture engaged his attention, and he built lofty towers in the morisco style, and added magnificent corinthian porticos to the Gothic abodes of his Ancestors. When this rage was subsided, the fury of antiquities began to predominate. Every corner of his domain was first ransacked for medals and tesselated pavements; then collectors were sent out to explore the most remote provinces of the Kingdom in search of rusty helmets, tattered shields, inscriptions and broken mile-stones. Meanwhile, commissions being sent to Sicily and Greece, whole shiploads of mutilated figures were landed at Alicant, and these pagan images scandalously usurped the nitches of the best Saints in the Calendar. When this passion had worn itself out, a violent admiration of paintings succeeded. Nothing pleased the Grandee but the productions of the pencil. He filled his appartments with the works of Raphael, Titian and Julio Romano at an immense expence, and constructed whole suites of rooms purposely to display them." (pp. 101-103).

He summed up his whole existence more pithily in 1781: "I fear I shall never be . . . good for anything in this world, but composing airs, building towers, forming gardens, collecting old Japan, and writing a journey to China or the moon."[6] As early as 1780, therefore, he saw himself as man-of-letters rather than writer, but even more as collector and dilettante. After the seventeen-eighties building, collecting and gardening predominated in his life to the almost complete exclusion of literary activity. The first record he has left of purchasing manuscripts and rare books is at the Crofts Sale in April 1783.[7] By 1784 he was deeply committed to the greatest love of his life when he attended in Paris

INTRODUCTION

the most important sale of the century, the Duc de La Vallière's, and made fine purchases in the teeth of the Holy Roman Emperor and the King of France.[8]

In *L'Esplendente* he dreamed of himself as an artist and imagined fascinating Romantic pictures. But since he could not paint, he turned to his Romantic contemporaries. In 1782 he was patronising J. R. Cozens, the son of his old drawing-master, Alexander Cozens who, next to his own father, was the most important influence on his youth. In 1783 he discussed commissions with old Joseph Vernet, who perceived him to be a true connoisseur of art. By this time, therefore, the picture of Beckford's life is complete except for his later passion for building and gardening.

To return to his second trip to Europe and first visit to Italy from June 1780 until April 1781. He kept a Journal of his tour which he wrote up as his first travel-book, with the intentionally Romantic title and atmosphere of *Dreams and Waking Thoughts*; my Chapter V discusses its suppression in 1783. This visit to Italy also gave him the finest friendship he ever had with a woman—the charming first wife of Sir William Hamilton, our Minister to the Court of Naples. But she increased his inner conflict by making him feel that his sentimental friendships with youths of his own class were "criminal passions" and by making him promise the impossible—their total renunciation.

By now he was confirmed in his fear of "English phlegm and frostiness" which nipped his enthusiasms in the bud. He found his contemporaries like Lord Morton, a friend to whom he had written delightful nonsense in boyhood, increasing "in stiffness every day".[9] Already he is more foreign than English. But from his earliest years he had felt lonely and isolated, and was only occasionally blest by a real and worthy friend (usually older than himself)—Alexander Cozens, Lady Hamilton, Dr. Verdeil . . . He was therefore never in a hurry to get back to England, to his autocratic mother and the daily responsibility of a large estate. So he dallied in Paris from February until April 1781, only returning because of serious legal trouble over his fortune.[10] In Paris he became rather too involved with a little penniless adventuress, Georgina Seymour, whose father was the lover of Mme. Dubarry. But for him such things were not much more than agreeable pastimes—until his partner caught fire!

He remained in England from April 1781 until May 1782. He started off by attending the London season, but at the end of June beat a hasty retreat to Fonthill for the rest of the year when he heard that the Seymour girl was coming over and was after him. His Coming-of-Age celebrations in September 1781 were worthy of England's wealthiest son and Lord Chatham's godson. But Beckford himself, contrary to such brilliant appearances, was dismayed at the prospect of adult responsibility and cried out in despair: "Don't call me *illustre ami* and *homme unique*. I'm still in my cradle! Spare the delicacy of my infantile ears. Leave me to scamper on verdant banks—all too ready, alas, to crumble, but rainbow-tinted and flower-strewn!"[11] Nevertheless, his strict upbringing and education had inculcated in him some sense of *noblesse oblige*, and he hoped to behave seriously whilst yet giving rein to his artistic side—"as flowers are strewn in the way of a grave and solemn procession, so do I ornament the road I mean in future to tread with solemnity".[12]

He held his own private celebration at Fonthill with a special group of friends that Christmas—a party which I discuss in Chapter VI because it sparked off the writing of his autobiographical novel *Vathek* and because too much has been suggested about Black Magic and other unhealthy practices. It was also notable for the presence of the sinister and quarrelsome Samuel Henley, who wormed his way into Beckford's confidence and then betrayed him, impinging periodically on Beckford's existence like a tiresome mosquito.

INTRODUCTION

After the party Beckford spent the season in London, interspersing brilliant incursions into Society with the composition of *Vathek* and additions to his manuscript *Dreams and Waking Thoughts*. He also wrote the music for Lady Craven's operetta *The Arcadian Pastoral* at the late Duke of Queensberry's house in Burlington Gardens.[13] Some of the "pigmy players" were adolescent sprigs of the aristocracy—sons of Lord Charles Spencer, Lord Paget and Lord Southampton. They were coached by John Henderson, the Shakespearian actor of whom Garrick was jealous, helped out in the ballet movement by professionals whom Cosway got from Drury Lane, and in the singing by Mme. Barthélémon, wife of the violinist, and by Pacchierotti. The B.B.C. have recorded Beckford's music from his existing score; it is in parts very Mozartian and charming.

From May to November 1782 he made his second tour to Italy, which was cut short by Lady Hamilton's death. He took J. R. Cozens with him as artist; the latter's sketches were worked up into some of his most famous water-colours. So he returned prematurely to England, where he remained until May 1783. He spent a quiet Christmas at Fonthill translating into French from an Arabic manuscript of the *Arabian Nights*, and then, as a contrast so typical of him, dashed into London society, where he was famous for mimicking Dowagers in a falsetto voice. His family wanted to rescue him from the emotional toils of Courtenay and Louisa and from the fast and unconventional women like Lady Craven, Lady Archer and Lady Clarges with whom he went about playing the fool. He was therefore married off in May to a blonde girl (he had dark hair with a white skin, so they made a good couple) whose brother, Lord Strathavon (later ninth Marquis of Huntly), he had familiarly known as "Strath" since at least 1775. She was Lady Margaret Gordon, daughter of the fourth Earl of Aboyne, and had powerful uncles on her mother's side—the first Marquess of Stafford, the fourth Earl of

ENGLAND'S WEALTHIEST SON

Dunmore (last Governor of Virginia) and the ninth Duke of Hamilton. They went to Switzerland for their honeymoon and only returned in mid-March 1784, after dawdling in Paris on the way back.

My Chapters VIII and IX deal with most of the subsequent events until Beckford's stay in Portugal in 1787. This was the period of his irremediable disgrace over Courtenay in October 1784 and his consequent retirement to Switzerland about July 1785. His wife's death there at the age of twenty-four in May 1786, after giving birth to her second daughter Susan (later Duchess of Hamilton), was a real blow to him and altered the course of his life. Henceforth he had no central rallying-point, no moral support, and became an embittered and solitary misogynist. Without her it was easy for him to plunge into stupid adventures; the married state had given some respectability and orthodoxy to his life and diverted a good deal of suspicion from him.

This was the time that his former friend Henley chose to deal him a treacherous blow by publishing anonymously, against his instructions and during his absence in Switzerland, the English text of *Vathek*, which he had been translating from Beckford's original French. Beckford wanted the English and French versions to appear simultaneously, if possible with the appended *Episodes of Vathek* (it may, however, be doubted whether a man of his reputation could have ventured to publish the *Episodes* in English). Worst of all, Henley in a lying Preface claimed that *Vathek* was a mere translation of an existing Arabic original: Beckford was robbed of his little masterpiece and of any credit for its originality. This was his second major literary blow in three years. Furthermore, owing to his reputation and extreme unpopularity in England, he could henceforth only publish anonymously as 'the Author of *Vathek*'; it is therefore possible that these setbacks caused his literary creativeness to evaporate. Beckford is so complex a character that such a guess may only be part of the truth. After

INTRODUCTION

Henley's treachery all Beckford could do was to get a French version of *Vathek* printed in Lausanne at the end of 1786 and then in Paris. To distract his mind from the loss of Lady Margaret (and probably of *Vathek* too), he travelled about Switzerland and then down the Rhone to Marseilles, sometimes making Journal jottings. He was in Paris over the New Year to arrange for *Vathek*'s publication, and then returned at the end of January 1787 to Fonthill, after an absence of about eighteen months. Under pressure from his family and adviser, Thomas Wildman, he sailed from Falmouth on 15th March, ostensibly to visit his plantations in Jamaica, from whence his wealth was drawn. But being a bad sailor, he got off at the first stop, Lisbon, and refused to go any further. His stay in Portugal until the end of November 1787 is discussed in Chapter X. The political background, which helped to make his friendship with a leading Court personage (the fifth Marquis of Marialva) one of the most curious episodes in Anglo-Portuguese annals, is outlined in my Introduction to his *Journal in Portugal and Spain*, 1787-88. He travelled on to Madrid, where he arrived in mid-December, to find a number of friends (like the Duchess of Berwick) whom he had known in Paris, and with letters of introduction to others from Marialva.

The excitement of his special situation in Portugal, combined with the narrowness of life in that "dirty fag-end of Europe", stimulated him from May 25th to keep, for the second time in his life, a regular Journal. But the social excitements and intrigues of Madrid were too much for him, so that the Journal soon petered out with the typically Beckfordian ending "I have acquired a confirmed habit of going to Mass". Even so, this private Journal of 280 printed pages gives him a high place amongst our diarists. It is strange that his dilettantism prevented him from repeating the performance or from acquiring the habit many years earlier, since he often made jottings which, though short and seldom finished, show real promise. He could not publish his Journal because of its intensely personal nature, its Roman Catholic bias and its anglophobia; for he never ceased to covet a peerage, which the publication of such a Journal would have made impossible.

But during the early part of the nineteenth century he produced a severely edited version, cast in Letter form, which was offered to Murray about the time of the sale of Fonthill Abbey in 1822.[14] It was published in 1834 as Volume II of *Italy; with Sketches of Spain and Portugal*. Ever since, he has been regarded as one of the best describers of the Portuguese scene in any language. The last two Letters in the Spanish section reprint (with a few trivial alterations) the two-day Journal he kept of his architectural-gardening rambles at the royal Palace of Aranjuez during the Court's absence in December 1795. The first five Letters in the Portuguese section, dated from Falmouth, are carefully edited from some of the fourteen real ones which Beckford sent to Thomas Wildman, Lettice, his mother and half-sister, Mrs. Hervey.

Incidentally, one of these unpublished letters from Falmouth contains the earliest reference to Beckford's gardening at Fonthill. He begs Wildman to secure the best greenhouse plants at the coming auction of the late Princess Amelia, George II's daughter: "the best opportunity to secure greenhouse plants offers next 23rd of April, when Princess Amelia's collection comes to market. Let me enjoin you, as you love Fonthill and believe in the excellence of its conservatory, to buy fifty or a hundred pounds' worth of the grandest orange, oleander and myrtle trees, that I may have less reason to regret Funchall and only hire my *hotel* there for a twelvemonth."[15]

His time in Madrid shows that he was attractive to women, since two beauties fell in love with him—the eighteen-year old Princesse de Listenais and the thirty-one year old Marchioness of Santa Cruz. Beckford liked playing with fire but was determined not to be

INTRODUCTION

burned; I do not think that such affairs are of much importance to his biographer, beyond shewing his cast-iron egotism, his ability to wound his friends and his irresponsibility; for example, when beginning to fall for the Princess he was almost as much interested in her brother, the nineteen-year old Prince de Carency (who had a shocking career and died insane), and her fourteen-year old husband. At the height of his intrigue with the poor misguided Marchioness he was noting a passionate affair with some youth. Was he merely reckless, irresponsible and promiscuous in his affairs? Several explanations might be equally true. But in the Portuguese section of his Journal one sees him looking on at the banquet of life, scornfully unable to appreciate some of the obvious human satisfactions, scoffing and cynical. He is like Mary Shelley's monster in *Frankenstein*, who said "Everywhere I see bliss, from which I alone am irrevocably excluded". He was therefore driven, Don Juan-like, to prove to himself and the world that his feelings and powers were like other men's, when, in fact, he was incapable of lasting feeling and possibly impotent.

His first stay in Portugal had an unexpected literary by-product. His *Journal* describes how he first met a seventeen-year old choirboy, Gregorio Franchi, and how their sentimental friendship developed. His respectable father sent Franchi to enter Beckford's service in Madrid in May 1788, accompanied by a touching letter. He later became Beckford's secretary at Fonthill and died in his service in 1828. Beckford wrote him, in their later Fonthill days, thousands of letters in Italian, a selection of the survivors of which form *Life at Fonthill, 1807-22*. These letters are highly original, unique as regards some of their subject matter, and give an extraordinary picture of Beckford's lonely, embittered but cultured existence in the Abbey. Franchi whisks in and out of some of my later chapters, so is introduced here.[16]

Beckford left Madrid for Paris in June 1788 and remained there, an interested spectator of the Fall of the Bastille, until the revolutionary crowds and junketings got on his nerves. He prudently withdrew to the safety and peace of Lausanne in August 1789. His devoted physician Verdeil and his Parisian bookseller Chardin, both ardent Revolutionaries, kept him informed of what occurred in Paris. His attitude to the Revolution and his Radicalism, as well as facts about his stays in revolutionary Paris are given in Chapter XI. That October he hoped to stay at Anspach with the Margrave's mistress, Lady Craven, but got no further than Basle when he was summoned back to England.[17] He remained barely a year at home, was back in Paris in October 1790, and only left it two days before Louis XVI's flight to Varennes on 21st June 1791.[18] These movements show that he was discontented with life in England and only left Paris when political trouble made him nervous. He was without an anchor of the soul, for at one time he seriously thought of settling in Portugal and at another in Jacobinical France—anywhere safe from Englishmen. He returned to Paris in November 1791 and remained until May 1793, except for political flights to Savoy and Switzerland from July to early November 1792 (and a lightning visit to Fonthill in October, when Meister saw him).

He was only in England for six months before sailing to Portugal in November 1793 for his second stay, which lasted until October 1795. This stay was packed with incident and interest, as Chapter X shews. Here for a time, surrounded by warm friends in a country at peace, he found his anchor as he tells us in his Journal of his trip to the monasteries of Alcobaça and Batalha: "These are the spots I peculiarly delight in, where I seem to breathe with greater freedom, and which the goats and sheep, whose bells I heard tinkling at a distance, love not better than I. How often, contrasting my quiet situation with the horrid disturbed state of almost every part of Europe, did I bless the hour when my steps were directed to Portugal. I looked round with complacency

INTRODUCTION

on a roof which sheltered no politician, on tables [upon] which perhaps no newspaper had ever lain, on neat white pillows which had never propped up the heads of financiers and schemers."[19] He cannot resist having a hit at Pitt. The life-long enmity between them probably dated from their boyhood days, when old Chatham foolishly commended Beckford as a model of oratorical brilliance to his own ambitious son. This early ill-feeling was fanned later by Beckford's Radicalism and their difference in temperament and wealth. Beckford was often exasperated and bored in Portugal, but the above diary-entry represents his settled view of her—"poor, beloved Portugal, my own true country" as he exclaimed when he learnt of our treacherous Convention of Cintra.[20]

Why, then, did he never settle in Portugal or Switzerland, Paris or Italy, the "great refuge for sinners of a certain sort"?[21] Two references to Italy in youth and old age give some of the factors which tied him to England in a grudging love-hate relationship. In 1782 he wrote to a friend, "I used to advise you to come to this fair region—for God's sake stay in England. There is more 'Vernal delight and joy' in one of our green lawns than in all the olive grounds and vineyards of Italy."[22] Ultimately, as this shews, he loved the unique landscape of England, still unspoiled, and its seasons. Later, when unwillingly facing the prospect of selling Fonthill, he wrote: "I fervently hope that the necessity of my position will not become so terrible as to exile me so far from human acquaintances as Italy. In order to prevent such a thing, I will conform to the most moderate system of expenses that can be contrived in Paris. I am frightened by the faraway-ness of Italy: as a place to travel in, well and good, but to live there continuously—God save me from it!"[23] He was a lonely man and without his childhood base of Fonthill and his familiars about him (agents and employees) he would have felt uprooted, without status and with no framework to keep him going. But when Fonthill had gone, why not Paris instead of Bath? Again one feels that the English landscape and seasons must have had something to do with it, as well as the general convenience of life in England—"the only country to live in", as he said on his last return from Portugal.[24] As so often with Beckford, there is no complete answer to this riddle.

He tried to travel to Naples from Portugal in October 1795 but was prevented and found himself, as already mentioned, for a few days in Aranjuez. He returned to Lisbon and landed again at Falmouth on 26th June 1796,[25] having been away nearly three years. He found Wyatt awaiting him with various plans for building, from which Fonthill Abbey developed. Its origin and early progress is discussed in Chapter XII. Henceforth building, collecting, gardening and forestry dominated his life. Foreign travel became more difficult and unattractive with the rise of Napoleon and the invasion of one country after another by the French armies. For years this essential outlet was denied to Beckford; after 1803 he ceased to travel at all, except for one stay in Paris for two months in 1814 and a lightning excursion in 1819. His collecting mania was typified by the purchase for £950 at the end of 1796 of Gibbon's library at Lausanne; but he was not able to see it until 1801, when he shut himself up with it and read himself "nearly blind". He spent the rest of his life wondering what to do with that hated library (he surely did not *give* it to Schöll, for gifts were hardly in his line).

This was an active period in Beckford's life. His literary activity temporarily flared up with the publication of two anonymous novels—*Modern Novel Writing* in 1796 and *Azemia* in 1797, which are discussed in Chapter XI. They contain some clever skits on contemporary writers and books, as well as Radical views on conditions in England, Pitt's repressive domestic policy and the current francophobia.

He had already in 1791 published anonymously as *Popular Tales of the Germans* his free translation (full of

INTRODUCTION

his own interpolations and fancies) of Musaeus' *Volksmarchen der Deutschen* (1787).[26] Beckford's book is the earliest collection of German stories in translation. It was reviewed favourably at the time, and according to Miss Stockley, one of our modern experts, compares well with many later translations; despite Beckford's free adaptations, she thinks that he knew German well and translated correctly.[27] Like his two later sallies just mentioned, it is very uneven. But it is often Beckfordian in its "odd mélange", its lapses into the "colloquial and coarse", its juxtaposition of "the humourous and the pathetic", its facetiousness, and its jumble of "the most risible absurdities of the Gothic Romance" with "beautiful descriptions and several novel images" and the bizarre; these are the words of a contemporary review,[28] in what amounts to a general description of the contradictions of Beckford's character, conversation and style. Since he could never keep his own image out of his works, *Tales of the Germans* has a perfect self-portrait: "He is shrewd, whimsical and fickle, petulant and rude; proud and vain, and so inconstant that he will be today your warmest friend, and not acknowledge you tomorrow; the distressed have sometimes found him kind, generous, and feeling; but he is at such perpetual variance with himself, that, like an egg put into boiling water, he proves hard and soft in a couple of minutes: and you will report him frank or reserved, mulish or pliant, just as the ignis-fatuus of his fancy whisks at first sight." (ii. 3-4). One of the remaining tasks of literary detection is the tracking of these little anonymous works—to which he challenged us so long ago: "If ever the world discovers the key of certain anonymous publications it will find I have not been idle".[29] The feeblest of them all is *Al Raoui* (1799), which he is said to have translated into German himself; but it had a (then) unprintable and lively counterpart, still in his Papers, from which I quote in Chapter VII.

He was also busy in the unsuitable field of diplomacy. He tried unsuccessfully to press his views, always sympathetic to Portugal, upon our Government after his return from Lisbon in 1796. From the summer of 1797 until the following March he worked to play the mediator between the French and English Governments and so end the war. He was genuinely horrified by the bitter struggle and the deplorable conditions at home which it caused, but he also had his eye on the limelight and social rehabilitation. The snub to his efforts and the death of his mother in July 1798 led him to sail for Portugal on 15th October 1798,[30] where he remained until July 1799. Only a few details of this third and last stay have been discovered (in Portuguese archives).[31]

His foreign travels were practically wound up by a long stay in France from the end of May 1801 (whilst the war was still on) to May 1803, when the renewal of hostilities made his final return unavoidable.[32] He went to buy pictures and other treasures, but above all to see Napoleon's new Museum at the Louvre, where the spoils of Italy were assembled—pictures never again to be seen together after their return to Italy under the Treaty of Vienna. Beckford, who hated the unskilled picture restoration and over-painting then prevalent, professed to be bitterly disappointed. He found Titian's *Martyrdom of St. Peter* (subsequently destroyed by fire), which he had known in Venice as "the finest picture perhaps in the world", now "almost covered with a glare of false colours", and Raphael's *Transfiguration* "patched like a sea chaplain's cassock at the end of a voyage round the world". "In short, most of these ci-devant masterpieces are like the French nobility and have lost their rank, their importance."[33] However, he found some consolation by getting a place in Napoleon's official procession of thanksgiving on August 18th 1802, to celebrate his birthday and the granting to him of the unique title of 'First Consul for Life', the restoration of peace and the anniversary of the official restoration of Religion.[34] Beckford's enemies at home gnashed their teeth and might well have exclaimed *Que diable faisait-il*

INTRODUCTION

dans cette galère? There was something irrepressible about him, as so often with *parvenus*! (He had already electrified the English world by entertaining at his unfinished Fonthill Abbey in December 1800 Nelson, the Hero of the Nile, and Sir William Hamilton and Emma, as I describe in Chapter XIII.)

His spirits were also revived when he broke his stay in Paris with a trip in the autumn of 1801 to Switzerland, "by far the most beautiful [country] in Europe".[35] Years later he sighed for its unique combination of the Sublime and the Picturesque: "How imposing and picturesque that castle with six towers between Sierre and Brig must have been, bathed by the Rhone and surrounded by varied hills. Beside these wonders of art and Nature, how miserable, common and *poor* is *wealthy* England with all its *mercantile* splendours!"[36]

When Beckford returned from France in 1803, the building of Fonthill Abbey was still dragging on and its plan being extended. He was not able to move into residence until 1807. The reasons for this delay and the dates of operations after 1800 are outlined in Chapter XIII. In preparation for his move he had several sales of effects and pictures, since the Abbey was to be furnished in an entirely different style, and anyway he had tired of some pictures and needed the money from others. His Christie sale in February 1802 included Cozens and two lesser contemporaries, Nicholas Poussin, a pair of Canaletto, a distinguished Rembrandt,[37] Claude, Murillo, a pair of Durer (then classed as Primitives), Hogarth's *Rake's Progress*, and Sebastiano del Piombo (sold on 27th March). The August 1807 sale was held by Phillips at Splendens (Fonthill House) and included an early Turner commissioned by Beckford, a fine early Canaletto now at the Soane Museum, two Nicholas Poussin, Ruysdael, Guerchino, L. Caracci, two Vernets (not those commissioned by Beckford), and surprisingly a *Ruines* by Robert (which one would have thought the height of Beckford's taste as a Romantic, and very

25

suitable for a Gothic abbey!). Then the house itself (except for its west wing or 'pavilion'), which was said to have cost his father £150,000 after the fire of 1755,[38] was knocked down to the dilapidators for £9,000. Characteristically, Beckford tried to double-cross the auctioneer just before the two 1807 sales by getting his furnisher Foxhall to sign an Agreement to buy everything, inside and out, for £16,000.[39] Presumably at the last moment he thought he could do better by letting the sales proceed. He had a further picture sale at his London house in May 1817, which included a few good pictures (if one could believe the attributions).[40]

One of Beckford's greatest worries in the early part of the century was the marrying off of his two daughters. Poor things—he was hardly an asset as a father-in-law, except for his money. This was the bait which the Marquis of Douglas swallowed in 1810, after nibbling at it for at least six years. Beckford made an offer, it was found insufficient . . . and so the sordid bidding went on, despite Beckford's increasing impoverishment through lawsuits over his plantations and the steady fall in the price of sugar. The old crotchety, hypochondriacal Duke of Hamilton (the "Snarling Dog", Beckford called him, as he snapped ferociously at his sons) and his unfathomable, 'cold-balled' son Douglas refused to recognise these difficulties, until Beckford exclaimed "I find it in vain to attempt persuading you that the state of my affairs, not their manager, not any other influence under Heaven, prevents my most cheerfully enabling D. to live in the manner he wishes."[41] Even as the date approached and the terms had long been more or less settled, they couldn't help wondering whether the Marquis might "renounce the alliance" . . . As Beckford's solicitor said, "whatever the private sentiments of the Marquis may be, he does not outwardly shew or profess an anxiety for dispatch".[42] Susan was safely married off to the Marquis in April 1810. Her elder sister Margaret took the law into her own hands a year later and married

INTRODUCTION

a penniless Colonel without prospects or connections, followed by a volley of oaths from her father, who could "swear most marvellously".[43]

The ordered framework of life at Fonthill is outlined in Chapter I and described in *Life at Fonthill* (pp. 24-25). His hundreds of letters in that book give a vivid description of his activities—continual building, avid collecting, some literary trifling and unceasing reading "pencil in hand", hard exercise and rural pursuits in order to keep at bay the demons within. But boredom and bitterness ("an indigestion of fruitless remorse")[44] were his chief enemies in the extraordinary vacuum of the guestless Abbey, and he escaped regularly to London to see the opera and vaudeville and comb the picture dealers, printsellers and book depots. When he was obliged to sell the Abbey in 1822, the same kind of life and activities continued until the end at Bath.

Whatever moralisers may like to think of Beckford's existence at Fonthill, they could not take a severer view than he at the end of his last Arabian Tale, composed in 1815 when he was fifty-five. His heroine Zinan-Adna is reading the works of a fictitious Brahmin, Behergir. "One evening, [said Zinan] thumbing them through, I was struck by these words [of the Brahmin]: 'For sixty years I have plumbed Nature's depths, I have examined the dogmas of every religion, I have grasped the varied secrets of Art. If I had not attained Truth, at least I was happy in the pursuit of her. But the Angel of Retribution appeared to me, saying "Behergir, do not flatter yourself that you will be Privileged at the Great Day of the renewal of life: a crowd of ignorant but charitable folk will be preferred before you. When Wisdom bears not the fruit of charity, she is a sterile tree whose cultivation is too agreeable in this world to find reward in the next" . . . "I read and re-read [said Zinan] these words which applied so well to my own situation. The gnawing worm of anxiety possessed me. Henceforth I continually reckoned these ten last years which I had barely perceived slip away, and I trembled lest they be my last."[45] Beckford is speaking of his own life at the Abbey, in which he had then resided for eight years!

But even his most severe critics must admit that Beckford was indomitable in old age and resilient in adversity. When his sugar fortune was crumbling and the impossible Abbey up for auction, his many enemies "flattered themselves that I had foundered, but they are deucedly mistaken—strong I breast the waves" (he boasted).[46] And so he built up again, in Bath, collections of books, pictures and treasures almost bigger and better than before, and caused the wilderness to flourish and towers to rise. In his seventies he produced books that caught on; in his eighties he was as mentally alert, and as astute and untiring a collector as ever.

Death could only rob him of his friends, one by one—the last Marquis of Marialva (Don Pedro of the *Journal*), the blaspheming Abbé Macquin who made little rhymes parodying the Mass;[47] a long string of devoted foreign physicians—the foul-mouthed and irascible Alsatian Ehrhart, Verdeil, and Schöll, who had attended at Lady Margaret's deathbed;[48] and, most terrible of all, the humorous, patient, kindly Chevalier Franchi, one time choir-boy and pianist. So naturally, there were moments when Beckford's spirits faltered at the end:

"Now Spring returns, but not to me return
   Those thrilling joys my vernal years have known"
he wrote in March 1844, as his woods at Lansdown (Bath) were tinged with green, the scent of violets blew, and he heard his lambs browsing the turf. But "in the midst of this sweet revival and of this pastoral charm I remain, alas, sad and sickly. I am not tired of life, but life is tired of me." This Spring elegy was his last formal composition[49]—and his last Spring. By May 2nd he was no more; his daughter Susan cut off a lock of his "precious hair",[50] and his servant Beckett told the printseller Smith that his "*excellent* Master" was dead.[51]

Chapter I

BACKGROUND

The Beckfords are one of those interesting families who rise suddenly from nothing, rapidly attain power and wealth, and produce in successive generations men of great ability, culminating in an eccentric near-genius. Then, with equal suddenness, they are extinguished like a meteor in outer darkness, leaving no male successor in the main line.

William Beckford, said to be the richest heir in England, could only trace back to his great-great-grandfather, a shadowy and humble figure in the purlieus of Clerkenwell, the dates of whose birth and death are unknown. It was his son, known as Governor or Colonel Peter, born in 1643, who went out to Jamaica as a young emigrant after the Restoration, and laid the foundations of the greatest fortune ever made in sugar.[1]

It would be pleasant to believe that this is a classic Success Story, so much in vogue today, and that he went out as an obscure young man without connection or advantage. But unfortunately, Beckfords were already well established in Jamaica when Peter was granted a thousand acres in Clarendon Parish by Royal Patent dated 6th March 1669.[2] There was Alderman Sir Thomas Beckford of Maidenhead, a self-made man mentioned by Pepys. He was one of the first of Jamaica's absentee proprietors; in 1670 he was drawing £2,000 a year from his Jamaican property. There was Richard Beckford, a Clothworker and citizen of London like Sir Thomas. From 1660 onwards he was buying up land, laying out mortgages and trading in Jamaica. He even granted land by deed to Peter Beckford in Jamaica in 1675 and 1676.³ There must be some connection between all these Beckfords. Yet the evidence in the Royal College of Arms shews that our Beckfords could not prove descent from this other branch.⁴

However, there is no doubt about the colourful character of Beckford's direct ancestors in Jamaica. The Earl of Inchiquin, one of its Governors, named Peter and two others as "the greatest incendiaries here", who encroached on the King's prerogative and revenue.⁵ This Governor Peter was ruthless, unscrupulous and violent. His immense success in administration and business went sadly to his head. He developed pronounced megalomania, "thinking himself the greatest man in the world, carrying and using, too, a large stick on very trivial provocations", knocking down Members of the Jamaican Assembly who presumed to disagree with him whilst he was Lieutenant-Governor.⁶

The manner of his death conveys the atmosphere of the whole family for generations—the violence, quarrelling and hub-hub which surrounded them, the tragedy with its dramatic but faintly ridiculous air. He died in 1710 as he came to the rescue of his son Peter (the third of his line of that name), who was Speaker of the Assembly: "During a warm debate upon the subject, Peter Beckford, the Speaker, repeatedly called [the Assembly] to order; and was at length compelled to force it by adjournment. But irritation had gone so far that, when he rose to quit the chair, the Members drew their swords and held him there while the obnoxious questions in debate were put and carried. The doors were barred; the uproar was alarming; and the Speaker's father heard the disturbance in the council-chamber. He recognised the voice of his son crying for help, and rushed into the Governor's apartment. Sir Thomas Handasyde seized his sword, ordered the sentinels to follow him, forced the door of the court-house and

BACKGROUND

dissolved the Assembly in the Queen's name. But the fray was fatal to the elder Beckford; in his agitation his foot slipped, he was precipitated down the staircase, and the effects of terror were deadly to his aged frame."[7]

The violent temper of the Beckfords, when they encountered opposition or apparent insult, led them even to murder. Speaker Peter Beckford, when a young man, shamefully murdered the Deputy Judge-Advocate in Jamaica, who was more than twice his age.[8] He worked himself up into an insane fury, just like his grandson William. Despite his violence, he died in his bed in 1735, reputed to be the richest subject in Europe.[9] In a family which produced a cleverer man in each generation, and which had become so exceptionally wealthy, it was fortunate that the principal heir, Alderman William (our man's father) was the ablest of them all—'the great Beckford, as he is usually styled';[10] and that he was not content to settle down quietly as an ineffective English country gentleman, like his younger brothers Julines and Francis.

Born in 1709, Alderman Beckford came over to Westminster, the most fashionable school in England, and then went up to Balliol. He represented the City of London in Parliament from 1754 until his death, and was twice Lord Mayor. He headed the West India interest (then our richest overseas possessions) in politics and finance and was the most valued of Chatham's supporters in the City, struggling with him and Wilkes against the Court party and the extension of George III's power. His moral courage and combative temperament have often enough been recounted in the incident of 1770, when he outfaced the young King and put him to silence, whilst presenting a Grand Remonstrance from the City. This made him a national hero, worthy of a statue in the Guildhall (an honour only shared with Wellington and the two Pitts); his untimely death at the height of his power was commemorated in the striking of medals.[11]

31

His opposition to the Court made his political outlook modern for the times, as a summary of one of his speeches as Lord Mayor shows: "The number of paltry rotten boroughs, the number of placemen and pensioners, with the corruptions of the electors as well as the elected, were the instruments that in time would effect the ruin of the country. To prevent such an evil, it was necessary [that] there should be a more general representation of the people, that the number of placemen should be limited by law, and that the servants of the Crown should be obliged to exhibit fuller and fairer accounts of the manner in which the public money was disposed of."[12]

His difficult position in English society as a 'Colonial' with an ugly Jamaican accent made him strongly anti-aristocratic. His family's position in Jamaica was at least as important as that of any of the great titled families in England, and he was wealthier than any of them. But he was cold-shouldered and regarded as an upstart; proud himself, he felt their insolent hauteur. His views on the nobility have an almost Socialist ring: "The sense of the people, Sir, is a great matter. I don't mean the mob—neither the top nor the bottom (the scum is perhaps as mean as the dregs); and as to your nobility, about 1200 men of quality, what are they to the body of the nation? Why, Sir, they are subalterns; I say, Sir, . . . they receive more from the public than they pay to it. If you were to cast up all their accounts and fairly state the balance, they would turn out debtors to the public for more than a third of their income. When I talk of the sense of the people, I mean the middling people of England, the manufacturer, the yeoman, the merchant, the country gentleman . . .; and, Sir, the people of England, taken in this limitation, are a good-natured, well-intentioned and very sensible people who know better perhaps than any other nation under the sun whether they are well governed or not."[13]

His ability and usefulness in Parliament were limited by some glaring but superficial faults—lack of charm, uncouth gestures, an inharmonious voice, a rapid utterance, ill-ordered and ill-digested thoughts, and an impetuous disposition which he was unable to check, and which led him into ridiculous situations. He was spoken of as one "whom no argument can convince, no defeat make ashamed, nor mistake make diffident".[14] He was forthright and uncompromising—"did what he said, and *said whate'er he thought*", as the poet Chatterton wrote in an ode on his death.

So he was the sport of the House of Commons and diners-out. His host Dodington treated him cruelly in front of Henry Fox, Richard Cumberland and others: "in the happiest flow of his raillery and wit [Dodington] combated this intrepid talker with admirable effect. It was an interlude truly comic and amusing. Beckford loud, voluble, self-sufficient and galled by hits, which he could not parry and probably did not expect, laid himself more and more open in the vehemence of his argument; Dodington, lolling in his chair in perfect apathy and self-command, dozing and even snoring at intervals in his lethargic way, broke out every now and then into such gleams and flashes of wit and irony, as by the contrast of his phlegm with the other's impetuosity, made his humour irresistible, and set the table in a roar."[15]

His tremendous surplus energy found notable expression in the number of his illegitimate children, on whom he doted. Until the Alderman's marriage late in life, his eldest bastard Richard, of whom he was particularly fond, lived with him at Fonthill and was a familiar figure in the neighbourhood.[16] His eldest natural daughter Barbara married a local parson, Wake, Rector of East Knoyle;[17] another son, Nathaniel, boarded with them. There was also John, being trained in the counting-house of Messrs. Hope & Co. of Amsterdam. Rose (a boy), Thomas, who matriculated at his father's old College, and Sukey (Susannah) were at boarding school. His principal mistress was Mrs. Hannah Thwaites, *alias* Maxwell;[18] another one evidently gloried in the name of Jennings, since his third son was known as Charles Beckford, *alias* Jennings, and lived in Wolverhampton.[19]

As far as his only legitimate child, William, was concerned, the Alderman's most important act was the purchase of the four or five thousand acre estate of Fonthill about 1736 (prior to entering Parliament for nearby Shaftesbury). This place traditionally had bad luck. It once belonged to Mervin, second Earl of Castlehaven, who was executed for sodomy in 1631 after being denounced by his son in one of the most notorious cases of the century (Beckford claimed descent from these Mervins, and took their motto, *De Dieu Tout!*). The next owner was Lord Cottington, from whom it was confiscated by the Commonwealth, in favour of President Bradshaw, who signed Charles I's death-warrant. At the Restoration, Cottington took it back by force; his family sold it to the Alderman. During the latter's ownership it was destroyed by fire in 1755.

He rebuilt it on such a lavish scale that it was nicknamed Splendens. On the new ground floor he constructed a vast, solemn and mysterious Egyptian Hall, from which radiated endless vaulted corridors and an interminable staircase lost in gloom. This led up to suites of stately apartments gleaming with marble pavements polished like glass; further flights of stairs led to galleries filled with curious works of art and precious cabinets. All this made an indelible impression on the young William and left its mark upon his Oriental tales.

Tourists were struck by the overwhelming display of immense wealth "almost too tawdrily exhibited".[20] The inmates boasted openly of "the immense sum" which this and that object cost, and of the State Bed "not yet finished, but it is said that it will be the handsomest in England".[21] The traveller Warner was almost epigrammatic, describing it as "one of the most splendid mansions in the Kingdom . . . where expense has reached its utmost limits in furniture and ornaments, where every room is a gold mine and every apartment a picture gallery".[22] Even in the Alderman's lifetime, few visitors came; the neighbours were put off by his morals and shunned him as a nouveau-riche 'radical'.

But he was unquestionably the most important influence in the life of his son, who drew an excellent portrait of him in the last of *The Episodes of Vathek*, as a buccaneering Merchant Prince, sending out ships in every direction, constructing canals, trying to forestall Providence and control the future by his speculations; attentive to business but not particular about religious observance; anxious to have a male heir and determined that he should grow up a potent prince, "he did not care by what means"; and importunate over women and other good things—"I shall certainly not wait a moment longer than I please".

The boy was particularly impressed by his father's terrible glance when he was angry. Speaking of the Gordon Riots, our Beckford said: "My God! . . . if my father had been Lord Mayor, in place of the stupid animal that then presided over the destiny of the city, he would have stopped this riot in a moment, aye almost with one of his own ferocious glances, under which the King himself had learned how to tremble".[23] So this is the source of Vathek's terrible eye, which so struck Sir Walter Scott!

One of Beckford's own characteristics was his love of towers, and this too (we shall see) was derived from his father. In fact, the figure of his lost father dominated his imagination throughout youth. When he dreamed of painting Salvator Rosa-like scenes of banditti, "his father, leaning on his spear, and giving orders to his warriors, was generally the principal object in these pieces, characterised by a certain horror, which those ignorant of such dreadful scenes fancied imaginary".[24]

The Alderman settled down to marriage in 1756, at the age of forty-seven, picking on the thirty-two year old widow of another City man, Francis Marsh. They did not have a child for four years, when, on Michaelmas Day, 29th September 1760, William Beckford was born in their rented house in Soho Square (now No. 22).

She came from a different class of society, her paternal grandfather being the Earl of Abercorn and a Hamilton. She never forgot it, as Beckford writes in his novel *Azemia* of Lady Arsinoe Arrogant, the wife of Colonel Brusque: "she never seemed entirely able to forget that Lady Arsinoe Arrogant had married a Commoner, though he was a man of family not very much inferior to her own. The Arrogant blood, however (in spite of the elegant refinement of her mind, and a *tint* of Methodism . . .), continually reminded her, at the head of this magnificent and well-furnished table, that Lady Arsinoe was *déplacée*".[25]

She also differed from her husband over religion. Whereas he admitted impiety[26] she was methodistically inclined and surrounded by 'methodistical dowagers', as Beckford called his aunts and her other friends (he was always making sarcastic hits at them and their Bibles). Here we have a vital influence on Beckford, and so must examine the rest of the evidence for her Methodist inclinations.

After her death, the problem of the education of Beckford's daughters at West-End (Hampstead) had to be considered (they had been living there in her household and under her charge). His former tutor Lettice proposed to undertake the job, but said "I cannot consent to go to West-End . . . unless Mr. Rowden with his flinty ill-humoured face and . . . morose and untractable spirit, be removed from the premises. Poor Mrs. Rowden, with no ill-meaning but a good deal of ill teaching to the young ladies in their childhood, and with her silly cant and methodistical whimpering, has been of irreparable disservice to Miss Beckford: and as she has at all times expressed more inclination to quit West-End than to stay, she cannot justly complain of being removed."[27] Mrs. Beckford also had Swiss Calvinist governesses for her grand-daughters when they were very young;[28] all this had a permanent effect on one of them, Susan (later Duchess of Hamilton), who was full of Calvinistic leanings.

Mrs. Beckford's greatest crony was Lady Euphemia Stewart, who was constantly interfering in Beckford's life, lecturing him, and trying to keep him on the straight and narrow path. Her letter home about his young wife's death in Switzerland has a strong Evangelical tinge; a month later, when he was still prostrate with grief, she wrote "It gives me great pain to hear your spirits are no better; pray, exert your great abilities to support what cannot be remedied, but by entire submission to the Will of Heaven; that renders light every burden; but it is not easily acquired; and impossible without Divine assistance, which, I hope, you pray for fervently, as I do, for both you and myself".[29] The sense of Fate and of the implacable Will of Heaven is a leading theme in Beckford's writings: with the accompanying sense of Sin and Judgement it was first imbibed at home, even before he became immersed in Oriental literature.

Mrs. Beckford's religiosity is also apparent from her choice of tutors for her son; Drysdale and Lettice were both good, pious and uninspired men. Of Drysdale, Beckford wrote to his mother: "your dearly beloved Mr. Drysdale [is] most compleatly hum-drum. I think for singing a babe asleep he need not turn his back to any old woman in Christendom and would be more useful in the Nursery at West-End than on board the *Julius Caesar*."[30] Beckford had to read a chapter of the Bible every day as a boy; later on he sarcastically mentions "not having a fine Bible to spare after the West-End fashion".[31]

Mrs. Beckford was a woman of determined character who usually managed to get her own way, by storming and threatening or by cozening and blandishments; her son nicknamed her 'Her Supremacy' and 'The Begum'.

ENGLAND'S WEALTHIEST SON

Throughout life, therefore, whenever difficulties arose, Beckford turned to some person (mother, tutor or friend) to extricate him: "devise some plan", he would say plaintively, "think for me—I cannot very well think for myself".

In order to keep him to herself and protect him from the world, she refused to send him to school or university. He was not grateful to her for this bondage. The portrait of her as Carathis in *Vathek* is not flattering, and she ends up damned. References to her in his correspondence are patronising, resentful and belittling; she is somebody whose whims have to be borne.

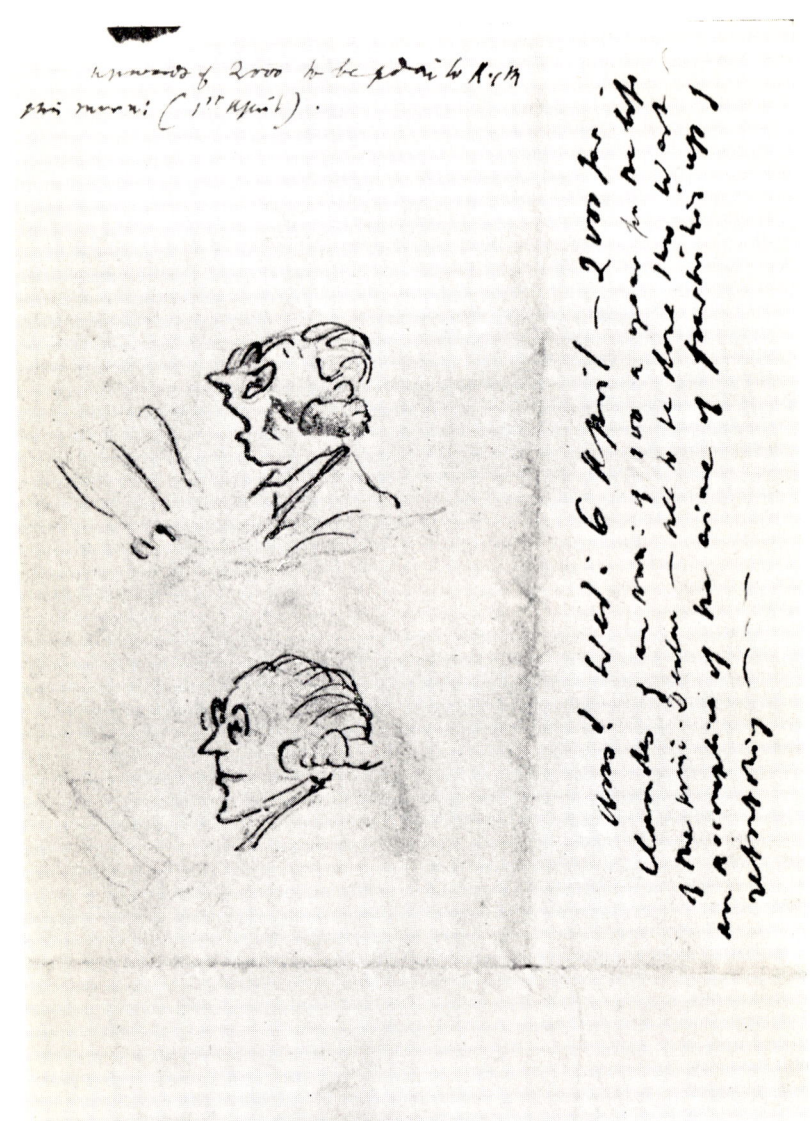

CARICATURE OF BECKFORD, 1803

Chapter II

EARLY YOUTH, 1760-1777

Memories of early childhood, though usually trifling, are often instructive. Beckford's Papers record three such incidents (apart from his lessons with Mozart), each indicative of his character. He wrote to his friend Pacchierotti, the famous *castrato*, "Good Night, may you sleep as soundly as I used to do at five years old after running about all day in the meadows".[1] Here we see him running about his beloved Fonthill like a Child of Nature, without a care in the world. Throughout life he looked back on Childhood as the only happy time, when the scales of Innocence had not yet fallen from his eyes and Dream had not paled before Reality. As he put it, *L'illusion est assise aux commencements de la vie, et quand l'age et la verité viennent, les illusions s'effacent et le bonheur s'eloigne avec la jeunesse*.[2]

The next recollection comes from Redding: "Among his diamonds were a number of very fine brilliants, unset and laid loosely into a beautiful ancient tazza. These he called the cat diamonds on account of the singular mode by which he had acquired them. A relation of his who had become very old was always surrounded by a parcel of cats of whom he was particularly partial. Mr. Beckford, then quite a boy, pretended to be also very fond of them and constantly paid them the utmost attention. In return for this, these diamonds were one day given to him, with the statement that they were presented to him solely on account of his attention to these favorite animals."[3]

Here we see his hypocrisy, his eye for the main chance. The actor in him was partly responsible for this trait: he could not resist playing up to his audience. There is a capital example when, shortly after his seventeenth birthday, he led on the Curé of Salève: "The old bigot, imagining he had a most zealous Catholic for his guest, began a long conversation about the perverse heretical dispositions of my countrymen. Unwilling to lose the opinion he had conceived of my *heureuses dispositions*, I began a pathetic harangue upon the separation of England from the Mother Church, the suppression of convents, the barbarous and ungentleman-like usage the blessed Virgin had endured, not to mention Thomas à Becket and fifty more sufferers on the like occasion. This fervor pleased *Son Reverence* vehemently; he had not met with so excellent an opportunity of displaying his rhetoric since the last Easter."[4]

The third recollection dates from his tenth year. A friend of the family twitted him about his great-great-grandfather, a shoemaker; he "by no means relished the thoughts of this plebeian descent" and flew into a temper. His father, amused, baited him by hinting at the lowly condition of another ancestor.[5] Genealogy became a blind obsession of Beckford's. His heraldic studies were inspired in the first instance by his father's ownership of Eaton Bray in Bedfordshire, an old castellated residence of John of Gaunt.[6] Henceforth he bent his efforts to tracing his descent from Gaunt!

The most important event in his childhood was his father's sudden death at the height of his fame in June 1770, when Beckford was nine. This shaped his awareness of the instability of human grandeur—"so many great characters . . . passed away like fleeting clouds, of which no traces remain".[7] His strong reaction is described in his unpublished early novel *L'Esplendente*: "I have pined after thee in this dreary solitude and have often wept thy absence; the silence of this vale is terrible when thou art away, and my heart has been chilled by the midnight gusts that blow from the mountains . . . thy dying voice seemed to be borne on the gales by my ear. My nights were sad and desolate, my mornings without consolation since thy departure."[8] This unexpected deprivation of a beloved figure helps to account for the underlying gloom of Beckford's character and an anxiety which always led him to expect the worst.

The Alderman's death changed the status of the family at Fonthill, particularly with the unedifying quarrels consequent upon his Will. Not until the heir came of age and was ready for a political career were there visitors of consequence and solicitations for his favour. This is the opening theme of his unpublished French story *Zinan*, in which the father has just died, and his widow and only child are soon forgotten! The latter, being of a studious and solitary nature, does not mind; but the mother, preoccupied with money and position, is determined that her child shall retrieve the family fortunes: "your father's death has plunged us into that *néant* which I detest, and we must escape from it at whatever cost". She therefore schemes, and forces her child into another kind of existence.

Meanwhile, "in his earliest childhood" Beckford browsed in the Alderman's library; there he acquired a taste for Oriental literature, particularly the *Arabian Nights*, "when other children are seldom of an age to do more than comprehend their letters".[9] He dreamed of the gorgeous, the fantastic, the horrible and the magical. He talked with evident satisfaction of the power of Eastern satraps, the servility of their subjects, the pomp of their attendants. He exacted similar obedience at Fonthill. His anger was unbridled when he was provoked or contradicted. He became imbued with the idea that he was descended from a race of Kings. Had he not been naturally humane, these dreams might have made him ferocious. After such reading, the Classics "fell flat upon his mind", and it was only gradually that their influence and his own enthusiastic love of nature provided some counterweight.

This was the child that the new tutor Lettice found about a year after the Alderman's death, late in 1771 when Beckford was beginning his twelfth year. Lettice arrived too late. The domination of his imagination by the Orient could not be broken.

At Lord Chatham's suggestion, Lettice compelled his pupil, when just over thirteen, to burn a splendid heap of Oriental drawings which he treasured. The trauma was severe. The scene is re-enacted in *L'Esplendente*, where he describes his hero's first rift with his beloved Mahometan father when the latter discovered him impiously drawing the human form and ordered him to "abandon for ever an art which some demon must have suggested to you in this retirement. So saying, he furiously snatched up the leaves [of the book] which were scattered about, and tearing them asunder, committed them to the winds and the torrent. The youth sobbed, not daring to reply or to make any attempt to save the children of his fancy. But the loss affected him more than can be imagined; he turned angrily from his father and, hiding his face with his hands, gave way to violent indignation. What can my father mean, what crime have I committed?"[10]

Even the unimaginative and pedantic tutor flinched at the severe course of instruction laid down by the exacting Chatham, who was Beckford's godfather. In his first report to the latter on the boy's progress, written after a stay with the Pitts, Lettice said that, without the example held out by Chatham's own family, he would not have thought that "it was practicable to adopt so severe a plan" at Beckford's age and that such studies would not have been profitable until later. At first it was painful up-hill work for tutor and pupil: "It was likely that our first setting out in this thorny path should prove rather irksome to so warm an imagination; and so, indeed, it happened. But we had been at Burton [Pynsent], and were fired by example too much to retreat, though little charmed with the rugged prospect before us. It is true, that for some time we scarcely took a single step on mathematical ground without stumbling, and I fear we trod but tenderly when we were last at Burton; but since our return I have had the satisfaction of concluding that the good impressions Mr. Beckford received there have had a lasting affect, from the unusual attention with which he has lately applied himself that way."[11]

A sustained attempt was made to divert the child from his natural bent, to convert him from a creative writer consumed with imagination and fire to a cold political animal, a gentleman fit to take his place in the ruling class. Beckford, of all people, was to be schooled to "look upon taste and sentiment as acquisitions of less importance than the right use of reason".[12]

This repressive effort failed; but the attempt imposed various strains upon him. It threw him back all the more upon the pleasures of the imagination, which were regarded as criminal by his elders. A dichotomy was created in him. He was forced to hide his imaginative life from the outside world, which he increasingly felt to be unsympathetic. He became a lonely moping soul, resentful of his elders and estranged from his contemporaries, who fitted more easily into the orthodox pattern. Feeling different from them, his outlook was tinged with contempt for his fellows: "State of Fonthill, 1779: The ladies are pretty, sentimental and dawdling. As for the men, I shall say nothing, but that I think them qualified to act the parts of Noodle, Doodle and Foodle in *Tom Thumb* [to] admiration. Surrounded by such an assembly, my situation (tho' not in Paradise) is as solitary as that of our first Parent when animals alone encircled about him."[13] This uncongenial system fostered in him a tendency to desultoriness in study and reading, so that later on he became a dilettante. "Beckford nibbled at the sciences, 'a mouthful of each and a bellyful of none'."[14]

He hardly knew, in his teens, the consolations of friendship. But his earliest draft letters are playful and affectionate scrawls to an Eton contemporary, Lord Morton, who was organising a puppet show there with another boy, John Penn, grandson of the founder of Pennsylvania.[15] The fourteen-year old Beckford advised them on their play: "have a very grand catastrophe, which I dare engage will surprise, if not please. This mighty catastrophe is to make the poor Knight swallowed up by an oyster and ordered to close confinement ... Be sure and make your oyster of a tremendous size with hideous gaping jaws, and let the Knight stand quivering on the edge till the oyster at one gulp sucks him in." For their grand finale he sketched the following scene: "It should represent a delightful garden. The side scenes composed of trees bending under a profusion of fruit and flowers; at the end a large rock partly bare, partly covered with bushy wood; a cascade streaming down its side. Above, a clear tranquil sky with domes, obelisks and other gay edifices just peeping over the top of the shrubs."

These early letters are full of Beckfordian characteristics, for example, his hyper-sensitive criticism, rather too supercilious. In April 1775 he attended a Covent Garden performance of Arne's popular opera *Artaxerxes*, which had an English libretto. He refers to "the miserable actors who roared out with great emphasis and consummate vulgarity the dull English recitative of the still more stupid opera of *Artaxerxes*".

His one real friend was Alexander Cozens, the artist, who had been drawing-master at Eton and was much in demand in Society as an instructor. He was born and bred in Russia, where he travelled widely and met Persians and other Orientals. Beckford's earliest mention of him is in the first letter to Morton written in April 1775. He appears as a familiar figure, nicknamed the Persian, so that Beckford must already have known him for some time, probably from about the age when he would have gone to a public school.

Their early friendship is described in *L'Esplendente*, in which Cozens appears as a venerable Jew, Ben Jacoup,

EARLY YOUTH, 1760-1777

"whose long residence in the Levant had familiarised [him] with its customs".[16] The Jew is at once struck with the precocious boy, who makes up to him, doing his best to flatter and impress him. His young fancy is fired by the Jew's stories of the strange foreign countries in which he had travelled; the Jew "loved to hear him ask questions in so animated a manner". He shows him some Oriental manuscripts "beautifully illuminated and glittering with gold and azure". Seeing them, and under the Jew's tuition, the boy develops a passion for drawing, which is at first opposed by his Mahometan family. But once he is allowed to continue, he says to himself "Now I shall give a loose to my inclination. I shall paint from noon till night and see all my fancies transfer'd upon paper—strange castles, and deserts skattered over with the tents; priests ministering at altars, and the antient King of China with his long nails, surveying his golden fountains." (p. 54).

Meanwhile the boy in *L'Esplendente* was living in the greatest seclusion with his family, following (except for his drawing) the orthodox lines laid down for him. But the Jew's stories gave him a whiff of the outside world, to which he wanted to escape and become an artist. There is now a secret rift between him and his family; their limited interests and outlook are no longer his. The Jew encourages him, ridicules their prejudices, and introduces him to Hebrew lore and the writings of Solomon.

Coming of a persecuted race, the Jew is an adept at deception, and advises "the utmost care with respect to affairs wherein Religion is anyways concerned". He recommends the lives of the Christian Saints and the Fathers of the Desert: "by such performances you will command the respect and affection of the circle in which you are about to move. For the future you must quit the appellation of Mahomed and, resuming that of Ferdinand, appear as much as possible in a Christian light." (p. 75). The Mahometan boy Mahomed has now changed his identity; the change is symbolised by his secret assumption of the *Christian* name of Ferdinand. This recapitulates Beckford's inner development at Fonthill in his teens. He was putting up with the rigorous Christian and Classical training of Lettice in his mother's evangelical household, whilst developing a secret dream-life of the imagination, centred on the Orient.

L'Esplendente mentions Mrs. Beckford's suspicion of Cozens and of his influence over her son: "She was not quite clear in her ideas about him and was half inclined to conjecture he was employed in magical researches. Mahomed quieted her suspicions as well as he was able and told her that he did not think him abandoned to the study of that pernicious art, but on the contrary a great philosopher." (pp. 51-52). This suggests that Cozens was interested in Magic. We cannot prove it, but it is not unlikely. According to Beckford, other artists whom he knew (Loutherbourg, Cosway and the architect Ledoux) were also adepts.[17] His influence on Beckford may not have been altogether healthy; he may have revealed an aspect of himself which he concealed from the Society ladies whom he also taught.

He gained a great ascendancy over Beckford's mind and was the repository of all his confidences and aspirations, as can be seen from the letters which Beckford later sent him from Switzerland. He alone saw the instalments of Beckford's second literary effort, *The Vision*. Beckford addressed to him other early literary fragments and his first Journal.[18] This was because he felt that only Cozens understood him and would not disapprove of his most secret thoughts; they were leagued together against conventional Society.

His feeling for Cozens is touchingly displayed in an essay which he wrote to him from Switzerland in 1777 or 1778.[19] Missing his company, Beckford recollects all that he had told him of his adventures in Russia. He recalls his stories of "gilded halls, bright lights and a

EARLY YOUTH, 1760-1777

long train of nobles led [out in the dance] by the Empress and moving majestically to Polish measures"; Peter the Great's funeral, "when you kissed his pale hand"; his audiences with a Georgian Princess, "surrounded by a melancholy Court in long black robes of mourning", and with a Tartar Prince, sad hostage amongst the Russians; his Persian friend, who presented him with curious drawings and girt on his side a Damascene dagger; a terrifying night in a large and desolate house in Petersburg, where "every gale seemed loaded with lamentations of unhappy Spirits or the cries of deceased magicians, whose voices were all vindictive Heaven had suffered them to preserve as memorials of their existence, and condemned their souls to wander without shape or form in the void of the air".

Cozens faded out when disgrace fell upon Beckford in 1784. But when the latter was an exile in Portugal in 1787, he did not forget his old friend, now dead; he associated him in his dreams with his young wife, Lady Margaret Beckford, who had died the previous year, within a month of Cozens: "The recollection of poor old Cozens took possession of my fancy. I seemed to hear him commending the oriental scenery of my apartment and the lulling whispers of the winds. I seemed to behold him seated at my feet, examining the sprigs of citron I had gathered, and saying with a smile: 'Shall I give them to Lady Margaret?' I woke from my trance in tears." (*Journal*, p. 165).

Beckford's first book was about artists. *Biographical Memoirs of Extraordinary Painters*, published in 1780 but written in 1777,[20] is a remarkable production for a youth of sixteen and is full of Beckfordian touches and topics—the terrible eye, St. Anthony of Padua, and Hell and Guilt. Here, guilt is associated with the young artist's innocent friendship with a girl, from whom he fled "like a criminal", lest his work be hampered. After he deserted her, "his dreams represented her . . . on the distant shore of rapid torrents, beckoning him to console her in vain; for the instant he attempted to advance, tempests arose and whirlwinds of fire snatched her screaming from his sight. Often he imagined himself reclining by her side in meads of flowers, under a sky of the purest azure, and suddenly she would become ghastly pale, and frowning on him, drive him to a flood that rolled its black waves between terrifying precipices, and dashing into its current drag him after her; and then he would wake in horror, crying, 'I drown! I drown!' Indeed he seems to have been selected as an example of divine vengeance." (pp. 54-55).

These are Beckford's own dreams. Most of the ones recorded in his Papers have the same theme: when he tries to make contact with the beloved object, the sky becomes overcast, the storm breaks, and the object is unattainable; the dream ends on a note of frustration, despair and guilt. This helped to drive him into the arms of his own sex, but denied him happiness there also, leaving a trail of broken relationships. His sense of guilt was represented by accusing voices: "In every passing wind, he fancied he heard voices upbraiding him with his crimes, and cries denouncing vengeance seemed to issue from every thicket he left behind." (p. 57). He felt he had to "expiate his baseness".

Beckford also enjoys the grotesque and the ludicrous. When mocking the finicky realism of Dutch masters like Gerard Dou, he describes an armchair of the richest velvet and a Turkey carpet painted by one of his heroes: "The exquisite drawing of these pieces was not less observable than the softness of their tints and the absolute nature of their colouring. Every man wished to sit down in the one, and every dog to repose on the other." The future devotee of St. Anthony of Padua describes a picture of the saint which the artist was commissioned to paint for the Pope: "he placed St. Anthony on a rock projecting over the sea, almost surrounded by shoals of every species of fish, whose countenances, all different, were highly expressive of the most profound attention and veneration. Many persons fancied they distinguished the likeness of most of the Conclave [of Cardinals] in these animals; but this is generally believed to be a false observation, as the painter had no pique against any of their Eminences."

Here he expresses the mocking spirit of the eighteenth century. But his Romanticism finds full expression in *Biographical Memoirs*, as when he describes a Hell-like landscape: "By night he was directed by the mournful light of those eternal fires which issue from the peak of the mountain, and by day a few straggling crucifixes, erected over the graves of unhappy travellers, who had perished in the expedition, served him at once as a mark and a memorial of the perils of his route. On the fourth day, after a night spent almost without sleep, he arose, and lifting up his eyes saw before him the mouth of that tremendous volcano, which the superstition of the times led him to believe the entrance of Hell. The solitude in which he found himself, the sullen murmur of the volcano, and all the horrors of the scene worked so strongly on his imagination, that he fancied he beheld strange shapes descending and ascending the steeps of the fiery gulph. He even believed he heard the screams of desolation and the cries of torment issuing from the abyss." (pp. 87-88).

His contemporaries did not know what to make of such writing. Some thought it a skit on the *Vie des Peintres Flamands*; others that it was levelled at certain contemporary artists. The *Monthly Review* for 1780 confessed itself baffled at "this strange work . . . we have consulted both professors and virtuosos concerning it; but still remain in the dark with respect to the author's real drift . . . On the first view of this performance, it naturally occurs that the author meant to draw some modern or living characters; but if such was his intention, we confess that we are not of that class of readers who can identify any one of them in this mingled mass of true and fictitious history." (p. 469).

It was wise for such a brilliant and imaginative youth to have a solid framework to his day, which began with a half-hour ride at seven with his tutor. They started work before breakfast with Latin and Greek grammar and a chapter of the Bible. Lessons continued until one, when they rode before dining at three. An hour and a half of work followed until some light reading before tea, "after which he chatted with the ladies or walked in the grounds if the weather permitted". They supped at nine and enjoyed conversation, music or singing until bedtime at eleven. This routine was imposed until Beckford was twenty. He maintained it practically unchanged (except for adult occupations) until he took to his bed to die. If anything, he was slightly stricter on himself once he was his own master—he rose at six in October, and was invariably in bed by ten, even when staying in London; and he bathed in the lake daily until November! This shews that he practised self-discipline and tried to counter his temperamental and constitutional weaknesses; perhaps, too, he was for ever clinging to his childhood!

Chapter III

FAMILY QUARRELS

The strife in the Beckford family stemmed from the Alderman's Will. If his son William, a delicate child, had no lawful male heirs, everything would go to the eldest bastard Richard and his male issue, failing which to each male bastard in turn. It was therefore possible that Fonthill and its Parliamentary seat at Hindon might pass to the bastard line; and this although the normal heir to William should have been his first cousin Peter Beckford, now grown up, or the Alderman's surviving brother Francis, with several sons. The Beckfords were a rising family of County status and national reputation, with political influence and Society marriages. As far as the senior line at Fonthill was concerned, all this would have been cast away had the estate passed to the bastards, and the whole family would have received a mortifying blow. The Alderman's attachment to his natural children must have been unusually strong.

The Executors of the Will were also guardians of the children during their minority. They were not the distinguished people named by previous biographers (Lord Thurlow, Lord Lyttelton and others), but Lord Bruce[1] and his father-in-law Henry Hoare of Stourhead, both of whom resigned; Sir John Gibbons, an absentee landlord from Barbados;[2] Dr. Wake, Rector of East Knoyle, who had married the Alderman's illegitimate daughter; and W. M. Burt, later Governor of the Leeward Islands.[3] During the heir's minority the executors had full control of all his father's estates, so that from 1770 one of the greatest fortunes in England was administered by three men—Burt, Gibbons and Wake.

But the great source of trouble was the Will's last principal clause, which recommended that all plantation produce shipped to London be consigned to the House of Collett, Evans & Co "until such time as any of my sons shall set up in the business of a sugar factor, then my desire is that the consignments may pass through his or their hands". This meant a commission of $\frac{1}{2}$% on insurance in transit and $2\frac{1}{2}$% for selling the produce. The clause gave no time limit, such as the heir's coming-of-age, so Richard tried to perpetuate this lucrative arrangement.

The trouble began at once, after the Alderman's death in June 1770.[4] Lord Bruce and Mr. Hoare found the Will impossible to administer and did not like what was occurring, and so resigned. This left Burt, the only other honourable executor, in an impossible position, outvoted every time by Gibbons and Wake. Gibbons was prompted to throw in his lot with Wake and the bastards through jealousy of Burt, the only other man of the world on the board, and through rivalry with him for the management of these vast estates.

Who, indeed, was to manage them? This was the first bone of contention and was of the utmost importance. It was generally agreed that Burt was the most qualified person, but when he subsequently sailed for Jamaica to take over management, Gibbons and Wake tried to get him stopped at law. Burt quite rightly said that the sugar-factors in London, Collett & Evans, were not the proper persons to administer the estates; it gave too much opportunity for abuse and mismanagement. But in fact one of them, David Evans, was directing the management from London from the day of the Alderman's death. As early as August 1770 Burt complained that he was not consulted, and he was gradually squeezed out. In the end, he refused to continue as executor because of the continued interferences of the sugar-factors and of Richard. Effective control was obtained by the business men, Collett & Evans, and by Richard, who joined them.

For Richard naturally took full advantage of his father's Will. In May 1771 he set up as a sugar-factor in partnership with Collett & Evans; thus, without doing any work himself, he got the large commissions on all the produce which arrived at the Port of London. Of course, shipments also came regularly to Liverpool, which the Alderman and Burt had preferred, and Bristol; but an increasing amount was diverted to London in the interests of the factors there. The Alderman and Burt had also thought it most profitable to sell all the rum in Jamaica, but it was now shipped over for sale on the London market.

There was also opportunity for dishonesty over insurance. And a fortune could be made by sending out to Jamaica an unnecessary amount of stores, which were charged against the London account and then sold on the spot. Finally, the local agents had their alleged expenses, which were paid for by Bills of Exchange issued in London; Richard paid these Bills from the London account without settling the Jamaican accounts. In this way a sum of £140,000 remained to be accounted for when Beckford came of age in 1781. In time, Richard became the nominal manager in London, and the two remaining executors, Gibbon and Wake, acted on the advice of him and his partners.

Young Beckford lodged a 'complaint' in Chancery on 1st October 1770 against his father's Executors and Richard and others, in order to get accounts and suitable managers. At the same time his mother ousted his guardians and had him made a ward in Chancery. Expensive proceedings dragged on for at least two years, and it was found impossible to dislodge Richard as consignee. All that could be done was to make him render annual accounts to a Master in Chancery and pay any balance into a bank. Although his father's

Will had only expressed a *desire* that he should become consignee at the Port of *London*, he boldly claimed the *right* "to the disposal of [all] the produce of the . . . plantations in Jamaica".

We can imagine the resulting publicity and gossip. The old wound was re-opened when Beckford made a second attempt to get control of his affairs when he came of age in September 1781. In preparation, he opened hostilities against Parson Wake, the only surviving executor, by ordering the agents in Jamaica, without Wake being consulted, to consign some of the produce to his own agents in London.[5] So there were now two rival consignees in London. Richard did not intend to forego a penny of his commissions, so tried to force Beckford to account to him for the rival consignments and sales. By acting promptly, Beckford had hoped to get control of produce which was still at sea after he had come of age. But Chancery proceedings were very slow, and after September 1781 Richard was still having sugar consigned to himself which had not even been shipped.

By mid-July 1782 Beckford won his case in Chancery. But the vindictive Richard, impervious to scandal, appealed to the House of Lords in February 1783, and finally lost. At this stage he was only claiming £1,647 for commissions allegedly due. Therefore his real purpose must have been to embarrass the legitimate family as much as possible and to perpetuate his consigneeship, which Beckford rightly claimed had terminated at his majority.

It would have been bad enough had there only been Richard to contend with. But the other bastards were just as grasping and dishonest, and everything was ventilated in Court. Young Nathaniel at nearby Knoyle, egged on by his sister Mrs. Barbara Wake, clamoured for his legacy of £5,000, on which he was getting 4% interest pending settlement, and he had the effrontery

LADY MARGARET BECKFORD, by Maria Cosway

to complain that it was insufficient. Master Rose Beckford was accused of overdoing the ordering of stores from England during his two years or so in Jamaica, and was apparently in trouble with the Customs.

The Alderman had done his best for his second bastard John. He had him trained with the sugar brokers, Hope & Co. of Amsterdam, and in Paris. He then tried to bribe him with £200 a year if he would go to Jamaica to take up the well-paid Secretaryship of Jamaica for seven years (really to act as Agent for his family). But Master John disliked the idea of Jamaica, and infuriated his father by buying instead a cornetcy in the Guards. His father recovered from his rage and gave the lad more money.

Now that his father was dead and as much as possible was to be got out of the Beckfords, John suddenly decided that, after all, he would take the post as his right; but he was not going to Jamaica—a Deputy was doing the work for him out there. Curiously enough, the Deputy was named Robert Evans—probably a brother of the sugar-factor David Evans, who was in league with Richard. He also claimed that his father had given him the two Jamaican estates of Stanton Harcourt and Harbourhead, worth £3,000 a year or more.

Beckford tried to dislodge him from his claims (which meant that he could administer the Alderman's estate in Jamaica, handling the profits) by bringing a case against him in Chancery in 1773. John appealed to the House of Lords in May 1774, but in February 1775 accepted their Lordships' advice to withdraw his appeal, with costs. He was declared to be "now of narrow circumstances", having dissipated the money which his father had given him, including a £5,000 legacy.

Almost worse humiliation and scandal followed. One of the Parliamentary seats at Hindon went with the Fonthill property. Richard Beckford resolved to intervene and oppose Mrs. Beckford's candidate, General Richard Smith (the most notorious of all the Nabobs),

ENGLAND'S WEALTHIEST SON

in the October 1774 election.[6] So Richard Beckford joined with Calthorpe (a local landowner, who controlled the other Hindon seat), and Mrs. Beckford put a second candidate in the field to oppose Calthorpe. Both her nominees won, but the losing candidates petitioned the House of Commons to declare them elected, alleging bribery by her candidates. A Select Committee reported in 1775, found *all* candidates guilty of gross bribery, and declared the election void.[7]

A fresh election was therefore held in May 1776, with General Smith again a successful candidate and Richard unsuccessful; the latter alleged corruption and malpractices by the General. Another Select Committee was appointed in January 1777, unseated the General a second time for corruption, but also disqualified Richard from taking his place, and declared the election void. A third election was held in February, which was not disputed; by this time Richard had given up.[8]

The constitutional historian Oldfield states that Hindon was no more corrupt than most of the other rotten boroughs, but that most of them escaped these Parliamentary enquiries because the business of corruption was usually conducted with more caution and secrecy. The flagrancy of the proceedings at Hindon was due to the bitterness of the vendetta between Mrs. Beckford and Richard. Oldfield also states that unsuccessful candidates usually hesitated to incur the enormous expense of petitioning Parliament;[9] yet Richard did so twice running. His campaign against the Beckford interest was conducted with Beckford money—what his father had left him in his Will, and his commissions and perquisites from the management and sale of Beckford produce.

The campaigning by each side in preparation for the October 1774 election began as early as February 1773. Every house was intensively canvassed by both sides; the bastard Nathaniel from Knoyle acted for his brother. Mrs. Beckford sent word that she expected her tradesmen to support her interest. But some of them favoured Richard because they had known him for twenty years—a great deal longer than Mrs. Beckford, they said; for he had been much at Fonthill, and they regarded him as a neighbouring gentleman, whereas the two opposing candidates had been brought in from outside.

General Smith, whom they nicknamed General Gold, started bidding at ten guineas a voter with £3,000 available. But Richard bid him up to 25 guineas a voter, with 4,000 guineas available for all expenses; these included sundries like three shillings a head per couple for drinks at pubs on voting day—when one could get "drunk for a penny and dead drunk for twopence" on gin. Parties were put up for the night before the poll in pubs and houses, eating and drinking their fill. Some of them stayed at Nathaniel Beckford's at Woodyate, where they found Richard with 4,000 guineas in his saddlebags, looking "as cool as a cucumber, and his nose was turned crooked in his face". On the great day he drove from there to Hindon in a chaise, stopping to shake hands with anyone he met on the road and throwing money to those who ran alongside.

Parson Wake was the local J.P., but was active on Richard's side. He had a party of voters along, where they got into liquor, Mrs. Wake serving the beer herself; as well as being promised 25 guineas a head, one or two yokels had gold and silver lace hats crammed on their pates as an extra inducement. At this date Wake was (with Gibbons) the only remaining executor of the Alderman's Will; we can guess whence he got the money for this corruption and later to suborn witnesses to give false evidence before the Select Committee of the House of Commons. The villagers had a wonderful time, taking bribes indiscriminately from both parties, and bidding them up against each other.

If we are to believe an unsigned and undated pamphlet in the British Museum, called *The Case of the Sitting Members for Hindon*, which is careful not to mention names, the fresh election of May 1776 was conducted amid scenes of extraordinary violence, perpetrated by Richard Beckford against Mrs. Beckford's candidate, General Smith. The latter and his colleague were returned by a majority of seven votes out of a total of 117.[10] They alleged that their majority would have been much greater but for the campaign of terror engineered by Richard or his agents. Before and during the election Richard "kept a mob constantly employed in endeavouring, both by menaces and open violence, to influence voters and the Bailiff". "Those who had the courage to withstand their insults were forcibly turned out of their houses, their goods thrown out of doors and strangers put in possession in order to vote for the petitioners." When the terrified Bailiff held a scrutiny of the poll in the presence of the candidates, Richard's mob threatened to pull down his house if he failed to return Richard and his colleague. After declaring the result, he prudently left Hindon until the violence subsided. When agitators were arrested, they were rescued by confederates who beat the constables. The mob was summoned out into the street by drummers, and the 'peace officers' were afraid to intervene. When Richard and his colleagues petitioned against the election result, his mob demonstrated, "daily declaring that if the petitioners do not succeed, they will destroy the town and all the Roundheads in it, to terrify anyone from appearing as witness for the sitting Members".

The sequel is unexpected. By 1791 Richard was as good as finished, despite having been an M.P. elsewhere continuously since 1780 and having married a wealthy wife. He had large debts in the City, where he was now partner in the West India merchant house of Beckford & James; he owed a considerable sum to friends on whom he had sponged, including Beckford's first cousin Peter; and his private affairs were "much deranged". His creditors were pressing him.[11] Only Parliamentary privilege saved him from imprisonment.

FAMILY QUARRELS

At this critical juncture he bethought him of his half-brother William and wrote a grovelling letter, no longer asking anything as of *right*. But he did expect that William's generosity would "enable me to pass the remainder of my life in comfort and to live in a manner becoming a brother of yours". Incidentally, he had to explain away little *mots* that he had circulated at his brother's expense in the House of Commons![12] Perhaps he had charm, perhaps his stammer was an engaging characteristic; anyhow, Beckford paid £500 down to quieten his most pressing creditors, and gave him an annuity of £500.

Just before Beckford left for Paris he allowed "poor Richard" to come to Fonthill, and affectionately acknowledged him as his brother. Somehow Richard persuaded Beckford that the numerous reports of his ill-will towards him were false. Characteristically, even then Richard did not fully explain the extent of his debts and difficulties; and he evidently got a further 'present' out of Beckford. But he was not going to acknowledge such generosity openly. He begged an intermediary (Sir William Hamilton) to keep it quiet, and particularly not to mention it to Peter Beckford, who was then in Italy, in case some of his City creditors pressed him further for payment![13]

The trouble with the bastards between 1770 and 1783 profoundly affected young Beckford. It influenced his outlook on sex, and made the pursuit of women seem ridiculous and even disgusting. It made him cynical, and anxious about money. The scandal contributed to that *mauvaise honte* which Lettice noticed in his pupil when he arrived in 1771. And it explains why his mother did not send him to Eton; how could he have endured public school life with such scandal going on?

Chapter IV

SWITZERLAND AND SAVOY, 1777-1778

Since Beckford never went to boarding school, the problem of the next stage in his education arose when he was sixteen. His mother was against sending him to an English University, "most probably from the dissipation into which a youth of his expectations and vivacious temperament would infallibly be led".[1] We can hardly blame her when we recollect what Gibbon said about conditions at Oxford. And she may have been prejudiced by the fact that one of her husband's bastards had gone up to his old College, Balliol. They were all a rotten brood, and, with the Beckford background, she could not be too careful. Since he had been brought up in a fatherless household, surrounded by elderly women and an old-womanish tutor, with every moment of his day organised, the change to the freedom and male-ness of a University would have been difficult.

The solution seemed brilliant. About midsummer 1777 he was sent with Lettice to Geneva, one of the intellectual centres of Europe. There he lodged with distant connections of his mother's family, the Hamiltons. They had been living in Geneva for two generations and knew everyone; no better introduction to this cosmopolitan society could have been found.

But Beckford's fate had to be fulfilled: his mother overlooked two things. Colonel Hamilton had served in India, and so would encourage the boy's interest in the Orient![2] And through his mother Hamilton was almost certainly a first cousin of Jean Huber, a brilliant

SWITZERLAND AND SAVOY, 1777-1778

but erratic agnostic. Beckford soon regarded the latter *in loco parentis*, and became friends with his younger son Jean-Daniel Huber, an artist whose lively imagination and satirical humour were altogether too like Beckford's. From the point of view of his family, this was the worst possible company for him.

His time was healthily divided between serious study, gay amusement, writing, and expeditions along the Lake of Geneva and in the mountains. Many of the parties were held during the 'season' at the neighbouring spa of Evian, which Beckford never tired of recalling in old age. "While there he rendered himself agreeable to everybody in a way scarcely to be believed. Was there a party of pleasure proposed on the Lake, he was always the gayest of the gay among those who composed it, doing the agreeable to the ladies in a manner singularly polite and gentlemanly."[3]

His red-letter day came when he and Colonel Hamilton held a fête on a natural terrace overlooking the Lake and surrounded by the Woods of Blonay.[4] At one end under an arbour was a cold collation of cream and brown bread and butter, with baskets of fruit; at the other, an irregular lawn, surrounded by firs, sloped gradually to the Lake; a cleft in the jagged rocks gave a distant view of blue peaks, and an invisible cataract thundered down the mountain. Along one side of the terrace, green damask cushions and seats twined with boughs and flowers were casually placed under the chestnuts.

At three o'clock music suddenly struck up, concealed among the firs, and the guests were galvanised into activity. The scene resembled a picture by Watteau or Fragonard. The ladies had towering plumes and floating veils, and the uniforms were resplendent with decorations. Silhouetted against the sky, like presiding genii, were two nuns "with at least 150 quarter[ing]s between them", their lawn robes bellying in the breeze. Forming a contrast was a German Baron, as fat as the famous

Mr. Bright, whose capacious waistcoat, a-glitter with gold like Surajah Dowlah's shield, could enclose seven or eight striplings.[5] Determined not to be outdone, he clambered about the precipices like an old goat, oozing with sweat. Beckford drew a caricature of him for his partner. Their music and laughter "attracted the peasants and all the people of the environs who, flocking with pleasure beaming in their countenances, joyfully partook of the cheer and by their queer figures and uncouth air showed powerfully the effect of contrasts".

Supper followed, but in no time the impetuous Beckford leapt up, seized a fern and stuck it in the plumes of his partner, "the beauty and heroine of the King of Sardinia's dominions". Out of deference to their host, the rest of the ladies submitted to the *ferne panache*, and the dancing was resumed with redoubled vigour. Even when the sun set and the deep azure of the distant mountains had become a misty blue, "the indefatigable dancers were still thumping the turf with their feet".

At length they heard the sound of oars, and barges arrived to take them back to Evian. "Everybody cast a long look on the woodlands of Blonay and lamented the lapse of such agreeable hours. 'It may be the happiest day of my life, such another may never return' was the explanation I made as I handed Mme. la Baronne to her barge." A Neapolitan lady and her musical dilettanti joined them; as the boat was pushed off from the bank in the azure twilight, they began to sing. The rowers rested on their oars. Not a breath of wind stirred. The moon appeared from behind a dark grove on the mountain, and rose above the mouldering turrets of Blonay Castle, casting a silver track upon the waters. The snows glistened on the peaks. The Neapolitan went into ecstasies. The peasants lit a huge bonfire on the shore. The leaping flames tinted the whole forest like enamel, lit up the figures gathered round, and gleamed in the water. Answering fires sprang up in every direction, illuminating mountain and glacier. Everyone was hushed and overawed.

SWITZERLAND AND SAVOY, 1777-1778

Fond as he was of gaiety, Beckford loved nature more—Mont Blanc as yet unconquered, and the Bossons Glacier with its "white pinnacles like Gothic spires". But he was most impressed by the Grande Chartreuse. Inspired by reading the life of its founder, St. Bruno, and by Gray's Ode, he made a pilgrimage there in 1778, following the footsteps of Gray and Horace Walpole.

As he was swallowed up in the noonday by its dark forests, with torrents roaring in his ears, he thought "how dreadful must be the despair of those who enter it never to return".[6] "Not a furlong", he said to Redding (and quoting Gray), "but would awe an atheist into belief".[7] The seclusion of the monastery, protected by almost impenetrable precipices, through which Napoleon later blasted a tunnel, appealed to him: "everywhere around appeared mighty barriers that seemed to have excluded for ever the rest of mankind. All was wrapped in sober melancholy."[8]

On his arrival he captivated the Carthusian friars. They were specially interested in him because he owned Witham Abbey, the ruins of the earliest Carthusian monastery in England. "The Secretary, almost with tears in his eyes, beseeched me to revere these consecrated edifices and to preserve their remains for the sake of St. Hugo, their canonized Prior. I replied greatly to his satisfaction, and then declaimed so much in favour of Saint Bruno and the holy prior of Witham, that the good fathers grew exceedingly delighted with the conversation and made me promise to remain some days with them. I readily complied with their request, and continuing in the same strain that had so agreeably affected their ears, was soon presented with the works of Saint Bruno, whom I so zealously admired."[9]

Beckford was genuinely interested in St. Bruno's life and was struck by the incident which caused him to retire from the world. Bruno was at the funeral of a saintly friend when suddenly, amidst general consternation, the corpse uttered the terrible phrases, "I stand before the tribunal" [of Christ] and "I am condemned by the justice of God".[10] Bruno picked on the site of the Grande Chartreuse because of the vision of his friend Hugo, Bishop of Grenoble, in which the very spot was designated and "declared to be for ever barred against the foot of the hunter and woman's allurements".[11] This visit was a turning-point in Beckford's life. It inspired his dream of a secluded Abbey set in Alpine scenery, which materialised twenty years later at Fonthill.

A few months before this, in the winter of 1777,[12] Beckford wrote an uncompleted story without a title, dedicated to Alexander Cozens, and first published in 1930 as *The Vision*. So it was composed during his first prolonged absence from his mother, when he was under new influences, had the usual adolescent conflicts, and was conscious of his homosexual tendencies. Permeated by feelings of guilt and couched in wonderful dream-language, it describes an adolescent initiation ceremony presided over by Moisasour and Nouronihar—God-like figures who are his parents.

Beckford did not emerge successfully from this ordeal into adult independance. For, as (in the story) he was following his own bent, he panicked, felt himself separated from the parent figures and was overcome by guilt. He came running back to his mother, who in Methodistical language warned him that he had very nearly been lost through "fluttering like these insects from one grove to another" (thus did Beckford castigate his independent excursions into the realms of the imagination). "Another hour", she said, "and never wouldst thou have seen me more. If thou hadst suffered any longer a voluptuous indolence to creep into thy veins, if regardless of his former goodness, thou hadst allowed the memory of Moisasour to have been banished from thy mind, thou must have been snatched from these delicious valleys and . . . awakened in the upper world with the bitter recollection of thy lost happiness to prey upon thy mind and punish thy ingratitude . . . These Beings were assembled to inspect thy conduct and mark the moment to separate us for ever. They were mourning with me thy frailty." (p. 75).

Beckford was also frightened by the imaginative life teeming in the Unconscious strata of his being, which he thought would swamp his rational and intellectual self. Thus there are caverns inundated by floods teeming with monstrous animal life, including "crocodiles whose eyes glared horribly and whose scales, reflecting every feeble ray of light, quivered thro' the gloom". Beckford's mother-protectress informed him that "the arrival of such uncommon shoals denotes the approach of a period when the meteors will be obscured and the plain deluged with rains. Then strange monsters will range the valleys and others will issue from the gulphs and even from the great deep, too horrible for mortal view. Let us retire then lest we should endure this inclement season and witness such ugly sights." (p. 80). The birds ceased to sing and the sky became overcast. The pair prudently retreated to a higher level!

In his writings Beckford prophesies his own doom. His later situation at Fonthill, cut off from the outside world but unreconciled to his lot, is exactly foreshadowed by the superior but depraved beings who degenerated into malevolent dwarfs huddled in the abyss: "In the profound abyss . . . the guilty race awoke to . . . all the horrors of conscience. The most dreadful silence prevailed throughout this gloomy space . . . Deprived of the gift of speech and fixed to the spot on which they had fallen, each creature imagined himself in an entire solitude. They had formerly heard of the idea of eternity. They thought that dreadful eternity arrived; an endless duration of darkness, solitude and silence, without a single object to divert the gloom of their situation or a being to whom they might have the consolation to complain. A thousand times they wished all the horrors of punishment at least visible, they wished even the cries of torture to sound in their ears, any degree of misery seemed preferable to this total inaction; for to a race whose limbs had always obeyed the vivacity of their souls and whose tongues had been accustomed to utter a million of thoughts which crowded their imaginations, what situation can be conceived more painful than this horrid calm of the body whilst the mind, doubly active, ranged over the former period of its existence, burnt to deprecate the power it had contemned, and found itself at once deprived of all the faculties of expression?" (pp. 52-3). The loss of their former position inspired them with malevolent hatred towards mankind, whom they saw as usurpers.

Beckford's descriptions of scenery are like John Martin's illustrations for *Paradise Lost* (published in 1831) or his pictures of the Last Day (painted in 1853). And there are the beginnings of the paraphernalia (so prominent in *Vathek*) which suggest the mysterious, the supernatural and the sinister—ebony portals which suddenly fly open, revealing terrifying flights of steps, etc.

In two unprinted fragments of *The Vision*, Nouronihar begins her own tale. The first opens with a situation familiar in Beckford's writings. Nouronihar is led by her 'unlucky Destiny' through a perilous desert. In the distance are "the marble palaces of African monarchs sited on the green margin of clear lakes, enclosed by wildernesses of palm and fig trees".[13] After a terrible night, floundering in the sands and parched with thirst, she and her companions see a mirage. Already they catch the cool gale from the groves and anticipate their shade. Already they hear the murmur of falling waters amongst the tufted orange trees; "we even hear a citron dropping from its bough". Then, without warning, as she was on the point of satisfying her wishes, a sandstorm engulphs her caravan. Everything is blotted out. Her companions are overwhelmed and their cries borne away by the wind. She is petrified with dread and falls to the ground in an agony of despair. When she awakes she again lives through "the horrors of her cruel disappointment". But she is comforted by finding herself in the consoling arms of an old family servant. Throwing her arms round her neck, Nouronihar says, "Dost thou once more assist that unhappy one whose tender years occasioned so many nights of affliction and anxiety?" There follows an independent jotting in which Beckford describes the emotional vicissitudes which he himself endured, "one instant frightened with the stern aspect of Cerish . . . and the next melted by the soft attentions of Lahina".

Without indulging in the horrors of Freudian jargon, one can see that this reflects Beckford's early relationship with his parents, and that at critical moments he was overcome by anxiety which led to frustration and insecurity.

The second fragment about Nouronihar's tale is the only piece of writing in which Beckford deals at length with sexual intimacy; this takes place in the burial vaults of Nouronihar's ancestors, amongst their tombs! Her consciousness of the sacrilege heightened her passion and delight, but at length she cried "I was alive to all my guilt . . . the cold hand of my Ancestor was upon me . . . I deprecated with bitter cries the vengeance of Heaven".

But though Beckford dreamed about heterosexual love under curious circumstances, in real life he experienced the usual adolescent 'crush' for some youth. He noted that the latter "seemed to hang on my words, whose eyes drank eager draughts of pleasure from my sight, whose inmost soul was dissolved in tenderness when by chance he touched me, whose countenance was flushed with conscious blushes, who feared to own the passion that stole into every vein and poisoned the serenity of his mind. How he lingered at parting from me, how he departed and returned, confused and not daring to confess for why . . . , but pined in solitude and consumed his hours in vain lamentations."[14] Significantly, his account of their calf-love served to record a similar experience when he was over twenty, and was kept to the end of his life in a special folder—for he never grew out of that stage. A year later he still pined after "that voice, whose thrilling accents sunk with such pleasing pain, such melancholy tenderness, into the inmost recesses of my existence".[15]

This was too much for Beckford's mother! Becoming anxious about him, she travelled to Geneva in the autumn of 1778 to bring him back, after he had only been away eighteen months. The stage which he had reached is shewn by his fantasy *Hylas*,[16] based on Theocritus' ode. Hylas, the youthful squire of Hercules, by whom he was beloved, went to a spring to fill his pitcher and was dragged into the pool by the lustful female Naïads; he never re-appeared and Hercules sought him in vain.

Beckford thus describes Hylas' situation beneath the water: "he perceives the features of the Naïads, flushed with desire. Fain would he fly from their importunities . . . In the midst of his afflictions, the well-known voice of Hercules descended faintly through the waters. Thrice did the lovely captive reply; and thrice did the unavailing sound rise bubbling from below. The malicious Naïads sported with his perplexity, and as he sat dejected on a mossy fragment, danced wantonly around. And now the moon, rising to illuminate that world to which he never could return, . . . darted her lustre on the humid realms below. Shadows without number, reflected from the impending vegetation, glanced on the playful group and chequered their lucid forms. But Cynthia, disgusted by their wantonness, soon lost herself in clouds. Hylas now mourned in darkness."

Beckford feared the crude desire of the opposite sex and having to reciprocate their feelings. He realised that, after advancing thus far, he could never return to the world of childhood and early adolescence, with its sentimental and romantic friendships. "The well-known voice of Hercules" would be heard but faintly through the muddy waters of desire! Soon he had his own little squire, whom he called 'another Hylas'—the pretty young William Courtenay.[17]

Chapter V

ENGLAND AND ITALY, 1779-1781

Beckford met Courtenay during the English tour which he made with his tutor Lettice in the summer and autumn of 1779. En route he stayed with his distant Courtenay cousins at Powderham Castle, near Exeter. William was eleven, a girlish boy of intelligence and sensibility, the youngest of thirteen children (all the rest were girls), the darling of the nursery. Beckford fell in love with him in a sentimental way.

This can be seen from the letter which he wrote to Alexander Cozens after Courtenay had absented himself from Westminster School to be painted in Romney's studio at Beckford's request:[1]

"I have seen him tho' it was but for an hour, and have now but too full an idea of the swiftness of happy moments . . . Judge how I felt upon his telling me that his head had run on nothing but me since we parted, that Fonthill had been ever in his dreams, and that when he crossed Salisbury Plain every distant wood or thicket seemed to belong to it . . .

"But all my miseries are renewed when I consider how seldom I am doomed to be with him, how little his father or mother comprehend the nature of my love. Who can enter into its refinements, who feel its ardour, who conceive its extent? I mourn single and solitary, without one friend but you to whom I can disclose my melancholy sensations . . .

"O that I could snatch up some inspired pencil, and dipping it in the most vivid colours of Heaven, paint his wild roving eyes instinct with the brightest fancy and yet softened by tears . . . His countenance one moment appeared as lively as light; the next, a dark shade came over it, and those eyes, which but the last instant sparkled with vivacity, now glistened with tears.

"In this wavering state the hour he spent with me was passed; and after a thousand transitory hopes and fleeting anxieties, after confused moments of the liveliest happiness and deepest dejection, he was summoned away. I followed him wistfully with my eyes and listened till his steps grew fainter and fainter. The door closed, and the sound of the carriage which bore him from me was lost in the noise of London.

"Then returning, melancholy and alone, I threw myself on the ground and wept like a poor miserable being cast away on a desert world, *deprived of the best part of its existence.*"

It is a pity that Beckford, with his eagle eye and diverse interests, had not yet started to keep a consecutive diary, but only managed an occasional jotting (apart from long write-ups at Plymouth, York Minster and Hackfall). For on this tour he saw a surprising amount of the new industrial areas, as well as the stately homes and some of the loveliest English scenery. He went over the Soho Engineering Works at Birmingham, where Boulton and Watt had recently perfected a steam engine to raise power in a factory for the first time. He explored a subterranean section of the Duke of Bridgewater's canal which connected Manchester and Liverpool; the greatest engineering feat of the day, it had only been finished in 1772 and had nearly made the Duke bankrupt. He saw French and Spanish prizes lying in Liverpool harbour; he visited Kedleston Hall, Chatsworth and Haddon Hall.[2]

On his way to the Lakes he travelled in the early morning from Lancaster to Ulverston in the Furness peninsular. At low tide he crossed the immense stretch of sand in Morecambe Bay:

"It was ebb, for the sands are flat as an oriental desert but hard, wet and trackless. The distant mountains of Westmoreland and Cumberland rose before us with their heads in some places veiled in mist, in others rising in an infinite variety of forms, colors and magnitudes. From the lower elevations they ascended in fine gradation until they were lost to the vision, while before us stretched an immense plain of sand crossed by shallow streams that reached only to the axles of our carriage wheels. Guides on horseback preceded us, for the passage was only practicable at certain times of the tide. Horrible were the stories told of accidents that had occurred from venturing across at the wrong time of the tide.

"There was nothing wanting to complete noble landscape scenery. The land bordering upon the sands consisted of corn fields, green enclosures and woods, while churches, villages and romantic old castles were well dispersed over the picture. Sometimes we saw fine woods of oak and beech descending almost to the sands and sloping upwards to the mountains. Here a group of rocks frowned over some pretty bay, within which green islands shot up, continually varying their forms as we proceeded. We passed close to reefs and shoals—dark, jagged and fully exposed by the recession of the tide.

"Now we crossed the estuaries of tidal rivers, by which were seen flocks of sea mews and other acquatic birds, stately herons and dark shags. Some were swimming, others on the wing, and vast numbers grouped and motionless. As we approached the opposite shore, the scene was enlivened by passengers—some on foot and some on horseback or in carriages, hurrying forward with the guides to reach the opposite shore before the flowing of the tide. Parties of fishermen too were setting their nets. The morning was fine; we had left Lancaster early and by ten o'clock had reached Ulverston in Furness.

ENGLAND AND ITALY, 1779-1781

"The sea came in quickly after we had crossed; it soon closed upon us and converted the vast plain of sand we had just before passed over into an ocean. We felt as if we were suddenly pent up in another world."[3]

This description is interesting because it was written so early. It is as good as an account of the return journey across the sands to Lancaster, published sixteen years later by the novelist Mrs. Radcliffe in her *Observations during a Tour of the Lakes*. Until Beckford's day the Lakes were unknown. He was one of the first of that spate of Tourists of the Picturesque who descended on them, with the recently published guide-books of West and Hutchinson in their hands.

The first Lake he visited was Coniston. Upon its shore, he spotted the Hall in its thick woods, "a ruinated place, as my driver told me, inhabited by a very antient man". He looked up the encircling mountains and "all down the steeps appeared trunks of decayed trees of the strangest shapes imaginable, whose appearance this misty and showery weather was almost formidable; they seemed to me like spectres frowning upon the pass below. Under one of the yews lay three black heifers that basked portentous and odd, as if they belonged to somebody I fear to name."[4]

The last Lake he visited was perhaps Derwentwater. He was pleased by its white cottages peeping out of oaks and hollies. They had trickling springs "conducted from the rock by a trough to supply little natural basons scooped out of the living rock, on the edge of which I noticed several bright jugs of earthenware, that reminded me of Patriarchal times and made me venerate these fountains".

He visited an ironworks in the wilderness. The torrent roared over the rocks and was overhung by oaks and mossy crags. "To the right, strange roofs and black wheels casting around them a perpetual rain. The hollow wind in the woods mixing with the rushing of waters, whilst the forges thundered in my ear. To the left, a black quaking bridge leading to other wilds. Within, a glowing furnace, machines hammering huge bars of red-hot iron, which at intervals cast a bright light and innumerable sparks thro' the gloom. Several boughs, fixed on a beam above, shook and trembled with the strokes." His tour in the North finished up at York and Hackfall, near Ripon.

Back at Fonthill with his mother, the old problems arose—boredom, restiveness and isolation. He fell back on the powers of his imagination. We can see his slim figure as he paced rapidly up and down the platform beneath the entrance portico of Splendens, gesticulating and declaiming in a falsetto voice, imagining himself some potent monarch of whom he had been reading in literature: "Last night, tired with Frenguis and Frenguism, I stole from the Saloon and, led by a glimpse of moonshine between the arcades of the Egyptian Hall, went out at the Southern Portal. The dissolution of the snows next the pavement had left round it a narrow circle of verdure beyond which all was white. A grey mist had risen from the waters and, spreading over the lawn, seemed to inclose the peaceful Palace on every side. Thro' the medium of these vapours the moon cast a dim bluish light just sufficient to discover the surrounding woods, changed into groves of coral. I was so charmed with the novelty of the prospect that, setting the cold at defiance, I walked to and fro on the platform for several minutes, fancying the fictions of Romances realised, and almost imagining myself surrounded by some wondrous misty barrier no Frengui could penetrate."[5]

He went up to London in June 1780 to set out on a Grand Tour, and saw the Gordon Riots, which left a lasting impression on him. He told Redding that "when young he had continually sought out scenes of an extraordinary character. He had indulged a fancy for the confused, the tumultuous and even the terrible. During the Gordon Riots . . . he sought to gratify this inclination by tracking the devastations of the mob, and witnessed many of the extraordinary scenes that occurred. He said that, apart from humane considerations, and looking with the eye of an artist at the vast conflagration, late at night, he should have felt a positive delight at the grandeur of the picture had not a sensation of horror intruded itself on account of the probable loss of life."[6]

He observed the irresolution of the authorities, which led to the situation getting out of hand; the calling out of the troops, who fired on the mob; the savage punishment meted out by his future enemy, Chief Justice Wedderburn; and the inhumanity of the King. The latter remarked to Beckford's uncle, Field-Marshal Sir George Howard, after he had ordered the shooting: "Ah, Howard, glad to see you—peppered them well, I hope—peppered them well—peppered them well".[7]

Beckford left for the Continent with relief and did not return home until the following spring, 1781. His travels gave him the material for his second published work, *Dreams, Waking Thoughts and Incidents*. This was printed in 1783, but before it was distributed Beckford ordered its withdrawal, and burnt most of the copies. His family were anxious for him to take his place as a politician, but he never would have been taken seriously in the House as the author of a romantic travel-book which began: "Shall I tell you my dreams?" etc. And so it never appeared until 1834, as Volume I of his book *Italy, with Sketches of Spain and Portugal*.

The suppression of a book of merit and originality was a serious blow. He put his Romantic feelings into it; if they could not find creative expression, they were likely to have a less desirable outlet. Indeed, the background of these travels cannot be guessed from the book. During his first stay in Venice in August 1780, when he was on his way south, he became involved with a youth of the aristocratic Cornaro family.

For the rest of his tour he knew no peace of mind: "Alas, I can find no distractions. Fate gives me no peace. Landscapes and the splendours of the setting sun have lost their effect . . . One image alone possesses me and pursues me in a terrible way. In vain do I throw myself into Society—this image forever starts up before me. In vain do I try to come up to the great expectations formed of me—my words are cut short and I am halted in mid-career. This unique object is all I hope for—I am dead to everything else."[8]

When he was staying with Sir William Hamilton, our Minister at the Court of Naples, he confided in the first Lady Hamilton, the predecessor of the notorious Emma. She spoke of the friendship with Cornaro as a 'criminal passion' and tried to help him to eradicate such feelings. We need not suppose they were 'criminal'; as we have seen, the same phrases in which Beckford described his innocent Swiss 'crush' were used by him in 1781 for this. But the point is that he now came to regard these feelings which came naturally to him as 'criminal'.

Consequently, they produced an incapacitating conflict in him. So much so, that during his stay in Venice in December 1780 and January 1781, on his journey home, he fell ill; his spirits drooped in a way quite new to him: "Among the Isles of Venice . . . he was found amid the chilly unwholesome atmosphere, landing on one and coasting another, until even his boatmen were fatigued, and complained. The consequence was that he soon began to suffer in health and, *what had never been observed before in any of his previous indispositions*, his spirits appeared to droop in an extraordinary manner."[9]

The conflict was due not only to his sense of guilt, but also to the impossible situation in which he was placed. He was beginning to realise that his feelings could not be indulged by anyone with his conscience in a Christian society. His dilemma is expressed in his translation of an aria sung by Marietta Cornaro, presumably the sister of his friend; her words threw him into a 'strange delirium':

"When sleep its magic balm instils,
The form I love my vision fills;
Swift flies each tort[u]ring pain.
Imperious God, Thy justice prove,
Ah, realise the dream of love
Or wake me not again."[10]

Beckford means that only in the dream world are his friendships with his own sex unimpeded. But they are so real to his nature, which he has been *given* and not *chosen*, that if his Creator is just He will either make them possible in real life or send him to the Grave, where the problem no longer exists. It seemed to him doubly unjust, because his nature placed him in difficulties unshared by most of his fellows, but for which he was blamed. This is one of the sources of that sense of Fate which dominated Beckford's thought, and which he shared with so many Romantics.

One of his dreams shews his subconscious awareness of the dead-end inherent in these friendships: "Yesterday, in my troubled dreams, I thought I saw your Adriatic Sea under a blood-red moon. I saw the porticos of that dark palace, which is only too well known to us, hung with mourning crêpe. The voice of lamentation was heard. I was being called. I ran up. I was about to touch the blond head of – – when a dagger pierced my heart. I awoke with a piercing cry, bathed in a mortal sweat."[11]

But he was no weakling and did not mope like a lovesick youth. He was always brimful of vivacity and curiosity, and single-minded in the pursuit of his interests. Venice gave him the first glimpse of his beloved East, and he hunted out any Orientals he could find in order to learn about Bagdad, Damascus, and Delhi; his enquiries were earnest and painstaking—unusual for a young English gentleman in the best society! Back in Venice on the return journey he was equally persevering in his chosen occupations: "I idle away my mornings in my gondola, wrapped up in furs, reading and making calls. My body is frozen, but my ardent imagination wanders in the Indies and frolics in the rays of its own sun. The night is spent in cafés and at the opera, where Bertoni's voluptuous music, supported by the artistry of the world's finest singer, makes me more than ever effeminate."[12]

While he lingered in Paris before returning home in April 1781, he was cured of his morbidity by his affection for William Courtenay: "I'm nothing less than cured. The first object of my thoughts is always my little C. Filled with thoughts of him, I spend hours at my clavichord, recalling moments—" (here he judiciously broke off).[13]

A new sense of spring-like joy filled him: "I rode to a wild bushy glade called the Bois de Boulogne, and observed with delight the first approaches of Spring; the birds were twittering in the brakes and the deer chasing each other down little turf paths sheltered by banks, where I expected to find some violets. After searching some time without success, I sat down and read a letter I had just received from my lovely William, so tender and affectionate, so elegant and childish that tears of joy and tenderness swam in my eyes. Then every object seem[ed] to acquire a secret charm; the twigs seemed covered with vivid buds; the air felt genial as the breath of May; and forgetting the season, I began to look about for cowslips. But my researches soon ended in the lines before me. I no longer sought for spring—'twas in my mind."[14]

Chapter VI

THE ORIGINS OF VATHEK, 1780-1781

Beckford had intended to remain on the Continent and return to Naples in the spring of 1781. But as we have seen, his advisers found that, if he was to get control of his Jamaican estates and their produce when he came of age on September 29th, preliminary action had to be taken against Richard Beckford. His presence in England by the Spring was therefore essential, and he unwillingly returned.

But whatever the trouble behind the scenes, no money was spared to make his coming-of-age celebrations worthy of the richest heir in England. He himself must have played a great part in their conception and production. For he loved theatrical effects, and wished to emulate the splendours he had seen in Italy and the descriptions of the Courts of China and Japan.

As evening drew on, a thousand lamps glimmered in the trees of the Park and the surrounding groves; they were reflected in the waters of the River Nadder and the lake in front of Splendens. Skiffs sped along its surface in every direction, recalling a Venetian regatta. The portico of the house and its sweeping colonnades were illumined by wax torches, which cast a wavering light on the groups lounging on the broad flight of steps below. Opposite the portico was erected an illuminated triumphal arch, so that a great piazza was formed in front of the house, reminiscent of St. Peter's. In the background three bonfires glowed on the Downs, reminding Beckford of Troy and Hector's funeral. At intervals fireworks exploded and Catherine-wheels burst in clusters of stars, which shed a bluish light upon all below; this was greeted with shouts by the tenantry, who were swilling beer in three great tents, each with its own band. By contrast, in the intervals wind instruments sounded, concealed in thickets. Then silence reigned whilst the greatest *castrato* in Europe, Pacchierotti, sang in a *terzetto* so seductive that Beckford nearly swooned.

At ten o'clock it was still as mild as May; Beckford and his most distinguished guests passed under the triumphal arch, the crowd dividing respectfully before them. They ascended a hill on the left of the house crowned by a classical temple in an oak-grove. It was lit up by "a continuous glow of saffron-coloured flame, and the throng assembled before it looked dark and devilish by contrast". When they stood under its portico and "looked down on the plain below, the scene was nearly allied to enchantment. The hum and buzz of such a multitude in groves but a few hours ago so solitary, struck me beyond expression. I could not believe myself at Fonthill. I rubbed my eyes and thought the whole a dream", wrote Beckford.[1]

In the midnight darkness a last display burst briefly upon wondering eyes before the gloom of an English Sabbath descended upon the company; the sky was filled with Catherine-wheels and elegant sprays of aigrettes. The evening, heightened by Beckford's imagination and backed by his reading, was enough to inspire *Vathek*.

The writing of this book was finally stimulated by a party at Fonthill that Christmas, to which Beckford invited a few friends—his cousin Louisa (Mrs. Peter) Beckford, her sister Harriet, a few boys and their tutor Samuel Henley, Alexander Cozens, the respectable daughters of Lord Dunmore (last governor of Virginia) and others.

Half a century later Beckford described it in glowing terms: "through all these galleries did we roam hand in hand, strains of music swelling forth at intervals . . . Sometimes a chaunt was heard, issuing no one could devine from whence—innocent affecting sounds that stole into the heart with a bewitching languour . . . Delightful indeed were these romantic wanderings; delightful the straying about this little interior world of exclusive happiness, surrounded by lovely beings in all the freshness of their early bloom, so fitted to enjoy it. Here, nothing was dull or vapid; here, nothing ressembled in the least the common forms and usages, the *train-train* and routine of fashionable existence . . . Even the uniform splendour of gilded roofs was partially obscured by the vapour of wood aloes, ascending in wreaths from cassolettes placed low on the silken carpets . . . I still feel warmed and irradiated by the recollections of that strange, necromantic light which Loutherbourg had thrown over what absolutely appeared a realm of Fairy, or rather perhaps, a Demon Temple deep beneath the earth, set apart for tremendous mysteries; and yet how soft, how genial was this quiet light. Whilst the wretched world without lay dark and bleak and howling, whilst the storm was raging against our massive walls and the snow drifting in clouds, the very air of summer seemed playing around us; the choir of low-toned melodious voices continued to soothe our ear; and, that every sense might in turn receive its blandishment, tables covered with delicious viands and fragrant flowers glided forth by the aid of mechanism at stated intervals, from the richly draped and amply curtained recesses of the enchanted precincts. The glowing haze investing every object, the mystic look, the vastness, the intricacy of this vaulted labyrinth occasioned so bewildering an effect that it became impossible for anyone to define at the moment where he stood, where he had been, or to whither he was wandering; such was the confusion, the perplexity so many illuminated storeys of infinitely varied apartments gave rise to. It was, in short, the realization of romance in its most extravagant intensity."[2]

From the nonsense that Louisa and Beckford scribbled to each other, it has been deduced that Black Magic was practised at this party. A typical sentence used in this argument (quoted from one of Louisa's letters) runs as follows: "My love, you are irresistable, and if I can but lure Harriot within the attractive sphere of your influence I do not doubt but she will fall into your arms an easy prey to your seductions and her own desires".[3] If this was to be taken literally, it would mean that Louisa was promoting an intrigue between her sister Harriet and Beckford, with whom she herself was in love! The following phrase in Beckford's letter to Cozens has also been thought significant: "That night in particular haunts my imagination, when we arrived from Salisbury and seemed transported to a warm illuminated palace raised by spells in some lonely wilderness". But we shall see that this merely refers to the effects produced by Loutherbourg's interior lighting and stage management at Fonthill.

Beckford thought, spoke and wrote all his life in these 'magical' terms. In 1779, for example, when he was overcome by the stained-glass windows of York Minster which filled him with religious feelings, he used words like 'magic', 'enchantment' and 'illusion'.[4] This *façon de parler* was part of that growing interest in the supernatural and the psychological, which produced the Gothick Terror novels of Mrs. Radcliffe and 'Monk' Lewis. It was also a literary style, inspired by the descriptions of enchanted gardens in Spencer, Tasso and Ariosto, and above all by Milton's apparent glorification of Satan in *Paradise Lost*. It would be ridiculous to assume that artists like Martin, who glorified Satan in their illustrations of Milton, practised Black Magic.

What Beckford loved at his party was the tender sentimentality; the presence of 'lovely beings' of both sexes in 'their early bloom'; the appeal to the senses made by fabrics, food and music; the striking contrast with the wintry world outside; the conspiracy of the young against their disapproving elders; the make-believe and, above all, the theatrical manipulations of Loutherbourg.

For he, and not Cozens, was the central figure at the party. Since his arrival in England in 1771 he had been chief designer of scenery at Drury Lane under Garrick and Sheridan. He revolutionised the art of scenery on the English stage, was a master of lighting, and invented most of the modern methods of reproducing the sounds of thunder, wind and wave.

At this party Loutherbourg may first have displayed the most original scene of his entertainment called "Imitations of Natural Phenomena, represented by Moving Pictures". Its mechanism, and the panorama, were known as The Eidophusikon. Pictures were moved on a stage; the changing atmospheric effects, which were its chief feature, were produced by the manipulation of coloured glass and gauze in front of lamps. The effect was heightened by appropriate sounds and music. Loutherbourg's exhibitions had their first two seasons in London in 1781, and ended just before he came down to Fonthill.[5] London was taken by storm. The scenes resembled the paintings of the elder Vernet and other contemporaries—Sunset near Naples, the Moon rising over the Mediterranean, etc., culminating in the finale, a Storm at Sea with Shipwreck.

The third season started soon after Loutherbourg left Fonthill. There was a new finale, called "Satan arraying his troops on the banks of the Fiery Lake, and the raising of [the Palace of] Pandemonium" in Hell; it was based on the First Book of *Paradise Lost*. The artist, W. H. Pyne, watched this and saw "in the foreground of a vista, stretching an immeasurable length between mountains ignited from their bases to their lofty summits with many-coloured flame, a chaotic mass rising in dark majesty, which gradually assumed form until it stood, the interior of a vast temple of gorgeous architecture, bright as molten brass, seemingly composed of unconsuming and unquenchable fire".⁶ The hues changed from sulphurous blue and lurid red to a livid brightness. The horror was heightened by peals of thunder and "a variety of groans that struck the imagination as issuing from infernal spirits".

Now Milton was one of the favourite poets of Beckford, who was always preoccupied with the theme of Hell. He thought of Fonthill during the party as "a Demon Temple deep beneath the earth"; he says that the scenery engineered there by Loutherbourg inspired his description of the Halls of Eblis (the Prince of Hell) in *Vathek*, written shortly afterwards. All this suggests that Loutherbourg first displayed this finale at Fonthill and perhaps devised it for the party; he may have got his inspiration from Beckford.

Loutherbourg must have been important in Beckford's life. But the latter's interest in light effects was innate, and developed independently, fostered by his love of Rembrandt and of pictures in general, and stimulated by his reading on China. As early as September 1778 he made a note of "the luxurious Emperor Ki who, deserting the career of government, buried himself with his Empress in a palace lighted with an artificial sun".

So, when he visited St. Peter's two years later, he saw himself as a Chinese Emperor, comfortably settled on its 'field of marble': "The windows I should shade with transparent curtains of yellow silk, to admit the glow of perpetual summer. Lanterns, as many as you please, of all forms and sizes; they would remind us of China, and, depending from the roof of the palace, bring before us that of the Emperor Ki, . . . for his Imperial Majesty, being tired of the sun, would absolutely have a new firmament of his own creation, and an artificial day. Was it not a rare fantastic idea? For my part, I should like of all things to immure myself after his example, with those I love; forget the divisions of time, have a moon at command, and a theatrical sun to rise and set at pleasure."⁷

He was determined to give concrete expression to his dreams, and his wealth enabled him to do so. According to *The Rambler's Magazine*, in December 1782 he prepared an entertainment which centred round the idea of an artificial sun: "Great preparations are making at Mr. B—'s for an entertainment in a new style. It is to be [as] perfectly Eastern as our climate and customs will permit. A large temporary building is to be erected in the pleasure ground, which is to be gravelled, and divided into walks, by the finest exotic shrubs. A clear sky, painted overhead, illuminated by an artificial sun, a gallery supported by pilasters, encrusted with mother-of-pearl, is devoted to the music; both the instruments and the composition Indian."

His idea of being immured in a strange and luxurious tower is frequently mentioned long before the building of Fonthill Abbey. These early references show that his later seclusion at Fonthill was not merely the result of social ostracism; it was the fulfilment of a dream, developed by his youthful reading. He noted the tower of the Chinese Empress Tan-ki, whose illumination counterfeited "the warm glow of an evening sky. By this serene light the Empress often passed six months in a continual round of secret and voluptuous pleasures, without beholding the sun. None but her favourites presumed to violate the retirement of these magnificent chambers, which were strewed every morning with fresh flowers and heaped with the rarities of distant Kingdoms."[8] The next sentence in the book tells us that "she used to assemble young people of both sexes, whom she made undress and herself excited to the worst infamies".

The Empress Tan-ki was the wife of the last ruler of the Second Dynasty, who reigned from 1154 B.C. They were an unspeakable pair, of a type frequently found in Beckford's reading. The Emperor was lively and a great talker, a cruel libertine with extravagant tastes; he artfully eluded the counsels he was given, and was adept at concealing his faults. The Empress was also avaricious and quickly dominated her husband. One of their hobbies was torturing; they invented a new machine and roared with laughter when watching their burning victims.

As he made notes from books by missionaries and ambassadors in China, Beckford identified himself with the scene. Here he is with the Russian Ambassador, Ysbrants Ides, being entertained in a sumptuous hall in Pekin by the Emperor's uncle, the Viceroy Sungut Doriamba: "I should have delighted in seeing that vast Hall, adorned with gilded statues and filled with tables covered with such a variety of exotic dishes, intermixed with pyramids of fruit and vases of flowers. What pleasure would the strange Chinese play acted during the repast have given me, and the silver brasiers smoking with oderiferous Kalemba. How I should have enjoyed myself when, seated with the Doriamba on sumptuous thrones spread with the skins of tygers, observing the agility of the dancers and hearkening to a concert of flutes and voices which animated their movements."[9] The dancers were "little boys dressed in girls' cloaths, who very skilfully measured their steps in proportion to the time of the song, and played on the flute, withal, distorting their bodies into antick postures, and playing with a fan in their hands".[10]

The despotism, magnificence and luxury of the Emperors chiefly attracted Beckford. But his satirical sense peeps out: "The Koutouchtou Lama was visited by two Siberian priests, sent by the Archbishop of Tobolski to propagate the Christian faith amongst the Mongalls. They found [him] in the midst of a vast encampment, seated on a cushion of State in a magnificent tent of China velvet, encircled by a multitude of Lamas—some reading attentively in certain mysterious books, others holding censers of perfume. The trumpets sounding, a crowd of votaries entered and, prostrating themselves before the pontif, offered tea, hydromel and sweetmeats in cups of the finest porcelaine, whilst the

THE ORIGINS OF VATHEK, 1780-1781

tents echoed with acclamations . . . After these transports were a little subsided, the pontif asked the missionaries several curious questions, such as if they could tell exactly the number of the Dead, etc.; upon which they begged to be informed of that of the Living."[11]

Beckford was particularly interested in Mulai Ismail, Emperor of Morocco (1672-1727), a ghastly sadist without a redeeming feature. His courtiers were abject, out of superstitious reverence for him as a supposed descendant of the Prophet. "These notions", Beckford notes with interest, "he takes care to maintain by artifice and hypocrisy, strenuously maintaining the Law of the Prophet and making it subservient to all his purposes. Often praying and prostrating himself on the ground in public, being desirous to persuade his people that in these trances and sudden fits of devotion he receives inspirations from on high."[12] Voltaire said of him "he cut off heads every Friday after prayers". He attacked his favourite, a young man, when in a rage, and then sent him a bag of money, desiring (too late) that he might recover. Beckford sometimes beat his employees and then, in a fit of remorse, sent them golden guineas!

The Emperor's troubled conscience made him rise early; after prayer, he visited his extensive building works, where all would "taste of his anger in their turns—beating, killing or giving good words, according to the humour he is in. This is one of his top pleasures." Like Beckford at Fonthill, he sought distraction in building, to which he was wonderfully addicted—"eternally building and pulling down, shutting up doors and breaking out new ones in the walls. But he tells them this is done to occupy his people; for, says he, if I have a bag full of rats, unless I keep that bag stirring they will eat their way through."

But in vain. The Emperor's attendants "report his sleep is often disturbed and full of horror; that he starts up and calls upon those he has destroyed, frequently asking for them; and if any answer 'He is dead', he presently replies 'Who killed him?'. To which they must answer 'God', unless they have a mind to follow." On one occasion his victim appeared to him in a dream and warned him that "there would be a time when God would judge between them both".

He was surrounded by Yes-men who cried out "God lengthen thy days, my Lord", and swore by Allah that he was right. Boys were educated from their infancy in the Palace to become his Bodyguard and obey his every whim. "T'is wonderful", notes Beckford, "to see the insolence, state and gravity of these young rogues; how they ape the old Emperor in the haughty phrases of command, and how familiarly they talk of strangling and extermination".

He was said to have 700 sons; when Beckford noted this, the shadow of his own father loomed over him! To his favourite sons the Emperor was most generous, like Alderman Beckford to his bastards.

Another figure who similarly impressed Beckford was Gilles de Laval, Marshal of Retz, usually called Gilles de Rais, the Bluebeard of Orleans. A brave soldier, he campaigned with Joan of Arc. He was burnt at the stake for alleged sodomy, witchcraft, heresy and murder; he squandered his fortune through love of ostentation, and resorted to magic to get it back.

Beckford read about him in a fine red morocco volume stamped in gold with Louis XIV's arms—Lobineau's *Histoire de Bretagne*. Lobineau states that he was a man of illustrious birth who came into his fortune as a young man, on his father's death. He refused to listen to his guardian's advice, and embarked on a career of extravagance and debauchery. He travelled about with a suite of 200 mounted men, which even the greatest Princes could hardly afford, and with a Chapel, complete with organ. This was served by thirty people, including choirboys, musicians and chaplains; they were clad in scarlet fur-lined cloaks with heraldic devices. The altar was covered in cloth-of-gold and silk; on it were censers,

THE ORIGINS OF VATHEK, 1780-1781

chalices, crosses and candlesticks. His table was open to all and loaded with exquisite dishes. In his private theatre he delighted in farces. He was not a frequenter of women, but smothered many a child with his infernal caresses; here Beckford notes that "the unfortunate victims of his lubricity only had an attraction for him at the moment of death". During his trial, he blamed his misdeeds on his upbringing, when pleasure and self-will were his only guides.

All this Beckford noted in French in the back of his copy,[13] which was then accidentally put in the 1823 Fonthill sale and bought by a journalist, whom Beckford dubs Mr. Cant, "one of the literary assassins". The latter at first asked £100 for it, but returned it to Beckford for 15 guineas, after being threatened with legal action if he dared to make use of the note.[14]

Beckford made a separate jotting about Lobineau's book and Gilles on the back of a receipt dated April 1790; so we cannot claim Lobineau as a source for *Vathek*, but it is typical of the reading which helped to produce the latter. Gilles was an important figure for later authors of the Romantic movement. But the first, and by far the earliest reference to him which Professor Praz notes is in the Marquis de Sade's *Justine*, published in 1791;[15] de Sade wrote much about him in at least two of his books.

It does not follow from Beckford's reading that he was a wicked or unpleasant man—any more than the millions who avidly follow Press reports of murders and trials; in doing so they participate in the drama and even identify themselves with one of the parties to the crime. For Beckford there is the excuse that this was the material for his creative work. Also, many of his contemporaries had the same love of the sadistic and macabre; this was the beginning of modern psychological interest in the curious by-ways of the human spirit, and was a characteristic of Romanticism, of which Beckford was a pioneer. Although he had been reading this ghoulish material all his life, it was particularly concentrated between 1778 and 1781, and formed the imaginative literary background for the writing of *Vathek* in 1782.

Chapter VII

VATHEK AND ITS EPISODES

It is not generally realised that Vathek was a historical figure (as Beckford proclaims in his opening sentence). As he said later: "I have truth to work upon in my dreams, and some truth I must have".[1] Vathek was the Caliph al-Wāthik Bi'llāh, son of the Caliph al-Mu'tasim Bi'llāh, and grandson of Harun al-Rashid. Beckford was attracted by the opposing character and career of father and son, and their similarity to him and his father.

There are many superficial points of resemblance between Vathek's historical father Motassem (as Beckford called him) and the Alderman. Both succeeded a brother, were intolerant and unorthodox, none too well educated, great builders, ruthless and aggressive, and millionaires with many children and slaves. Motassem is said to be the first caliph to add the name of God to his own, the suffix Bi'llāh meaning "he who is preserved and defended by the Grace of God", and his successors did the same. This is reminiscent of the megalomania of the Beckfords, who thought of themselves as a race apart, and of our Beckford's attitude to St. Anthony of Padua. Beckford was so interested in Motassem that he devoted a special *Episode of Vathek* to him, which he subsequently destroyed as improper.[2]

The son of Motassem was an unworthy weakling: Vathek was neither soldier nor statesman, but he was interested in poetry, singing and sensual pleasures. He was liberal to the poor and would have no beggars in his realm. He had a short and undistinguished reign, dying in his thirties in 847 A.D. D'Herbelot adds that he was superstitious and a patron of letters, and describes his terrible eye.

Vathek is clearly autobiographical. There are also independent indications of this. In his youth Beckford wrote of himself as he did later of Vathek. For example, about 1780 he noted: "My apartment shall be in the highest story of the tower . . . from whence I may observe the course of planets and indulge my astrological fancies. Here I shall esteem myself under the peculiar influence of the stars." Vathek too built a tower in order to penetrate the secrets of Heaven and divine his fate.

Secondly, Redding noticed that Beckford sometimes thought of himself as Vathek, and that other people got the same impression and felt that he personified Vathek.[3] Redding also noted that all the strange stories about him at Fonthill had one feature in common—they equated Vathek with his creator: "differing as they did, there was one point upon which all [these stories] agreed; and that was that Mr. Beckford was the type of his own Vathek—a half human, half demon sort of being".[4]

Lastly, Beckford was particularly touchy about any criticism of *Vathek:* "He was never displeased at wonderments spoken or written about him[self]. On the contrary, he was generally disposed to laugh heartily at them when they only attacked himself; but he did not like for his writings to be censured. *Vathek* was his favorite. To abuse *Vathek* he deemed a personal insult; his pride took the alarm and he could scarcely restrain his anger, so fierce when aroused, though evanescent."[5]

The autobiographical character of Beckford's writings is most easily analysed in his three *Episodes of Vathek*, which are appendages to the main story and were intended for publication with it.[6] The first Episode, *The Story of Prince Alasi and the Princess Firouz-kah*, shows the development of his friendship with Courtenay. The early editions of *Vathek* in French were more honest over the title, referring to it as *Histoire des deux princes amis, Alasi et Firouz!* As its text stands, Beckford lost his nerve and deferred to his readers' prejudice half-way through by turning Prince Firouz (Courtenay) into his sister Firouz-kah. But she looks exactly like him, and later dons male attire again!

The story opens with Alasi in a position similar to Beckford's after he had come of age. Alasi is unattracted by the idea of marriage, although he allowed his parents to arrange an engagement for State reasons. All he dares do is to delay his marriage. "With this almost misanthropic repulsion from the ordinary ways of men, I had to ascend a throne, to govern a numerous people, to endure the ineptitude of the great, and the folly of the meaner folk, to do justice to all, in a word, to live among my subjects."

Beckford was always afraid of being committed emotionally, and so the friendship with Courtenay was at first innocent enough: "Love, which in its own shape would have been repelled, took Friendship's shape, and in that shape effected my ruin," says Alasi. We can understand Beckford's yearning for the *disinterested* friendship which Courtenay seemed to offer: millionaires are usually lonely people, surrounded by sycophants and unable to tell who loves them for themselves rather than their money. "At last", says Alasi, "Heaven has hearkened to my dearest wish. It has sent me the true heart's-friend I should never have found in my court; it has sent him to me adorned with all the charms of innocence —charms that will be followed, at a maturer age, by those good qualities that make of friendship man's highest blessing, and, above all, the highest blessing of a prince, since disinterested friendship is a blessing that a prince can scarcely hope to enjoy."

We even get a disguised account of Courtenay's first impact on him: "The sound of Firouz' voice, his words, his looks, seemed to confuse my reason, and made my speech come low and haltingly. He perceived the tumult raging in my breast, and, to appease it, abandoned a certain langour and tenderness of demeanour that he had so far affected, and assumed the childish gaiety and vivacity natural to his years; for he did not appear to be much more than thirteen."

When Beckford married in 1783 he still retained his affection for Courtenay; as Alasi says to Firouz: "What is there in common between the affection I shall owe to my wife, and the affection I shall ever entertain for yourself". But Firouz became increasingly tyrannical; he was spoiled and arrogant, with an essentially bad heart. Although Alasi perceived this, he was powerless. Firouz "played upon me as he listed. Besides, he had himself well in hand, knew how to act so as to excite my sympathy, and to seem yielding and amenable, as it served his purpose." For an irresistible force compelled Alasi to love him; but he could not understand his feelings, so contrary to reason and good sense: "Friend of my soul, Fate alone can be answerable for the strange and unaccountable feelings of our hearts".

Firouz' character is painted black, and he is seen as the corrupting influence. Was it that Beckford turned round and blamed Courtenay for his own fate and his own weakness? All that we subsequently know of Courtenay, and the portrait of him by Romney in 1791, support Beckford's judgement. In the parallel case of Oscar Wilde and Lord Alfred Douglas, we know that it was the latter who was the corrupter and who exploited his older friend's weakness. Beckford had projected too much upon Courtenay, as he did on every new friend. But long before the scandal he feared that the most careful tutoring "will not prevent his being a trifling inconsistent character".[7]

The turning point in Alasi's life came when he believed the deceitful youth at a critical juncture, in preference to his fiancée; after that, she was compelled to abandon him to his fate. Perhaps Beckford thought that his own marriage gave him the opportunity to transfer his affections and loyalties in the usual way, instead of shilly-shallying between the two. Then, when he let that golden opportunity pass, he was unable to escape from the net of ambiguous entanglements. Thus, when Alasi was bound by crime to Firouz, he felt that he could not retrace his steps or take a different road; he had already chosen between God and His enemies. " 'O Mahomet! . . . thou hast forsaken me utterly and without hope! What refuge have I, save with thine enemies?' . . . I could not recall the past, probably I should not have recalled it if I could. No course was open to me save to leap, with eyes self-bound, into the yawning abyss of the future." (p. 46).

Now, on their way to Hell, they were committed irrevocably to each other: "It was already night when we came to the Terrace of the Beacon Lights; and, notwithstanding all that we could say to one another of endearment and encouragement, we were filled with a kind of horror as we walked it from end to end. There was no moon in the firmament to shed upon us its soft rays. The stars alone were shining there; but their trembling light only seemed to intensify the sombre grandeur of all that met our gaze. We regretted, indeed, none of the beauties, none of the riches of the world we were about to leave. We thought only of living in a world where we should be for ever inseparable." (p. 47). Beckford wrote similarly about preferring the company of young pathics "to all goods or titles and to all glory present and future".[8]

But even this was an illusion. Beckford foresaw that the punishment of those "criminal souls" was "the final extinction of every feeling save hatred and despair". For at the end Alasi says: "What a god have we served! What a fearful doom has he pronounced upon us! What! we who had loved one another so well, must our love be turned to hate? We, who had come hither to enjoy an eternity of love, must we hate each other to all time!" Whatever we may think of this as a prophecy of the ultimate outcome of such attachments, the fact remains that these friendships of Beckford's did end in frustration and recrimination.

The second Episode, *The Story of Prince Barkiarokh*, is the most horrifying thing that Beckford ever wrote. The Prince has no redeeming feature and revels in evil. He is an adept at concealing his real character: "To veil their vices from the sight of the good is the only resource of those who are not blind, and know themselves to be vicious. Thus was I confirmed in habits of hypocrisy." (p. 58)

The divided character, warring against itself, is portrayed when Queen Gulzara describes the shock she receives on re-meeting her old 'flame', Prince Tograi, whom she now finds ruthless, unscrupulous and cruel: "I thought I saw before me Tograi, amiable and compliant, as when . . . he came to say good-bye to me seven years ago; and then that old Tograi vanished, and behold the new Tograi, overbearing and perfidious, took his place and gave me advice . . . unrighteous and dishonourable. Never, never, will these two images cease to haunt me. Death alone can deliver me from them." (p. 95). She takes this terrible change, this double image to heart: "See that Gehanguz [my steward] makes the interior of my palace as sad and sombre as is my heart."

Barkiarokh is often brought to a standstill by the inner conflict between his 'criminal desires' and his conscience; the latter is pictured as 'the wand of remorse', the wand of the good fairy (the Peri); it strikes him a crippling blow, without warning, as he is about to indulge himself. The resulting tension and inhibition are so frustrating that a violent explosion, a fit of temper, follows.

On one occasion, Barkiarokh was about to enjoy the fruit of his crime: his two sisters-in-law had for his sake and with his connivance despatched their husbands;

they came to announce it; but as they spoke, he was struck down by remorse; he then arose in a rage of mingled self-hatred and frustration: "I was alone with the two wretches, and coldly listening to the recital of their accursed crime, when the Peri's wand struck me with such force that I fell down as if killed. A moment after, I rose from the ground in an inconceivable fury, and having seized my two accomplices, I pierced them through and through again and again with my dagger, and cast their bodies into the sea. To this involuntary act of justice succeeded new transports of despair. I yelled imprecations against myself till my voice failed, and I fell into a swoon." (p. 144). This perfectly describes Beckford's own famous rages.

This recurrent cycle develops into a process, a hardening of the heart. At length Remorse degenerates into Despair. Barkiarokh's fairy wife Homaïouna, whom he has so often deceived and deserted, leaves him. He sinks down into Hell, blaspheming horribly, and is told that "henceforward the rod that will beat upon thy heart is the rod of Despair; and thy heart, hardened as it is, will be broken and crushed throughout every moment of a frightful eternity". (p. 160).

In *Barkiarokh* Beckford introduces a well-known perversion (necrophilia), which must be one of the earliest examples in Western fiction, although later Romantic writers also describe it. Gazahidé, deeply wronged by Barkiarokh, fell into a death-like swoon when surprised by him. "So dire an accident ought to have been as a curb to my passion; on the contrary, it acted as a spur . . . [*sic*]. Ashamed and despairing, I issued from the apartment, hiding my head with the skirt of my robe . . . This first visit was followed by several others of a similar kind. The woman I sought to embrace was always inert and seemingly dead,[9] and I always quitted her with horror. Often, after issuing from Gazahidé's apartment, I rushed away to the mosque, and there beat my breast with such violence that the spectators were lost in admiration at seeing a king as zealous, as much a martyr in the cause of penitence, as the most enthusiastic of fakirs." (pp. 128-9). One recollects Beckford's interest in the perversion of Gilles de Rais, and the love-scene in the burial-vault which he wrote at the age of seventeen.

There is a dreadful refrain of Voices calling down Vengeance: "suddenly an infinite number of voices rang through the palace: 'Vengeance! Vengeance! Let all doors be closed, let every sword be drawn! . . .' I made all haste to get out of the palace. But every avenue was closed; swords swept glittering in all directions." (pp. 122-3).

The third Episode is *The Story of the Princess Zulkaïs and the Prince Kalilah*, concerning the Princess' inordinate affection for her twin brother Kalilah, and her father's vain attempt to separate them. As a forbidden relationship, it corresponds to Beckford's with Courtenay. If the latter was like this, it was not sexual but emotional. The childish dream in which Beckford often indulged in his reveries about Courtenay occurs here—the desire to take a drug that "will lull us painlessly to sleep in each other's arms, and so bear our souls imperceptibly into the peace of another existence!" (p. 189).

The story opens with a superb sketch of Alderman Beckford as a buccaneering Merchant-Prince, under the guise of the Emir Abou Taher Achmed. The boyhood of his son, Prince Kalilah, is remarkably like Beckford's. Kalilah's father was over-anxious for him to be outstanding, and subjected him to a rigorous course of study above his years. The fears and disappointment of the Beckford family during his youth and when he was later dallying with Courtenay are exactly expressed in the story: "Must the sun, as it rises and sets, see you only bloom and fade like a weak narcissus flower? Vainly do the Sages try to move you by the most eloquent discourses, and unveil before your eyes the learned mysteries of an older time; vainly do they tell you of warlike and magnanimous deeds. You are now nearly thirteen, and never have you evinced the smallest ambition to distinguish yourself among your fellow-men. It is not in the lurking haunts of effeminacy that great characters are formed; it is not by reading love poems that men are made fit to govern nations! Princes must act; they must show themselves to the world." (p. 184).

In the story, Beckford (now under the guise of Zulkaïs) is encouraged in his rebellion against his family and his forbidden love by a sinister figure who must represent Alexander Cozens. The portrait of Cozens is far from flattering, and is similar to that of the old Jew in *L'Esplendente*, but now he is an avowed practiser of magic, a perverted servant of Eblis, the Prince of Hell. He advises Zulkaïs to call to the Spirits for aid to further her connection with her brother.

The story breaks off unfinished, with one of Beckford's most imaginative and striking pictures. Zulkaïs, under the guidance of the old man, has descended into Hell in order to join her love Kalilah:

"A solitary taper of enormous size, fixed upright in a block of marble, lighted up a vast hall, and discovered to my eyes five staircases, whose banisters, made of different metals, faded upwards into the darkness. There we stopped, and the old man broke the silence, saying 'Choose between these staircases . . .' He [then] disappeared, and I heard a door closing behind him. Judge of my terror, you who have heard the ebony portals, which confine us for ever in this place of torment, grind upon their hinges! . . .

"Suddenly a voice, clear, sweet, insinuating like the voice of Kalilah, flattered my ears. I seemed, as in a dream, to see him on the staircase of which the banisters were of brass . . . 'Zulkaïs', said Kalilah, with an afflicted air, 'Allah forbids our union. But Eblis . . . extends to us his protection. Implore his aid, and follow the path to which he points you.'

"I awoke in a transport of courage and resolution, seized the taper, and began, without hesitation, to ascend the stairway with the brazen banister. The steps seemed to multiply beneath my feet; but my resolution never faltered; and, at last, I reached a chamber, square and immensely spacious, and paved with a marble that was of flesh colour, and marked as with the veins and arteries of the human body. The walls of this place of terror were hidden by huge piles of carpets of a thousand kinds and a thousand hues, and these moved slowly to and fro, as if painfully stirred by human creatures stifling beneath their weight. All around were ranged black chests, whose steel padlocks seemed encrusted with blood."

On and off between about 1780 and 1783 Beckford worked hard upon a famous group of Arabic manuscripts of the *Arabian Nights*; they had been brought back from the Near East by Edward Wortley Montagu, son of Lady Mary. Beckford translated a number more or less freely into French, and at the beginning of 1787 publicly announced that he proposed to publish them in due course.[10]

Had he published them in English, he would have been the first to translate stories from the *Arabian Nights* into good literary English and from the Arabic instead of from the French translation by Galland, which was first printed in 1704. It was Galland who introduced them to Europe, where his version reigned supreme for more than a century. Additional tales were published in French as late as 1788 and in English in 1794, and Galland was still being translated in 1811. This shows how early Beckford was in the field. Why didn't he persist? Perhaps he was too dilettante; perhaps he was prevented by the sale of the manuscripts in 1787 to the Professor of Hebrew and Arabic at Oxford. It is remarkable that a young man in his position should have tackled such a difficult job; it shows his talent, industry and originality.

VATHEK AND ITS EPISODES

The manuscripts were described in 1799 in Sir William Ouseley's *Oriental Collections*; and it was known that their new owner, Jonathan Scott, was planning to translate them. So Beckford hastily printed the only story which he had already translated into English as well as French. It was called *Al Raoui*, and was the last 'Arabian' tale of any sort that he published. He had translated it in 1783, after finishing *Vathek*.[11] It is a feeble story, but Beckford translated or composed in French a short *Suite* or tail-piece, which is far better. Unfortunately he could not print it because it contains a homosexual episode, which is erotic but not pornographic.

In this particular episode in Beckford's story the narrator is a disconsolate young man who tells of his recent encounter with a beautiful youth. He had just met him, and was making advances to him. The youth suddenly broke away, saying he wished to leave. The young man was beside himself. He abjectly offered the youth all his wealth, if only he would remain. The youth agreed on condition that he would allow himself to be shaved so that they both appeared equally young. The young man submitted, and was impatient for the youth to finish shaving him. " 'I was expecting', said the young man, 'to pluck the soft fruit of my complaisance. But when he had finished shaving me, the youth stared at me, burst out laughing and, going behind me, gave me such a kick in the arse that I fell on my face. He disappeared'. . . At this point in the story, the Emir of Grand Cairo [to whom Al Raoui was retailing it] laughed so heartily that he fell backwards into his sofa. At length, he said to Al Raoui, 'But what became of Feidah?'. 'She was no better than the youth and the blind man',[12] replied Al Raoui: 'Eblis and his friends were let loose that evening. For no sooner had the young man finished telling me this story, than Feidah too disappeared, giving us a great box on the ears'. The young man and I were dumbfounded. We stared at each other and separated without uttering a word—thoroughly resolved to support solitude in the future and to remember the saying *He who cannot relish his own company risks falling into bad company'*."

Here we see the frustration of something keenly anticipated, and are uncomfortably aware of the sardonic beholder who, although driven to these sensual pleasures, sees through them as ludicrous. Beckford was similar. His sardonic eye, his conscience and his inhibitions prevented him from becoming a regular homosexual.

BECKFORD'S BOY FRIEND IN PARIS
Self-portrait of the Chevalier Sequeira, 1826

Chapter VIII

1784: WAS BECKFORD GUILTY?

Beckford's writing was combined in 1782 and 1783 with strenuous attendance at the London season and a second journey to Italy; on this he took a large suite which included Lettice and the artist J. R. Cozens, Alexander's son. The speed with which he travelled and the magnificence of his *equipage* caused him to be mistaken for the Emperor of Austria, who was expected incognito on the same route. This "had the effect of giving a very imperial aspect to the charges on the road. No pains were spared—but in vain—to undeceive the innkeepers, who stoutly resisted every attempt to convince them of an error that must be followed by a reduction of their charges."[1]

But however much he threw himself into the activities round him and the composition of Arabian tales, he could not escape the misery of his equivocal friendships. To some he was like a living parable—a Midas with whom a peasant would not have changed place: "His destiny appears brilliant, for he has a great fortune and talents supposed to be marvellous, and he is young and his own master. How much enjoyment may he not expect from such a fine life! . . . Yet a fever consumes his powers, and up to now nothing stops its progress . . . Mr. Lettice is with him as preceptor, Governor and principal valet-de-chambre—a disagreeable enough combination. And then there are the travelling companions one gets, thanks to money: carriage, horses and innumerable servants—a useless show. Mr. Beckford leaves our Court, his suite astonishing all our countrymen. The least one among them who is in good health and his right senses can congratulate himself a thousandfold."[2]

His family hoped to save him from himself by marrying him off in May 1783 to a young woman nearly his own age, whom he had known for some years—Lady Margaret Gordon, daughter of the Earl of Aboyne and sister of the future Marquis of Huntly. Beckford was not in love with her; but he became attached to her as someone necessary in his life, a tutelary Deity in the background. He even admired her blonde and healthy beauty: "There are not many with whom she need dread competition: she is become slender and delicate, her arms have whitened and their smoothness equals that of your own; the colour which glowed so ruddily in her cheeks is softened into a bloom, like the innermost leaves of a blush rose; the more she pines the lovelier she looks."[3] She was a charming person, artless and uncomplicated; she had no pretensions to intellect, and was an outdoor type.

They spent their honeymoon until February 1784 in Switzerland and Savoy, which once more gave him one of the happiest times of his life. He whipped out his green pocket-book, laid aside since his last visit in 1778, and jotted down accounts of his long expeditions in the mountains round Mont Blanc. His guide was Dr. Michel Paccard, "who seems to have lost almost every trace of that simplicity for which the cottagers of Chamonix were a few years ago so justly distinguished".[4] Three years later Paccard won immortality as the first climber of Mont Blanc and, like Sir Edmund Hillary, became unwillingly involved in a dispute as to whether he or his porter had got there first.

Beckford noticed everything. Near Sallanches he visited the Cascade du Bon-Nant: "from the summit of tremendous cliffs a rapid stream pours down full 500 feet; the gulf which receives it is concealed by a hilloc of greenswerd where I reclined, enjoying the cool spray falling in silver mists from this giddy elevation; a little modest rainbow, its span about ten feet, lurked in the sheltered spot which the waters perpetually freshen, and delighted me with its vivid tints."

The highlight of this summer tour was the exploration of the source of the Arveyron in its ice-cavern beneath the glaciers:

"We leaped several rapid branches of the torrent, and advancing between huge masses of crystalline ice, saw the enchanted grot of the Arve[y]ron full before us. It had not been open, according to the account of our guides, above ten days, and was widening every hour. Large glittering drops were tricling from the azure vault, and every now and then a fragment, detaching itself, fell with the sound of thunder into the torrent. We were too much absorbed in contemplating the celestial blue of the arch to notice for some time the rapid increase of the waters around us; but at length, half stunned with their roar, we made a precipitate retreat.

"A crowd of peasant children met us immediately upon our return into the forest of pines. Some had baskets of strawberries, others cristals; and others little bundles of genista, a plant which the Savoyarde mountaineers (both men and chamois) peculiarly esteem for its medicinal virtues, and which grows alone on the peaks of the loftiest mountains."

Little is known about Beckford's wife, but we get a glimpse of her on these expeditions. Beckford walked and scrambled in the company of an unnamed young American and somebody called Le Fort. Whilst they told each other ghoulish stories, and the lightning played before their eyes, "the guides stood aloof, leaning against the black decayed skeleton of a pine and swallowing our discourse with avidity". Lady Margaret Beckford was very much in the background, although they had only been married two months. But from time to time she asserted her presence and surprised them by her boldness in gamely following them over glaciers and up mountains: "Lady M[argaret] surprised our guides by her courage and activity; she crossed the glaciers without making a false step. I confess myself to have been much less alert and far more inattentive. The glittering rocks dazzled my eyes, and my senses, lulled by the silver sound of the waters, were lost in a pleasing delirium. I hardly knew whether I was in the Lord's world or in that of Monsieur Bourrit when I reached the extremity of the glaciers and landed in a grove of pine".[5]

However, as winter drew on, Lady Margaret wrote a happy letter to her aunt about the pleasant evenings spent *en famille* with the Hubers; her *chere mari* sang, or the old man read aloud one of Goldoni's comedies.[6] But there were always young men round—in this case Huber's two sons, whom Beckford had known during his first stay.

The Hubers recalled that happiest time in his life. Then, the crowning moment was the fête which he gave in the Woods of Blonay. Now, he saw them illuminated:

"For six years I had been wishing to see the Wood of Blonay illuminated, and this evening my inclinations were satisfied. A vast floor was laid on the terrace above the Lake, shaded by ancient chestnuts which seemed growing out of it. At the extremity of this verdant gallery rose a pavillion composed of glasses, reflecting with a sort of magic confusion the long perspective of the woods, the steep green banks, the Lake and the mountains. Cristal lustres and garlands of flowers depended from every bough. The solemn verdure of the spruce fir was enlivened by braids of vine and festoons of roses. Enormous tapers, such as decorate the altars of a cathedral, appeared springing from the topmost branches of the chestnuts, many of which rise 50 feet without a bough. The broad green leaves, gilt by the setting sun, checquering a sky of the purest azure, formed our canopy. Thousands of peasants from the mountains of Switzerland, Savoy and the Vallais, in their gayest attire, were

1784: WAS BECKFORD GUILTY?

spread over the side of the hill. No tapestry could have a gayer effect.

"When I entered the wood about five in the evening, the crowd being kept at a distance, the platform was distinctly seen and produced the most majestic effect. I ranged then with perfect freedom under arches formed by the venerable chestnuts, enjoying the cool breath of the Lake, and gazing around me in a sort of delirium. The gay embroidery of flowers, the lustres which appeared as if composed of sparkling gems, and the tapers of pure white wax contrasted in the strangest and most striking manner with the rough trunks and savage branches of the trees which supported them. I could hardly help thinking myself under the influence of enchantment . . . The interesting glow of sunset . . . tinted the spacious floor and the rich masses of foliage with those saffron hues we are so fond of. This golden haze contributed not a little to give the whole scene an appearance like that of the Gardens of the Hesperides.

"Numbers of Savoyardes and Genevoise of the first distinction, many of whom were remarkable for beauty and elegance, were parading up and down the floor, as if conscious how much their charms were heightened by the soft evening light."[7]

In 1784, when Beckford and his wife were back in England, all seemed to be set fair. He sat as M.P. for Wells for a few months; but he soon tired of Parliament and sought a barony with the title of Lord Beckford of Fonthill.[8] It was to be obtained through the influence of his friend Lord Thurlow, the Lord Chancellor. But the clubs were sceptical: at Brooks', Mr. Edward Fawkenor bet Mr. J. M. Smith ten to one that Mr. William Beckford would never be made an English peer.[9] However, the newspapers gave his name as due to appear in the coming Honours list,—and the patent was made out.

Meanwhile, in September and early October he and his wife stayed at Powderham Castle, the home of

William Courtenay, who was now seventeen. Other guests included Courtenay's aunt Charlotte, and Lord Loughborough, who had married her not long before as his second wife; he was more than twice Beckford's age and seventeen years older than Charlotte. Beckford had been mortally afraid of him for a long time. Beckford was the kind of man to whom some people took an instant dislike, which he unwisely exacerbated by his sarcasm and nicknames and by mimicking them and their accent behind their backs. Loughborough, a hard-bitten, rising Scottish lawyer, probably despised Beckford and had been provoked by him. There were other reasons for his hatred. His wife Charlotte had been intimate with Beckford before her marriage and probably in love with him; above all, Beckford was the protegé of his hated political and professional rival Lord Thurlow, whom he later succeeded as Lord Chancellor. Everyone knew that Beckford's coming peerage was due to Thurlow's influence; the latter could be wounded through his protegé's disgrace.

Some untoward incident during Beckford's stay was twisted by Loughborough into a circumstantial story that Beckford and Courtenay had made a "grammatical mistake in regard to the genders".[10] For many months Loughborough applied extreme pressure to the effeminate and cowardly boy, but could not get sufficient evidence for a court of law. Meanwhile, he saw to it that rumours were circulated in the family circle. Lady Margaret's brother, Viscount Strathavon—the 'Strath' of Beckford's boyhood—came down to Fonthill to drag his sister away. He slapped Beckford's face, hoping to provoke him to a duel.[11] To his surprise, his sister refused to leave her husband or side with her own relatives against him; by taking this line, she put herself entirely in Beckford's hands.

Lady Margaret's letter to her aunt seems to prove that nothing wicked happened at Powderham:[12] "I flatter myself you cannot dissaprove of the part I have taken, nor of my conduct; sure, I was not to abandon *a man* who had always *behaved to me* with the *greatest tenderness and affection*. The satisfaction I feel at having acted in the manner I did, is not to be expressed; I every hour see fresh proofs of gratitude and affection from my dear husband. The affection you have always shewn, my dear Lady Gower, makes me believe you will now shew it and stand forth as my friend, now that I want your assistance; and shew by your goodness to me and my husband [that] you do not believe the half of what has been said. I wish it was in my power to persuade you to come down here. I am not well enough to write, and yet have so many things I wish to inform you of, relative to Lord L[oughborough]'s behaviour, that I should take it as the greatest favour in the world; would you but come and see me, I am at apt to think I should convince you how much to blame my brother has been."

After Strathavon's visit, a family council was held to see what could be done. It was decided to send Beckford abroad; his wife could not accompany him because of her pregnancy. He got as far as Dover on October 29th; but he realised that to flee abroad would play into his enemies' hands and vindicate their charge. So he returned to Fonthill. We can imagine his state of mind, alone at Dover, separated from his wife. But even in these circumstances he noticed everything and was amused by the vagaries of human nature: "I rambled about the Port with heaviness of heart, the weather as gloomy as my spirits; passing along the beach, I came under the perpendicular cliffs crowned by the Castle. Snug under one of these I found to my great surprise a little green spot, enlivened with mignionet and gilly flowers; steps cut out in the rock, leading to strange dens with something like gothic entrances, to which an old sea-captain often repairs in the summer months to carouse with a few boon companions. Beneath, lie plains of sea; above, nod the Castle walls, and many a crag mottled with samphire. A little boy showed me about, who seemed to delight greatly in Captain Smith's vagaries—for so is the old man called."[13]

So far, Loughborough had not got much satisfaction. But he was determined to ruin Beckford. At least six weeks after the trouble at Powderham, he unleashed an anonymous Press campaign, towards the end of November. The Press had far more latitude in those days, the law of libel being different. It was enough to ruin a man like Beckford, and it did. Supposing that he had felt able to face the unpleasantness, why did he not bring an action for libel? In such matters he had no chance against an enemy as powerful and experienced as Loughborough, who was Chief Justice of the Common Pleas. And he was prevented from doing so by the existence of "certain dangerous papers", which will be discussed later.

The scandal was now aired in public. The teacups began to rattle. A mere agent, suitably named Beldam(e), wrote to his master in Bath: "The tea-tables are full of the detection of B-kf-d in a scandalous affair with a boy at Mary[le]bone School. It is remarkable how many detections of this sort have happened of late."[14] The pompous bluestockings, whom Beckford had mimicked, shook their heads with an I-told-you-so air, and scribbled with glee to their cronies. Mrs. Elizabeth Carter wrote to Mrs. Montagu, Beckford's neighbour in Portman Square:[15] "I had received an account of B-'s horrid behaviour, but did not know, till by your letter, what was become of him. Poor Lady — is indeed greatly to be pitied. Are you at all acquainted with Lady —? I hear she does not design to quit her wretched husband? This young man at his first setting out, appeared to have such uncommon parts and so much knowledge, that it might have been reasonably hoped, that when the coxcomb was outgrown, he would have made a very distinguished figure in society. When he afterwards so extravagantly and ridiculously addicted himself to music, all prospect of his becoming great or respectable was over; but till this last sad story, I never heard that his conduct was vicious."

The news was retailed overseas. Sir William Hamilton at Naples was sent a highly coloured version about the 'operation' being watched through a keyhole by the boy's tutor, who was delicate enough not to interrupt.[16] Sir William's informant was his nephew, Charles Greville, who had taken the low-born, illiterate Emma Hart off a friend's hands, and was soon to sell her (more or less) to his uncle.

This malicious gossip plunged Beckford into despair. As he read about an outlandish tribe in Siberia, he reflected: "In this despairing mood I wished for one of those mushrooms with which Youkaguirians intoxicate themselves, that I might fancy myself of gigantic size and indued with powers so horrible as with one sweep of my arm to crush my enemies to atoms."[17]

The passage to which he refers is typical of the quaint information given in contemporary travel-books. This nomadic tribe drank more heavily, according to the author, an Anglican clergyman, than any other Northern nation. They distilled wine from a special mushroom, and, when drunk "imagine themselves to be of a gigantic size, and that they possess immense riches. Some lying on their backs sing songs full of lively images; others utter the most extravagant prophecies and rave about futurity. At the height of their rage they make a dreadful noise till they fall fast asleep. Some cannot bear the effect of these mushrooms, being so violent as to produce frenzy and downright madness; and they tell you that this dreadful effect is the certain consequence of enjoying a woman when drunk; therefore the soberer people do all they can to prevent them from indulging both these excesses at once."

Beckford's feeling of helplessness was increased by his Byronic sense of Fate. There was nothing he could do, he felt, to placate the stern and unjust Divine Power

which had given him his strange and complex character:
> "And Fate directs th' event; nor the bent knee,
> Libation pure, or supplicating tear,
> Can sooth the stern rage of those merciless pow'rs
> In whose cold shrine no hallowed flame ascends."[18]

There was reason to despair. When his old friend Huber saw him in 1785, he commented to Mme. de Stael: "This fellow Beckford really is a subject for a moralist. Extravagant conduct, arising from a Don Quixote-like character rather than any depravity, has lost him beyond hope—however exemplary a life he later leads."[19]

*   *   *   *

Was Beckford guilty? He was accused of buggery, as the crime was called in Henry VIII's statute, under which it first became punishable by law in England. (The lesser homosexual practices, known as 'gross indecency', were only recognised by our laws in 1885.)

There is one clue to the evidence which Loughborough obtained against Beckford. In 1789 the lawyer Wildman was urging Beckford to remain abroad, saying that if he returned to re-instate himself in society, his enemies "would have every justification from circumstances for interfering, and as effectually as they might chuse". Beckford angrily commented: "the only method of my enemies interfering effectually would be to produce the wretched book in open daylight; and to such an exposition I am certain L[ord] C[ourtenay] would never consent".[20] (Beckford's former friend William had recently succeeded his father as Viscount Courtenay.)

What was this 'wretched book' which was the only evidence Beckford's enemies had against him, but which so compromised Lord Courtenay that he would not consent to its use? It could not have been a confession wrung from the boy in 1784 that Beckford had criminal relations with him. For then Loughborough would have used it to bring Beckford to trial and have him hanged or, if the feelings of the Beckfords and their friends had any weight with him, to force him abroad at once, for good and all, as the only means of avoiding trial.

But this 'book' may have contained originals or copies of Beckford's high-flown letters to or about the boy. It must be the same as the 'dangerous' and 'obnoxious' 'papers' which Loughborough refused to give up to the boy's father in 1787, for return to Beckford, who considered that their retention by Loughborough prevented him from 'smoothing' his way home to England.[21] The description of them as 'obnoxious papers', which Beckford and his lawyer Wildman had some right to expect back, supports my suggestion that the 'book' was a letter-book of Beckford's letters to or about Courtenay. Once the latter had come of age, his permission for its use would have had to be obtained.

This fits in with the version of the affair which Beckford's mother gave Benjamin West many years later.[22] She mentioned a secret correspondence which young Courtenay's carelessness allowed to fall into their enemies' hands. Of course, she could not admit that they were love-letters to or about a boy; so she pretended that they concerned his aunt Charlotte, Lady Loughborough. It was true that she had been in love with Beckford and that he had written to her intimately about her nephew. So, as we might expect, truth and half-truth were mingled in Mrs. Beckford's version. She may therefore have been correct in stating that Beckford, furious at the boy's blunder, went to his room, locked the door and beat him; the boy screamed; the door was found locked; Beckford was in an awkward position!

If the only independent evidence that Loughborough could obtain was love-letters, we can understand how the Powderham affair remained a matter of unconfirmed Press reports. If Beckford brought a libel action, the letters could be produced; their nature would make everybody assume the worst, and his name would not be cleared; at the same time, he could not be convicted by them. As Sir William Hamilton said later: "no direct accusation lies against him [Beckford], and it is now 20 years since an unfortunate suspicion arose and was maliciously encouraged".[23]

One piece of evidence strongly suggests Beckford's innocence, and shows that he thought that he had been 'framed' in 1784: he followed an unusual trial and considered the case of the victim, Forreste (who was prosecuting), so similar to his own situation in 1784 that he procured a folio manuscript of the trial and placed it in his collection of treasured Manuscripts.[24]

Forreste and his wife, happily married, were intimate with her relations, Edwards and Col. Passingham, who seduced her. He and Edwards then made a conspiracy to force Forreste to agree to a separation and pay his wife a large maintenance, "by charging him with crimes of the most abominable kind". First they circulated reports, then put about letters, and finally produced witnesses on oath and obtained a warrant for his arrest. He was foolish enough to flee, but was caught on the Kentish coast. Fortunately the principal witness broke down and confessed that his evidence was false. Forreste was, as a result, able to bring this action for conspiracy against Passingham. In the witness box "he was frequently so agitated as to be deprived of speech, particularly when the subject of his wife and children was called in question". The evidence revealed many circumstances "at which human nature must shudder," and the jury found Passingham and Edwards guilty of a wicked conspiracy against the innocent Forreste.

It is also fair to conclude on general grounds that Beckford was not guilty of sodomy in 1784 and may never have been, *as far as youths of superior upbringing were concerned*.[25] His inhibitions on religious and emotional grounds were too strong. He was in love with youths like Courtenay, Franchi and Cornaro; but these were romantic and sentimental attachments, usually kept within certain bounds (far though he went). His

1784: WAS BECKFORD GUILTY?

Journal was a very private document, in which he noted all his feelings and experiences. It does not contain a shred of evidence to incriminate him, beyond one incident of kissing.

In fact, this question seems beside the point when we read of the effect of boys on him. Nothing could be more charming than his account of his first meeting with the twelve-year old Mohammed, brother of the Tripolitanian Ambassador in Madrid: "There is a languid tenderness in his eyes, a softness in the contour of his face, and a bewitching [   ] in his smile that enchanted me . . . I was seated on the carpet like an Oriental, to the great delight of . . . little Mohammed, who kept whispering to me with a tone of voice that went to my soul, and pressing my hands with inconceivable tenderness. I thought myself in a dream—nay, I still think myself so, and expect to wake. What is there in me to attract the affection of these infidels at first sight, I cannot imagine. Mohammed and I continued drinking each other's looks . . . with such avidity that we forgot how the time passed, and were startled upon quitting one instant the contemplation of each other to find the saloon illuminated with three vast lustres, the musicians placed in due order, the pages standing in solemn rows."[26]

Considering how natural to Beckford these feelings were, he seemed to be caught in the toils of Fate. The hopelessness and danger of his situation comes in a dream sent to the Countess Rosenberg after his return from Italy. He recollects the hours spent with her and an unnamed 'child' (*ma chère A*); as soon as his feelings are aroused, everything becomes stormy, the face of the beloved is blotted out, and he finds himself stretching out his arms to a brazen and indifferent sky. "Still, in my dreams", he writes, "I range over the lagoons by the gleam of the reddish clouds reflected in the water. The gondolas flash past like arrows; Fusina's shore is almost lost in the mists of sunset; . . . I hear the mournful pealing of the bells. You are stretched beside me, your face lit up by the reflection of the blood-red clouds floating above our heads; . . . I am about to speak of *ma chère A* . . . when a storm rises and the transparent beauty of the sky is darkened. The waves boil and our boat is engulphed. You perish before my eyes. I myself feel the agonies of death. I awake, crying out and raising my arms to a God who no longer desires to hear me."[27]

As he became older and more cynical, his tone changed; his letters from Fonthill Abbey are coarse and libidinous. But his complaints about lack of physical satisfaction at Fonthill show that down there, amongst his valets and stable-boys, nothing happened; he wrote obsessively about sex because he was repressed and possibly impotent.

What really happened is described in one of his letters to Franchi from Fonthill. Franchi was jealous of his boys; up in London some gossip had told him . . . So Beckford explains: "Dearest Gregory, your 'little bird' is wrong. I am not doing anything more than I did when you were here, I assure you. I love 'the Countess', as you know. I talk like the Duke of Lafões used to (*toujour galant, toujour aimable*), and do infinitely less than he; 'words, words, words', that's all, I swear to you."[28]

Probably nothing happened during his trips to London, when he visited abominable 'sinks' out of curiosity.[29] The danger of blackmail and prosecution was too great. His letters about the tight-rope walker Saunders in 1807 are sheer fantasy; even whilst he wrote, he never expected anything to happen. Had he suddenly been confronted with the opportunity, he would have gone cold. These letters concern his attitude to youths of the lower classes; if he was inhibited with them, how much more so with his equals! Even in old age, when he was sixty-four, he liked his little fantasies and we can see how harmless they were: "The new groom is nice, but not Patapouf. I have not yet spoken to him, but they say that he speaks as he looks, with the utmost sweetness and openness. Milan I am sure has the justest reputation of being and of always having been a great refuge for sinners of a certain sort. The tumult of the English (curse them!) going to the Jubilee (Ah, what a Jubilee I would give them if I were the Holy Father!) must have been odious—I would never have been able to stand it. In every other respect nothing would have delighted me more than to see what you have seen. Ah, my dear Gregory, when one reads letters like yours—letters which make everything appear before my eyes as in a *magic dream*—it is cruel to awake and find oneself surrounded by the vilest and most stupid beasts!"[30]

Chapter **IX**

FLIGHT, 1785-1786

After the broadcasting of the scandal in November 1784, Beckford and his wife stuck it out at Fonthill until July 1785. They were confined there by the general social ban; only their relatives called. Lettice advised him to remain quiet until the storm had subsided and effective representations could be made; this suggests that there was no real case against him. Lettice was probably right, for once Beckford left England it was difficult to return; his 'flight' seemed to substantiate the charge. But Beckford had no patience, he was proud and unable to hide his feelings. He whined, blew hot and cold, lashed out against friend and foe in the most pitiful way, and finally decided to leave "the dismal winding-sheet of Salisbury Plain" for Vevey, on the shores of the Lake of Geneva.

Life there was no longer the idyll it had been during his honeymoon, eighteen months previously. He had no intentions of shutting himself up in 'the dreary castle' of La Tour de Peilz, where they lived. So he had to overcome the prejudice which met him on his arrival. This meant overspending on lavish hospitality, which was his weapon for overcoming prejudice against himself abroad amongst foreigners and at home amongst the poor. But he usually remained afraid, or uncomfortably aware, that the respect and kindness which he received were due to his fortune rather than himself.

The most galling thing was that his wife's relatives wanted to send out, as a kind of Resident at his Court,

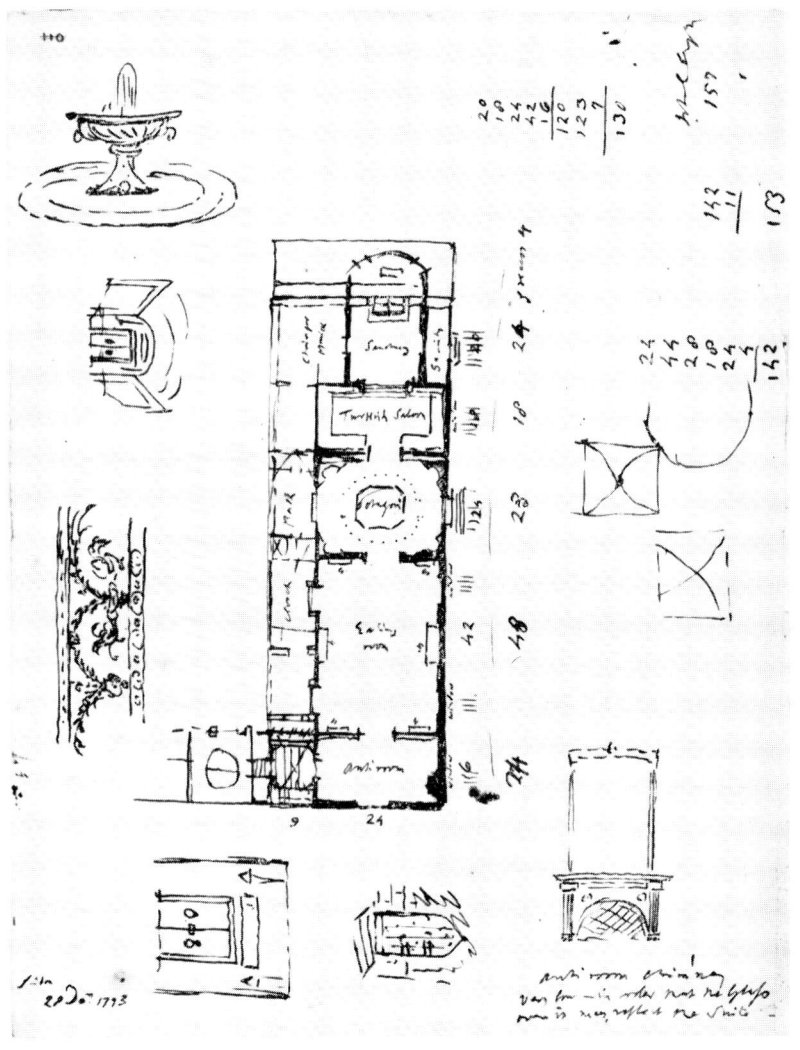

BECKFORD'S OWN PLAN of his Lisbon house, drawn by himself

FLIGHT, 1785-1786

the methodistically-minded Lady Euphemia Stewart. She was a typical aristocrat: "We have raspberries and currants in profusion a full month longer than our neighbour," said Beckford; "this I attribute to the scarecrow presence of Lady Euphemia. The birds keep aloof whenever she makes her appearance. No wonder that such a phantom parrading along the terrace in dismal weeds with arms akimbo, and that eagerness of eye, that sharpness of nose you but too well remember, should bring all the terrors of beaks and claws before their little imaginations."[1] She was to supervise them and choose their friends, and send back reports on his conduct.[2]

Bad as this was, it seemed preferable to a return to England. "I have [been] too vilely used by the English public ever to throw myself again on their mercy," he wrote, thinking of the horrible squibs in the Press, which had the cruelty to print his name *in full* in scandalous verses.

However, when Lettice came out in May 1786 he found everything transformed; prejudice was evaporating and Beckford's behaviour exemplary.[3] This may have been due to the influence, charm and good-nature of his wife. But she died of puerperal fever on 26th May.

Beckford constantly lived over her last days. Nearly a year later, as he lay becalmed at Falmouth, he wrote: "Revolving in my mind Clarence's dream, I take a melancholy walk on the slippery groundwork of the hatches, whilst the storm blackens in the North and shrill winds whistle in the shrouds. Sometimes folded up in myself, I think over the sad occurrences of last May when I lost all I doated upon, when my peace was destroyed for ever, and I beheld the object of all my tenderness in the last ghastly agonies. Never shall I forget those dreadful days of sunshine and spring without, death and gloom within. How dreadfully did the pale lights of a sick-room contrast with the mild breezes and blue sky of May!"[4]

Lady Euphemia Stewart arrived on the day of her death: "When I arrived yesterday, she was in the agonies of death, so that I had not the consolation of her knowing me, or hearing her talk; but I had that of hearing from Mr. Lettice and Mr. B. and the maids that were about her, that she prayed fervently, declared her full trust and faith in her Saviour, and her hopes of Heaven, and that she was in peace with all the world and had no resentment against anyone . . . Poor Mr. B. is inconsolable; I hope, my dear, you will get the C[hancello]r and Lord Stafford, my brothers and brothers-in-law to forget the past, as he is certainly quite changed and cares for nothing but what she valued."[5]

The month of May was strangely important in Beckford's life; he died on the 2nd and was married on the 5th, his wife died on the 26th, and his favourite daughter Susan was born on the 14th. We do not know how long Lady Margaret could have kept him from dangerous entanglements, but there is no doubt about the importance of her steadfast moral support.

Remorse and memory made Vevey intolerable. Beckford quitted it for ever. But he could not return to England without first enquiring about his reception; Express letters were sent to powerful relatives, but he had to wait until mid-June for the reply.[6] Meanwhile, the faithful Lettice whisked him about from beauty spot to beauty spot to divert his mind. The reply was so unfavourable that he felt obliged to remain abroad.

Lettice was then sent to England to make further representations on his behalf, but Lady Euphemia advised Beckford to brave the opposition and return: "Were I you, no revengeful opposition, however inveterate, should prevent my going to Fonthill. If your dear little Margaret could speak, I dare say she would bid me say a great deal to her Papa."[7] This suggests that his enemies had no case against him.

But he cannot be accused of cowardice, since there was nothing he could do to stop the Press campaign against him; it reached new depths in accusing him of being responsible for his wife's death. This aroused so much indignation in his Swiss neighbourhood that twenty-four of its leading personalities spontaneously presented him with a signed Memorial recording their horror and testifying to his admirable conduct as a husband and a man of honour.[8] These men, of the highest standing, had reputations to sustain; their unsolicited testimony can be set against the anonymous accusations in the English Press which had caused his downfall and prevented his return.

In their conduct these foreigners compare very favourably with Beckford's fellow-countryman Gibbon, who not only banned him from his society, but remonstrated publicly with Englishmen who dared to call on him. In 1792 'Buck' Whaley spoke enthusiastically of Beckford's entertainment of his party, which included ladies. Gibbon replied in a loud voice "that it was astonishing any Englishmen would visit a man who lay under such an imputation as Mr. B – – did; that even supposing him innocent, still some regard was due to the opinion of the world; and he would venture to say, that I [was the only one] among my countrymen who had ever paid that man the smallest attention since his banishment." Whaley made a tart reply and walked out amidst general consternation.[9]

Whaley's is one of the few contemporary accounts yet published which enlarges upon Beckford's position and the reason for it. Whaley implies more than once that there was only 'the bare accusation' against Beckford, and that it was 'a suspicion'; even Gibbon does not suggest more than this. Beckford characteristically revenged himself on Gibbon by buying up his library after his death and locking it away out of everyone's sight, unused even by himself. For Gibbon had told his Executor, Lord Sheffield, that he wanted it to be dispersed by auction amongst book lovers; and not "to bury my treasure in a country mansion under the key of a jealous master".

The accusation in the English Press about his wife's death was the cruellest blow Beckford ever suffered and a milestone in his life, converting him into a bear at bay, for ever snapping at his enemies. After that, he could never forgive Englishmen and was cut off from them and from English life: "I am extending my forests and sticking them full of hideous iron traps and spring-guns, that snap legs off as neatly as Pinchbeck's patent snuffers snuff candles. In process of time, when my hills are completely blackened with fir, I shall retreat into the center of this gloomy circle, like a spider into the midst of his web . . . If I am shy or savage, you must consider the baitings and worryings to which I allude—how was I treated in Portugal, in Spain, in France, in Switzerland, at home, abroad, in every region. You was in Turkey or in Lubberland when the storm raged against me and when I was stabbed to the heart by the loss of Lady Margaret. And what was the balm poured into my wounds—a set of paragraphs accusing me of having occasioned her death by ill-usage. Allowances were to be made for former attacks, but none for this; and I will own to you that the recollection of this black stroke fills me with such horror and indignation that I sigh for the pestilential breath of an African serpent to destroy every Englishman who comes in my way."[10]

This was written several years after the event. His reaction at the time is revealed by his jotting when reading de Lussan's *Histoire et Règne de Louis XI:* "Fatal as the rat-huntings of Louis the 11th, shut up in his iron castle of Plessis, a prey to remorse and the darkness [viz, darkest] suspicions. In his breast the worm that never dies seems to have taken up its residence. At night, by the gleams of torches, fierce half-starved cats hunted this loathsome vermin along the galeries, whilst the Tyrant, in robes of flame-coloured satten lined with sables, looked on and encouraged the huntsmen—Le Dain, Doyac and the physician Coctier."[11] As he read,

Beckford identified himself with Louis XI and projected his own state of mind upon his terrible Hero.

Beckford was attracted to Louis by similarities of character and habit so numerous that only a few can be mentioned here—plain and unfashionable dress, but spotlessly clean; a simple bed of yellow and crimson damask; favourite spaniels and greyhounds which slept on cushions and had collars studded in gold; a superstitious parade of devotion to saints, oaths in whose names were binding; constant preoccupation with health and a dying fear of being confounded *in aeternum*. Louis' favourite motto was *Qui nescit dissimulare, nescit regnare*. He was covetous and suspicious, and ranked money next to intelligence.

Louis, too, struggled against the English and was forced to fly from them! He married a Scottish Margaret and had two daughters. He was a bourgeois King, allied to City men, and had middle-class advisers, often foreign. But Louis was what Beckford never managed to be—'the terrible King' who ground down the hated nobility, even forbidding them to hunt without his permission. He lived in savage isolation in his castle at Plessis.

Louis' isolation and bitterness was partly caused by his remorse over his relationship with his father, Charles VII, with whom he had been at mortal enmity, and whose death he had impatiently waited and been unjustly accused of causing. Beckford too was filled with remorse—that he had been a Prodigal Son and was dissipating his patrimony.

For all these reasons, the image of Louis XI sank deep into Beckford's consciousness. This helps to explain similarities between the Castle of Plessis and Fonthill Abbey. Plessis was girt by dark forests, full of traps for intruders; it was surrounded by a 'Barrier' wall topped by *chevaux-de-frise*, and was called The Spider's Web (the very phrase which Beckford used of Fonthill). An undated press-cutting states that "like Louis XI of

France, Mr. Beckford always carried about him a small image of the saint [Anthony]"![112]

Meanwhile, in the winter of 1786, after the loss of his wife, Beckford sneaked back to Fonthill, only to be winkled out again in a few weeks, as we shall see.

Chapter X

PORTUGAL

There are three things for which Beckford is still remembered—*Vathek*, Fonthill Abbey, and his letters from Portugal. Yet he arrived in that country by sheer accident! Hardly had he returned from exile in Switzerland, than his family decided that he was best out of the way in Jamaica. There may have been something sinister about this, since it was engineered by the family adviser and agent, Thomas Wildman.[1] He and his brothers completely controlled Beckford's affairs; if the latter was far off for a year or two, they could be all the more easily 'managed' to the Wildmans' satisfaction.

So Beckford was sent to Falmouth at the beginning of March 1787, where he had to wait until the fifteenth for a favourable wind. He was seasick on board, even in harbour; he hinted in his letters from Falmouth that for this reason, and because of the hurricanes and earthquakes in Jamaica, he was not likely to get further than Madeira, and might even stop at Lisbon.[2] He did not mean this very seriously; but after nine days' misery at sea,[3] he could stand it no longer, and landed at Lisbon.

His ship, the *Julius Caesar*, was part of the Beckford fleet which brought sugar and rum from Jamaica and returned with plantation stores and timber. When Beckford went aboard he found geraniums in full blow, his books and china admirably arranged, and "powerful fumigations of burnt lavender water and sealing wax" to prevent sea-sickness. He was disgusted by the cockroaches, which "have not as yet displayed their taste for literature by gnawing my books to pieces, but amuse themselves with parading up and down the varnished paper of the cabin, like fashionable gentlemen who have no employment".[4] As he was composing one of these letters at Mr. Blundstone's inn, "chickens on the point of embarkation just under my window, and old women complaining that I have swept off all the poultry at Falmouth, make such a cackling that I have lost the clew of my epistle".

He felt incongruous amongst his uninteresting companions—Captain Collett of the West India merchant house, his Swiss physician Verdeil, his former tutor, dry-as-dust Drysdale, and the ship's captain, Gomm. He listened sardonically to the cross-currents of conversation round the breakfast table at the inn; he jotted down the broken threads of small-talk with a wry but mischievous grin: "Is the *Diana* gone up? . . . *Oui* . . . There's no swell . . . no wind's a good wind for sitting still . . . Fisherman fish today . . . catch whiting . . . Have they turbot here, Cap'n Collett? . . . John dories . . . Turbot keeps deep water . . . no Bay . . . not a Bay . . . *J'ai rencontré un de mes compatriottes et j'ai eu une longue* confabulation. *Il est passager, et reste ici pour gagner une guineé pour porter à Londres . . . une guinée* . . . Ah . . . N. by S.S.W.—South-South-West . . . I believe there's an east wind at London and on the east coast . . . No hunting today . . . *Avez-vous entendu hier au matin* . . . You-You-You . . . Good butter here . . . don't always look well . . . [*Verdeil:*] What do you see, Mr. Drysdale? [Drysdale:] . . . *Ni le Diane ni le Jules Caesar . . . les deux Danois . . . mynheer yong frow* . . . Ah . . . (a cockrell crows) . . . *Coupez le chanson de ce petit Coq* . . . broke the thread of his discourse . . . [*Collett:*] Pray, Sir, help me to a bit of crust . . . [*Drysdale:*] . . . Hoot . . . *le croute demi le croute* . . . The old Scotchman went for himself to Philadelphia all the time of the War . . . got money and lost it . . . I mean he was well off . . . His friends gone . . . he was a sufferer amongst the rest of the good people . . . but got his passage home for nothing . . . Here's a boat . . . comes or goes from the South . . . See Cap'n Gomm, Sir . . . what says he to the wind? . . . *J'aimerai mieux le pain tout croute—plus sain que l'autre parce qu'il est toute mie* . . . A little more, Cap'n . . . I see the *Diana* now . . . could not see her before."[5]

As day followed day and the wind still shifted, he hoped that he might be reprieved and allowed to sneak back home. "After waiting and waiting, day after day and week after week I think it quite honourable to allow oneself vanquished and make the best retreat in one's power. I am now furnished with a very tolerable excuse, and if you chose, you might let me off without any discredit to myself or advisers. Tho' I do my utmost to keep up my spirits, I cannot help confessing that no one ever embarked even for transportation with a heavier heart. The more I hear of Jamaica, the more I dread the climate, which I fully expect will wither my health away . . . you must excuse my going any further than Madeira. From Madeira I will return to England or to any other place you choose to appoint."[6]

Pathetic language for a man of twenty-six, master of a great fortune and a fine estate, Member of Parliament, once the friend of distinguished men! But worse was to follow. On arrival at Lisbon he expected, in the usual way, to be presented to the Queen of Portugal by the British Minister, the Hon. Robert Walpole, cousin of Horace Walpole. This alone would have enabled him to attend diplomatic banquets and other functions frequented by the small international Society of those days, in which he and his name were well known. It was particularly important for him to accept invitations from this circle, for every time he was not included, the humblest gossiper in the English community knew why, and raked up the Powderham scandal. Besides, it cut him off from cultured people in the capital like the

French Ambassador, with whom he had many acquaintances in common. Reports would soon be carried back to England, and strengthen the hand of his enemies.

But Walpole refused to present him to the Queen. This was probably not so much because of Beckford's reputation as because of a quarrel between them. They would instantly have disliked each other, and Beckford could not resist being sarcastic in retaliation for Walpole's hostility. Both were proud, choleric and touchy; after the first quarrel it became a personal vendetta, with their prestige involved. Walpole was well entrenched: his first and second wives had been daughters of British merchants in Lisbon. He thought Beckford easy game; the sneers and slander of "the scrubs and scrubesses of the English Factory" would soon make his position intolerable and drive him out of the country.

Beckford had every reason to be aggrieved, particularly because Walpole was acting outside his competence. This is clearly shown by the diplomatic correspondence[7] which resulted from Beckford's official presentation to the Prince Regent of Portugal early in May 1795 in an unorthodox manner—that is to say, not by Walpole. The latter was enraged, and wrote a curt Note to Pinto, the Portuguese Foreign Minister, demanding an explanation. Pinto forwarded this Note to Almeida, his ambassador in London, and asked the British Foreign Secretary, Lord Grenville, for an immediate explanation of Walpole's behaviour; Pinto suggested that satisfaction should be given for such rudeness and interference. Almeida went to see Grenville, who pointed out that Walpole had interfered unjustifiably and should not be regarded as having acted officially; he almost certainly promised to reprimand Walpole. Meanwhile, the latter saw Pinto in Lisbon, and told him that his Note was merely personal and unofficial; he retracted and apologised. Both Governments thought it best to leave the matter there, and to treat the incident as if it had never occurred.

PORTUGAL

Returning to 1787, we can imagine Walpole's mortification when the defenceless 'puppy' was unexpectedly taken up by the Queen's favourite, the Marquis of Marialva. The Marialvas were then the most important family in Portugal, and were Hereditary Masters of the Horse. Beckford's friend, Diogo, was in daily attendance upon the Queen, who valued him for his devoutness, his honourable and sympathetic character, and his conscientiousness. The Portuguese nobility were very exclusive; they married within a narrow circle and were nearly all inter-related. They avoided foreigners, and hated the English for their arrogance and anti-Catholic prejudice. Beckford's friendship with Marialva, who was twenty-one years his senior, is one of the strangest episodes in Anglo-Portuguese relations. Marialva became so attached to Beckford that, in order to keep him by his side, he tried to marry him off to his eldest daughter Henriqueta; she was as good as engaged to (and after Beckford's departure married) the Duke of Lafões, a member of the Royal Family, with the Court title of 'Uncle of the Queen'. Marialva even hoped to marry his only son and heir, Dom Pedro, to Beckford's infant daughter.

Marialva's affection, revealed in his letters, is pathetic. They are full of extravagant protestations of love and loyalty, but demand full reciprocity from Beckford. This was impossible because of their difference in age, temperament and taste, and because Marialva was driven by an irrational force over which he had no control. Beckford had the friendship thrust upon him; it was one of those curious accidents which happen to a man of his sort!

Marialva's ideas for their friendship were inevitably different from Beckford's: "For me, my dear friend, the sum of my pleasure would be to live in a quiet corner of the world, enjoying the tender company of my Only Friend. I still have a strong hope that this may come to pass; meanwhile, I will ask God to give you his

Grace and fill you with that lasting happiness which never fades."[8] Beckford had been suffering from three years of social ostracism, and was hardly likely to welcome this! Marialva was very jealous, and tried to keep his friend to himself.

The emotional pressure exerted by Marialva upon Beckford was enormous and made the latter restless and bored. He would never have stood the strain so long, were it not for the fascination of his situation, his interest in the Marquis' young son, and the hope of revenge upon Walpole. In fact, as soon as it was plain that Marialva could not present him to the Queen, Beckford left Portugal and did not return for six years, despite Marialva's tender entreaties. As long as he remained, he was in a false and dangerous position. But it needed courage and energy to tear himself away; at the last moment he was reluctant to leave.

For Marialva was an attractive man, an unswerving friend, ready to take risks and infinite pains for those he loved. The whole Marialva household was fond of Beckford—the nonagenarian Abbé Xavier, the portly and benevolent Grand Prior of Aviz, the two eldest children, and even the two little girls in the nursery. Consequently, Beckford never wrote so happily and engagingly as in his Portuguese Journal. His egotism did not prevent him from perceiving the family's sterling qualities—they come alive in all their charm and simplicity.

Beckford was introduced to the Marialvas by the Abbé Xavier, who appreciated his devotion to St. Anthony of Padua (the patron Saint of Lisbon), and his enthusiastic attendance at Mass. Even as a boy Beckford had been interested in St. Anthony; no wonder he felt that Fate directed his steps: nothing could have been more calculated to commend him to the devout Marialvas!

The friendship with the Marquis developed as rapidly as it had started. Soon Beckford made his first call at the Marialva Palace on May 25th, the day he started

PORTUGAL

his Journal.⁹ One can see why he began it then. He had arrived in Lisbon tired and unwell and was disgusted by the Portuguese landscape and the Lisbon climate;¹⁰ and his spirits were finally sunk by Walpole's conduct and by the lack of society in the English community. Consequently, his hopes were at once raised by Marialva's friendship and the unexpected change in his fortunes; everything took on a new air, and his days were full of interest and novelty.

Once Marialva took him up, it was more than ever necessary to be presented to the Queen; otherwise the incongruity of his position was too marked and would cause a scandal. So Marialva's prestige was involved in the struggle with Walpole. At this level, the question became a *cause célèbre*. It involved the Prime Minister, a former Secretary of State, the leader of the nobility, the Comptroller of the Queen's Household, and many others. The Queen was interested, and her heir, the Prince of Brazil, took Beckford's side. The nobility were divided into pro- and anti-Beckford factions, depending on their attitude to Marialva, with whom most of them were related: those who were at enmity with him refused to receive Beckford and cut him dead; those who valued Marialva's friendship invited Beckford to their drawing-rooms, where Englishmen were never seen, and least of all the hated Walpole.

It looks, then, as if Beckford did have the talk with the Prince of Brazil, which he describes in Letter XXXI of *Portugal*. We know from the *Journal* that the Prince was anxious to meet him, and that Beckford was on familiar terms with the Prince's *aide* who arranged it— perhaps only to satisfy his master's curiosity; but once the latter started to harangue Beckford about politics he may have become indiscreet, since Beckford had liberal-minded friends with the same outlook as the Prince. Beckford probably passed on these indiscretions to Marialva, and not to Archbishop S. Caetano (as he claimed later); this removes the one improbability in the story.

Some of the details are very convincing, and would hardly be mentioned unless true; for example, the sudden appearance of the Prince, who was on a shooting party in the wilds: "A little door in the ruined wall, against which an awning was fixed, opened, and there appeared a young man of rather a prepossessing figure . . . who . . . moved his hat in a dignified graceful manner." Some parts of the account may be fabricated, such as the paragraph in which Beckford raised conservative objections to the Prince's reforming zeal. This was most unlike Beckford at that date; he probably added this for the post-French Revolution public, as well as to enhance his own importance at the meeting and to make the most of his story. But on the whole it seems a true account of what happened.

Certainly during his later visit Beckford knew the Prince's younger brother João. The elder Prince died of small-pox in 1788 and was succeeded as heir by the younger, who later became King João VI, and effectively ruled the country from the Queen's madness in 1792. After presentation to him in May 1795, Beckford landed in England direct from Lisbon in June 1796. He claimed that the Prince had "charged him with a particular mission to the King", which the British Cabinet prevented him from delivering.[11]

Beckford's claim is difficult to believe, but on 14th July he had an interview with the Home Secretary, the Duke of Portland, a Conservative Whig of Burke's type, concerning Portuguese affairs and personalities. When Beckford reported this in a typically self-centred, peevish and uninformative letter, Marialva replied that the Prince wanted Beckford to continue his 'good offices' in the interests of Portugal.[12]

Marialva's letters also show that he and the Prince asked Beckford to send them anything he could learn about the Cabinet's intentions and deliberations regarding Portugal;[13] perhaps they thought that Beckford could get secret information through bribery in the

PORTUGAL

right quarters. At any rate, they enjoyed receiving his professions of esteem for Portugal and her ruler: "My beloved friend, . . . never a Packet arrives without the Prince asking me at once, 'Has good news of Becford come?' And I thank him heartily on your behalf for his inquiry, and shew him the letter you have sent me, which he reads thoughtfully, rejoicing in your expressions about him; and sometimes he has said to me: 'He is your friend, but he is mine too'."[14]

Although Beckford was genuinely interested in Portugal, his chief concern was his social rehabilitation in England and the acquisition of the English peerage lost to him in 1784. For years he hoped that this could be brought about through recommendations at the Court of St. James' by the rulers and ambassadors of Portugal. As each new ambassador was appointed, he was instructed by Marialva, who had the Portuguese Regent's ear, to press Beckford's case. One of them, later Foreign Minister, wrote back to Marialva, diplomatically hinting that one had to "take into consideration the trend of public opinion in this country [England], which, notwithstanding its laxity in many matters, shows in others an inflexibility for which no other reason can be found than those of public opinion and habit".[15]

Whenever an ambassador arrived in London with recommendations for Beckford, the latter's old wound was re-opened. They had known him in Portugal as the wealthy friend of Marialva; there it was easy to suggest that only Walpole's personal malice placed him in an invidious position; there, they could not realise how isolated and uninfluential he was in England. But now, in London, they saw his real position, and later returned to Portugal to spread different ideas about him. One wonders that he ever had the courage to go back there.

He also toyed with the idea of settling in Portugal, provided he was given a title and not obliged to turn Catholic.[16] He despatched his Portuguese friend Franchi to Lisbon about January 1790 to negotiate.[17] Marialva was always pressing and sanguine; as Horne, Beckford's agent in Lisbon, wrote: "A few days ago the Marquis of Marialva called on me, and in our conversation said Her Majesty had no doubt to grant every indulgence to Mr. Beckford on his arrival here, provided he would naturalize himself a Portuguese. He went so far as to say she promised to give him a Title and a Place about her person. I represented to him the absurdity of such ideas, and that it was more honourable to be a Commoner in England than a Grandee and Lord of the Bedchamber to a despotic princess; and I leave you to reflect how chimerical the Marquis' notions are."[18]

But when it came to the point, Beckford could never make up his mind to leave Fonthill for good. In any case, in moments of exasperation he professed his readiness to settle anywhere—even in Jacobinical France—provided that he was cossetted and protected from English insults. When he was in Portugal he was often bored and exasperated; but years later, at Fonthill Abbey, he often had *saudades* of Portugal—"memories of Portugal will always be the memories nearest to my heart".[19]

Beckford was drawn like a magnet to Portugal, partly because of the impregnable position of people of rank there.[20] Hence his ironical remark on the fate of the Duke of Marlborough, whose extravagance and collecting mania had led him to a bankrupt's auction: "What is happening in the case of the Duke of Marlborough shows very clearly the consequence of incurring debts, etc., in a country which, unlike Portugal, does not enjoy the benign power of royal proclamations, with their paternal advice to people of the lower orders to leave untroubled the repose of the heroes of the upper classes."

Beckford's second stay in Portugal lasted from November 1793 until October 1795, when he attempted to go to Naples to stay with Sir William Hamilton and Emma, but was turned back to a Spanish port by a French privateer, and finished up again in Lisbon.

PORTUGAL

Either he intended to settle there or to stay regularly. For he built a house in the Rua da Cova da Moura, near the Necessidades Palace, which he expected to finish by the end of October 1795. The original house on this site had belonged to his agent Horne, who left it on his death to his cousin and partner Joseph Sill, from whom Beckford bought it in 1794; this was almost certainly the 'pasteboard habitation' in which Beckford first stayed in Lisbon.[21] So the site was dear to him for the memories of 1787, and the erection of a fine new house on the same spot was a typically Beckfordian way of symbolising and consolidating his social triumph in Lisbon. Its influence on Fonthill Abbey will be discussed later.

Whilst this house was being built, Beckford rented the Quinta of S. José de Ribamare at Alges, a Western suburb of Lisbon. Besides its lovely situation, it had the advantage of being near the Marialva Palace and the Royal Palace of the Ajuda. From the summer of 1794 he also rented Monserrate, beyond Cintra, from the millionaire English merchant Gerard Devisme, who built it in 1790. Beckford was doubtless chiefly attracted by the lovely grounds and views, but it is interesting that Devisme constructed it as a mediaeval castle flanked by twin round towers (in which were most of the important rooms), and that its two principal entries gave on to an octagonal vestibule. Whatever Beckford chose to say later in his own defence when this baronial building was decried, he liked it enough to acquire it on Devisme's death in 1798 (during his third stay in Portugal).[22] Byron called it "the most desolate mansion in the most beautiful spot I ever beheld".[23] In every way it seems to have foreshadowed Fonthill Abbey.

Monserrate later fell into ruin, like a place accursed. This was what it seemed to Byron, who, in a moralising way connected its fate with Beckford's bad reputation:

ENGLAND'S WEALTHIEST SON

"There thou too, Vathek! England's wealthiest son,
Once form'd thy Paradise, as not aware
When wanton Wealth her mightiest deeds hath done,
Meek Peace voluptuous lures was ever wont to shun.

Here didst thou dwell, here schemes of pleasure plan,
Beneath yon mountain's ever beauteous brow:
But now, as if a thing unblest by Man,
Thy fairy dwelling is as lone as thou!
Here giant weeds a passage scarce allow
To halls deserted, portals gaping wide . . ."

Beckford's first stay in Portugal gave us his *Journal*, and his carefully edited excerpts from it, *Sketches of Spain and Portugal*. His second stay was responsible for his *Recollections of an Excursion to the Monasteries of Alcobaça and Batalha*, which he began to write in 1834, when he was 74. In the preface he states that "the other day, in examining some papers, I met with very slight notes of this Excursion . . . I invoked the powers of memory and behold, up rose the whole series of recollections I am now submitting." This is true; for these 'very slight notes' are in his Papers in the form of a diary which he kept spasmodically during his trip to the monasteries in June 1794.[24]

The *Recollections* tend to magnify his importance in Portugal, and discreetly veil his personal problems. But there is one striking passage which reveals one of his life-long preoccupations: "Throwing myself on the solid ground, I kept intensely poring over the stream, lost and absorbed in the train of interesting yet melancholy recollections which all that had occurred to me since I first entered this fair realm of Portugal was so well calculated to excite. I thought (alas! how vainly now!) of offers I had slighted with so much levity; of opportunities which, had they been grasped with a decided hand, might have led to happy results, and stemmed a torrent of evils. Since that period, the germ of destructiveness, which might then have been trodden down, has risen into a tree fraught with poisons, darkening the wholesome light, and receiving nourishment, through all its innumerably varied fibres, from the lowest depths of hell." (Eighth Day).

Beckford has in mind the results of the French Revolution, the passing of the old order, the rise of scientific materialism and the political misfortunes of Portugal; he hints that he might have played a part in the country's history! But Redding realised that this passage has a more personal significance, and says that it was "written under the influence of that impatient feeling, with which at times he was possessed, of his not having done enough in the way of acquirement, of his having thrown away his times and opportunities."[25] This was the world's judgement of Beckford; and it was his own.

But the passage can also be taken as a metaphor of the development of Beckford's inner life after 1787. 'The germ of destructiveness' in him was that spirit of discontent, that inability to accept his own character and situation; this led to bitterness, which poisoned his whole life. We have only to compare his later letters to Franchi in *Life at Fonthill* with the *Journal*. In 1787 hope was not yet quenched; he could still respond in a positive way to new friendships and new experiences. 'The germ of destructiveness' in him was also the coarser aspect of his perverted urges. Their force would have been less had he enjoyed normal social outlets and an established position. Looking back in 1794, it seemed to him that these blessings were in his grasp in 1787, had he been more skilful and resolute, and more appreciative of Marialva.

Little is known of his third and last visit to Portugal, to which he sailed in October 1798, after his mother's death. His characteristic return to Fonthill in July 1799 is described by Lettice: "I got safe to Fonthill on the 12th instant, but Mr. Beckford was not arrived, nor has any intelligence been received of the *Prince of Wales* Packet from Falmouth. I had not got quite thus far [with this letter] when I saw . . . the sudden movement of a vast crowd near the Lodge, [and,] in a few minutes two or three carriages driving rapidly through them . . . A few minutes brought Mr. Beckford and his suite to the door of the Grecian Hall, where I was happy in receiving him safe, and as well as could be expected after what he always suffers at sea. He expressed himself with great feeling and affection on seeing me . . . The Fonthill Association went a mile or two beyond Hindon to meet Mr. Beckford on the Downs, with drums beating, colours flying, and the music of his military band (about twenty performers). They returned about an hour after him, and have been manoeuvering on the Lawn, and their music playing all this afternoon. All the surrounding villages flocked in with them to partake the good cheer and jubilee of the day."[26]

Chapter XI

FRANCE AND RADICALISM

Portugal was Beckford's favourite country, but Paris his favourite capital. He loved its gay cosmopolitan society. He liked the interest in the occult, simmering below the surface; the restlessness and curiosity of its people corresponded with his own. He liked its culture, its opera, its food.

But as the Revolution gathered force, it had a special attraction for him. Anyone with ample foreign exchange could command what he liked, as France's currency fell catastrophically and the printing-presses worked overtime on the production of worthless paper *assignats*. World-famous sales of books and pictures took place as aristocrats emigrated, financiers were ruined and monasteries were pillaged by revolutionary commissars. One cannot help admiring Beckford for remaining in Paris during some of the stormiest periods because of his "love of rare and precious books" and of the Louis-period furniture now available through the dispersal of the Royal *garde-meuble*.

This collecting mania involved him in real danger as events reached a climax after the execution of Louis XVI on 21st January 1793. On 1st February, France declared war on England and Holland. Pitt's counter-measures included the passing of the Traitorous Correspondence Act; this would have made Beckford liable to prosecution for treason had he remained on enemy soil, especially since he was an M.P. Now that he was a rich enemy alien, with no Ambassador to protect him and with many treasures to be sequestrated, denunciations were prepared against him by Frenchmen. So he went underground! His bookseller Chardin disguised him as a clerk, and he worked for several weeks in Mérigot's antiquarian bookshop.[1]

At the beginning of April, if not before, Beckford tried to reach the safety of Lausanne; but as an enemy alien he was evidently turned back. He next attempted to escape across the northern frontier at Arras. Here he was arrested with his valet on the charge of putting the latter into a green livery, 'a symbol of feudalism'.[2] Was it a coincidence that green was the colour of the Revolutionaries, first worn by the extremist Desmoulins? He got out of this scrape, probably with the help of bribes and friends in high places.

Then, in the last week of April he joined the pitiful queues of those clamouring for passports. We get a novel picture of this imperious man, attending at office after office, arguing with petty bureaucrats and putting up with their insolence and procrastination, whilst his specially chartered ship lay waiting at Calais: "I have been for more than these ten days past in a constant course of solicitation in order to obtain my passports. The laws are positive against their being granted to any subjects of countries at war with France, and it was not without the most perseverant exertion that I have at length procured an exception in my favour. My application to my Section or Parish was the first step, from thence to the Revolution Committee, then to the Committee of Surveillance or Police, who referred me to the Committee of Publick Safety. After tedious, tumultuous and desultory debates at all these assemblies, the business was brought before the Maison Commune, ci-devant Hotel de Ville. Here I found tenfold opposition; a thousand strangers, English, Dutch, Spaniards, etc. had been applying for 6 weeks past in vain. Your letter of the 9th was produced, and in consequence of its proving the risks that my fortune would run by a longer stay in this country, the passport was issued".[3] The passport was signed by Lebrun, the Foreign Minister, and endorsed *étranger que Paris voit partir avec regret*. But in spite of this, he was detained at Calais until the Convention was referred to, and two of his riding-horses were confiscated for work with military baggage-trains! He was at last allowed to sail when the Committee of Public Safety reported on his Francophil 'love of liberty'.[4]

Beckford's library and treasures in his house in the Rue de Grenelle, in the fashionable Faubourg St. Germain, were looked after by Chardin. This was a dangerous and thankless task; sure enough, Chardin, in spite of having been A.D.C. to Robespierre's colleague Henriot, was denounced by Dr. Leymerie as an English agent, and as having appropriated Beckford's library and horses. He was thrown into jail with the extremist Chaumette and other 'criminals'; during his trial he was venomously attacked by Leymerie; the latter was a dangerous and unscrupulous man, who had been physician and secretary to the bloodthirsty cripple Couthon. Chardin was acquitted; the official Report of the Commission appointed to investigate the affair mentions Beckford's Republican sympathies. Consideration of this takes us back to the beginning of the Revolution.

Beckford says that "at first he felt all the enthusiasms of the time in favour of liberty, an enthusiasm quickly checked by subsequent events."[5] This is more than likely, since he followed his father's Radicalism, and his enthusiastic temperament was roused by the first stirring days of the Revolution. He moved in liberal circles which included Necker, a popular hero, and artists, who are often left-wing. One of his closest friends was his Swiss physician Verdeil, whose letters from Paris are full of revolutionary fervour.

On his travels, Beckford noticed whether the land was well cultivated, how the peasants were clad and housed and whether they seemed happy. Not content with the outward appearance, he peeped inside their cottages:

"The outward appearance of the houses in this village [of Lumiares] is tolerably neat, the walls whitewashed and vine arbours projecting before every door; but within, all kinds of filth is heaped up in profusion and every sort of vermin encouraged."[6] In France in 1819 he noticed "everywhere my eyes turn, *squalid misery*. Just as certain insects take their colour from the leaves they eat, so the people, who, alas, only have but stones to eat, are the colour of their own dwellings. Everything seems to be falling into ruin, nothing announces a ray of hope or prosperity."[7]

In his books he makes out that he was against the coming French Revolution, and perceived its evil consequences for established religion and society. But this was written long after the event, to make him seem a respectable member of orthodox society and a prophetic genius. He was in Paris when the Bastille fell on 14th July 1789, and remained for about a month during the mounting tension and disorder. The scene appealed to his artist's eye and his Romantic imagination, but he was too intellectual and sensitive not to be afraid of disorder. A Paris friend wrote to him at the end of August about the mob processions, and Beckford replied, from the peacefulness of Lausanne, that such things are all very well, "but I prefer to imagine them than to see them. I still shudder at the recollection of the Kalends of July; and when I think of the midnight processions on the eve of my departure, I am transported in imagination to the Temple of Vitzlipochtli rather than the Dome of St. Geneviève."[8]

Before he left Paris in such a hurry in August 1789 he said that if the Portuguese would not have him as an emigré on his own terms, "I shall accept the propositions of the National Assembly and fix myself in France."[9] This was not because of any love of 'liberty', but through pique at his position in England. Also, he was a born actor and loved taking people in; he could not resist playing up to their expectations, until he was identified with his part and imprisoned by his own role. It was as amusing and exciting to take in Revolutionary leaders about his Jacobin principles as it was to deceive Portuguese prelates about his devotion to St. Anthony. So, using his money, his hospitality and his tongue, he found the Revolutionary leaders as easy game as the Portuguese: "Two or three Deputies are chattering at one end of my room and swilling tea and observing that, since the introduction of this English beverage, *on pense plus librement*, etc., etc.—a deel of French stuff."[10]

All this explains the account given of Beckford in the Report (mentioned above) which examined the accusations against Chardin: '*cet Anglais était généralement estimé pour ses principes revolutionnaires . . . . . Inspiré par l'amour de la Liberté, il voulut par la suite acheter un Domaine national, afin de se fixer entièrement en France, mais n'en ayant pas trouvé a sa fantasie, il fut forcé, par une fatalité de circonstances, de retourner en Angleterre. Il partit, accompagné des regrets des sansculottes et de l'estime des autorités constitués de Paris.*' It adds that Santerre presented Beckford to the revolutionary committee which ruled France, and that its President, Destournelles, gave him the 'fraternal kiss'.[11]

It is amusing to see one rogue hoodwinking another; the thought of the *arriviste* Beckford embracing the proletarian, profiteering brewer Santerre is irresistible. But his cynicism and heartlessness are horrifying. This is how he saw life in post-Varennes Paris: "Happy, aye, thrice happy are those who in this good Capital and at this period have plenty of money; their Kingdom is come, their will is done upon Earth, if not in Heaven. By St. Anthony, my dear friend, I never was better amused since I existed. I have the most delightful appartments and the best cook and the best wine and the best Bristol water and the best everything . . . The finest linnen which ever Flanders or Saxony produced is scarcely thought worthy to garnish my sideboards, or to be spread under my boots when I return in all the majesty of mud, from dashing in the most invincible manner thro' the sloughs of the Bois de Boulogne, attended by half-a-dozen Captains and Lieutenants of the Garde Nationale. Don't suppose I wait one instant for my carriage at the Opera (where, by the bye, I have taken possession of the Prince de Condé's box)—not a bit—down drives my coach upon the slightest signal, and in I jump to the admiration and desolation of pennyless Dukes, Counts and half-pay Ambassadors."[12]

Under the shadow of war with revolutionary France, Beckford published *Modern Novel Writing* in 1796 and *Azemia* in 1797—two anonymous novels with Radical views in their second volumes. The first novel shows him to be anti-Establishment (as we say now); he lumps together "placemen, [Government] pensioners, peeresses, loan-mongers, bishops and contractors" (p. 232), and in another place "lords, aldermen, Parliamentmen, crimps, Justices of the Peace, Bishops, Deans, Arch-Deacons and Attorneys (pp. 98-99) who, like his mock-hero in the novel, "had at all times a proper contempt for the hunger and sufferings of the poor." At the end of *Modern Novel Writing* he has "An Humble Address to ... *The British Critic*",[13] in which he ironically approves of his critics' outlook—their support for the Treasonable Practices Act and Seditious Meetings Act of 1795; their contempt for any books which vindicate "the hoggish herd of the people" or dare to censure "the just and necessary war"; their courage in defending "the exclusive privileges of the FEW against the vulgar attacks of the MANY" (pp. 219-30). In a dream (pp. 99-101) he satirises Pitt's England as "The Isle of Mum", an island of "famine due to monopoly" (presumably a hit at the new class of millers and corn merchants[14] rather than at the Corn Laws), where the people's "just remonstrances [are] deemed seditious and treasonable". As a result of the repressive legislation, there was "a dead silence throughout the nation, and order and tranquillity pretty generally restored". This was in fact prophetic, since the Corresponding Societies and similar clubs were cowed and hamstrung by the Two Acts of 1795 (following on the suspension of Habeas Corpus in 1794).

The second volume of Azemia castigates the idle and wasteful rich who live on their rents at the expense of the poor and arrogantly trample them underfoot—"the horses and the dogs of lords and gentry are a great deal better off than their poor neighbours" (p. 75). He is shocked that in a few hours' amusement a hostess can spend as much as would make many nearby starving families happy for years. He perceives that the poor have no redress, since even rich men were ruined by the expense of Chancery suits. "Never talk of the equality of our laws, while a Chancery suit is ranked as an evil of as great magnitude as a fire, an inundation, a descent of the enemy or an earthquake; and really as to the ruin they produce, I see but little difference." (p. 156).

Not only had the poor no redress. Pitt's Cabinet aimed repressive legislation at their defenders, the reformers, who were prevented from meeting and talking and were tried for sedition as if they were dangerous pro-French revolutionaries. Beckford hits out at this repression and, speaking of the poor, opens his fourth chapter with a couplet from Charles Churchill

> Like *us* they were design'd to eat, to drink,
> To talk, and (every now and then) to *think*.

Unlike Pitt, Beckford was not mesmerised by the growth of revenue, trade and commerce, or by the apparent prosperity brought by war-time inflation. He perceived that the status of yeoman farmers, cottagers and agricultural labourers was rapidly declining. In answer to the current patriotic jingoism that we had never had it so good as during "the just and necessary war", he asks "how it happens, that while the rich are better, the poor are worse off than they were twenty years since? And why, if our trade and manufactures are so flourishing, and our resources still so immense, it happens that our gazettes are full of bankrupts, our jails full of debtors; that our feelings are continually shocked by public executions, and that our poor are literally perishing with hunger in their wretched cottages?" (p. 112). He roundly declares "that the distress of the middling and lower ranks has increased, is increasing, and certainly ought to be diminished." (p. 112). This is a brilliant parody of Dunning's motion in Parliament in 1780 that "the influence of the Crown has increased, is increasing, and ought to be diminished".

Beckford was far ahead of public opinion in his attitude to public executions, prisons and the gaoling of debtors.[15] But the reformers were only advanced in certain directions and did not attack property. What they chiefly wanted was a better life for the underdog. As Beckford says, "I would not have the rich live much worse than they do, but I would have the poor supported a great deal better". (p. 160).

His Radicalism is remarkable because there was then only one other Radical novelist in the upper classes— Charlotte Smith, the daughter of a Sussex landowner. All the rest came from the lesser classes and were often of Dissenting stock. Godwin was the son of a Dissenting minister; Amelia Opie was a doctor's daughter and was converted to Quakerism from Unitarianism. Holcroft was a shoemaker's son, and Mrs. Inchbald a farmer's daughter who turned actress. When they wrote, they had mutual support. Godwin married Mary Wollstonecraft and was Shelley's father-in-law; Mrs. Inchbald and Mrs. Opie were friends of Godwin and Holcroft.

By contrast, Beckford was completely isolated. We can guess the attitude of his neighbours from the character of the Tory Mrs. Albuzzi in *Azemia*. Her "eyes flashed fire as indignantly she looked at her old acquaintance: scorn and anger mingled on her brow, whilst she exclaimed, 'And it is thus, *in good time*, that persons who

FRANCE AND RADICALISM

have degraded and debased themselves by their profligacy, and dissipated their fortunes, have recourse to *levelling* schemes, *I think;* so that their apostacy really *frights* one. *Such* a man we all agree to loathe, *I believe*, and, with one consent, detest his conduct, while we abhor his principles'." (p. 38). Mrs. Albuzzi (i.e. All-Buzz) is Mrs. Piozzi, better known as Hester Thrale, the friend of Dr. Johnson!

Beckford's social radicalism is not inconsistent with his political conservatism. He had the paternalist outlook of the pre-French Revolution Whigs, who did not consider 'the people' as a political entity entitled to a voice in politics; affairs should be managed for them by their betters. He was confirmed in this attitude by his experience of mobs during the Gordon Riots and the Revolution.

As a Man of Property he could not help thinking of its safety; so in old age he became a reactionary. The 1832 Reform Bill was his bugbear: "Where will this end? Will life and property continue safe? Shall we not have a revolutionary outbreak? . . . All one's old feelings are sneered at. Respect for fine old families is gone; even the King with his pineapple head is leading the movement. What a hurried state of things we live in, what a hopeless future to look forward to! Well, God knows I do not care much about these matters now—these trumperies. The Reform Bill is only an amusement for the people, but it will give the commercial interests a lift. The sight of a fine old picture, reading, rummaging over my exquisite *Heures de Marie de Bourgogne* . . . anything married to literature or art affords me more enjoyment fifty times than attending to the noisy political demagogues of the day."[16] There is a certain astuteness in these remarks; for the Reform Bill did put the middle classes and commercial interests in the saddle, in place of aristocracy and land; the turn of the people had not yet come.

We could hardly expect Beckford to belong to the 'Young Jacobin' type of the 1790's, thrown up in English literary circles by the French Revolution. For one thing, he was too old; the leading representatives of the Young Jacobins were much younger—Wordsworth ten years, Coleridge thirteen, and Southey fourteen. It was difficult for Beckford to share some of their views. Unlike them, he had known the pre-Revolution Courts of Versailles, Madrid, Lisbon and Naples; he had enjoyed the pomp and music of their Catholic worship; he could not therefore be anti-King, anti-priest and anti-Church. They were also anti-slavery, which we could not expect of him. Nor could he remain indifferent to the revolutionary barbarism which destroyed an artistic heritage by melting down Church treasures, cutting up copes and altar-cloths for soldiers' shirts, and auctioning ancient churches to profiteers who wanted their materials and sites.

What effect did this Radical theorist, this generous but erratic employer have upon his working people? Loudon visited Fonthill in 1833 and asked Mr. Joy, agent of the new owner. Joy said that Beckford had ruined the workers with generous wages and the bounties which he added when pleased with their work; it was all spent on drink! Was Beckford to blame?[17]

It happened that his building, from 1796 to 1822, coincided with a disastrous transition for the English rural labourer and yeoman, who were pauperised and nearly starving from the combined effects of a series of changes. These were the enclosures and the decay of cottage industries; rising prices and population; the exceptionally bad harvests from 1792 to 1813; the Corn Law of 1815; the forcing down of wages; the post-Napoleonic depression and upheaval; and the Speenhamland system, first introduced in 1795. The latter was a sliding scale which fluctuated with the price of bread; in accordance with it, wages were supplemented out of parish rates. All this was enough, and more than enough, to drive the labourers to drink.

Indeed, in the very paragraph in which Loudon suggests that Beckford was responsible for the degradation of the poor, he adds, referring to the Speenhamland system: "The labourers, however, generally in this part of the country are deeply degraded by the system of making up their wages from the poor's rates; so much so, indeed, that many of the married men drink every shilling that they earn, and leave their wives and children to be supported entirely by the parish; declaring, what indeed appears to be their belief, that there is a law obliging the parish to provide for their families, and that they are only bound to take care of themselves."

Beckford's departure from Fonthill was deeply regretted by the country folk. Thirty-six years later, an observant traveller, who was not prepossessed in his favour, found that "his name still lives in Wiltshire . . . as a solitary severe man who lived for himself, yet was kind, generous and a great employer of the poor". This man chatted with one of Beckford's old keepers, who had been in his service all his life; the latter still spoke affectionately of 'Master', and all that he said tended towards "rather a more kind and familiar view" of Beckford than the traveller had anticipated.[18] This was also the opinion of C. F. Porden, the architect, as a result of his visit eighteen months after Beckford's departure: "my revisit has more than ever confirmed me in my opinion of the high respect in which the Founder, its only true and proper Lord, is and will be for ever held; all seem to regret his absence, and let who will possess the domain, their name must be eclipsed by that of Beckford".[19]

Beckford's Radicalism made him mistrust the future of 'feudal' Europe but look forward to that of America, a country "apparently destined to become the first in the world, the grandeur of whose maturity may well be augured from a state of adolescence which has produced characters already revered as the benefactors of Mankind". He was writing to a distinguished and enlightened American, James Wadsworth,[20] who wanted his opinion on the encouragement of European immigration into the States. His letter shows that he had read a rather specialised book[21] just published, which discussed the extraordinary growth of population in America. He himself attributed this to her freedom from all that Europe had so long suffered—"the luxury of the rich, the extreme poverty of the poor, long, frequent and bloody wars, large fleets and standing armies, celibacy enjoined by monastic institutions, servitude of peasantry and other feudal oppressions". Consequently, he thought that America would be unwise to accept colonists from "an old decrepit world, whose principles, moral, religious and political, are universally shaken and unsettled and too generally changed and corrupted, if not in many countries intirely annihilated."[22]

He was ready to back his judgement in a practical way. In April 1799 he bought for £9,400 (47,000 dollars) from James Wadsworth a tract of 23,000 acres of unsettled wilderness on the Genesee River in North Western New York State;[23] he even considered purchasing, for its landscape merits, 10,000 acres in the area of West Mountain, near Hartford, which later became the Wadsworth country seat known as Monte Video.[24] In reporting these transactions, John Trumbull, the American artist, said "should the confusion of Europe increase much further I should not be surprised to see Mr. Beckford establish himself in the U.S."

It is interesting to find Beckford involved in one of the great land speculations of the day. His acquisition on the Genesee was a residuary part of what is known as the Phelps-Gorham Purchase. In 1788 the State of Massachusetts sold six million acres of wilderness to a syndicate of this name, just when the post-War of Independence boom in unsettled territories was beginning. The land-bubble was pricked in 1796, and some of Phelps' fellow-speculators were imprisoned for debt. One of the big purchasers had been Jeremiah Wadsworth of Hartford. He involved his cousin James, who, with other Americans and acting as his agent,

BECKFORD'S DWARF
by the PRESIDENT OF THE ROYAL ACADEMY (Benjamin West)

came over to Europe in 1796 to interest foreign capitalists in the great blocks of land which were now overhanging the market! So, as always happens to amateurs, Beckford got the raw end of the deal.

The only sphere in which, though a Radical Whig, he seems to have been really illiberal, was his steady refusal to support the prohibition of slavery and its traffic. The third Lord Holland, whom Beckford admired as "the finest gentleman in England", was anti-slavery and, as a result, lost most of *his wife's* income from Jamaica! But Beckford's attitude to money was different. He was riddled with anxiety and terrified of being in debt. He had before him the example of his first cousin, William Beckford of Somerley, the historian of Jamaica, who spent several years as a debtor in the Fleet prison and dunned him for money.[25] He also had the innate Jamaican fear of a negro rising, strengthened by the continual example of San Domingo (Haiti) from 1791 and the Maroon rising in Jamaica in 1795-6.[26] He was also influenced by his hatred of the 'bible-mongers'—the Evangelical Clapham sect, whose 'methodistical' religion and outlook on life he detested. He was not, however, unsympathetic to negroes, as is shewn by his note on them in his copy of Henry Wansey's *Excursion to the United States in 1794*.[27] The conflict in him between humanity and self-interest, between his outlook as a radical and his position as one of the greatest slave-owners of the day, increased the anxiety and sense of guilt which was his most fundamental characteristic.

Chapter XII

THE ORIGIN OF FONTHILL

Beckford's most remarkable but least enduring achievement was the building of the 'gothic' Abbey of Fonthill over a period of twenty-two years from the winter of 1796. Building became a mania, which also seized many of his contemporaries. But he was not merely doing something which was 'in the air' during the period; he was carrying out a dream which began in his earliest years. It started as a tower, it continued as a baronial hall, it finished as an abbey.

His Chinese reading notes, made in his teens, show how much the idea of voluptuous and despotic seclusion in a tower appealed to him. *Vathek*, written in 1782, opens with the same theme. His compelling interest in towers was derived from his father: "He seems first to have thought of a tower on the summit of a high hill [Stop's Beacon], . . . being nothing more than the continuation of a building of which his father the Alderman had laid the foundation. It is very probable that from this work of his father's he imbibed this fondness for towers which seems to have so much distinguished him . . . With Mr. Beckford a tower in a picture was to the last an object of interest. At an exhibition of paintings, wherever a tower was delineated, he always ran to look at it first, and dealers have said that he purchased pictures, sometimes of inferior merit, because they chanced to contain well invented towers. Almost all the sketches he made from imagination had in them a lofty tower placed on a mountain or high over a foaming

THE ORIGIN OF FONTHILL

river, and when he showed them his first remark generally was, 'Look how admirably that tower comes in; what a fine effect such an object always produces in a picture'!"[1]

As Beckford passed from childhood to youth, his dream developed with his reading. Arthurian legend, mediaeval ballad, Spencer and other authors fired him with the idea of building a baronial hall.[2] When he was in his eighteenth year he foreshadowed Fonthill in a prophetic essay-letter which he wrote from Switzerland to Alexander Cozens:[3] "the time will arrive when we may abstract ourselves at least one hundred days from the world, and in retirement give way to our romantic inclinations . . . There we will execute those plans you have imagined, and realise in some measure the dreams of our fancy . . . we shall ascend a lofty hill, which till lately was a mountain in my eyes. There I hope to erect a Tower dedicated to meditation, on whose summit we will take our station and survey the vast range of countries beneath . . . At midnight . . . we will recline on stately couches placed on the roof of our Tower, and our eyes shall wander among the stars. We will then hazard our conjectures of their destination and audaciously wing towards them our imaginary flight."

From this there is only a short step to the superstitious Vathek on the summit of his tower. Indeed, during this 'literary trance' Beckford ranges freely on semi-magical ground—Pharoah's magicians, the Old Serpent, the Tower of Babel, the Solomonian and Apocryphal literature, etc.

After their excursions, he and Cozens return to the Tower along an avenue such as he later planted. Already, in his imagination, the Fonthill that we know has been built. As he and Cozens approach, "the painted windows of a hall high above in the Tower will gleam with the light of many tapers, and summon us to our evening's repast. We shall ascend the hundred steps which lead to the spacious Hall, wainscoted with cedar, whose arched roof will be strangely sculptured with gothic devices. The pavement is ruddy marble and the seats are painted with achievements; the tall windows are crowded with gorgeous figures coloured in antient times. Here are Knights, and Sovereigns clad in rich mosaic, Saints distinguished by their glories, and divers quaint forms unintelligable to modern Ages. Above the great window and below the others, is a broad and ample Gallery inclosed with gilt lattices and supported by thin-waisted pillars fretted with scrupulous dexterity. The doors of old oak are large and folded; in the huge chimney . . . will be placed grotesque vases of antique china, filled with Tube roses, and in the Gallery you will find stout coffers of cedar whose laborious carvings will amuse you for some moments. Open them and you will discover robes of state, rich chalices and censers, glistening apparel, coral rosaries and uncouth trinkets, the treasure of the imaginary Lady of the Tower . . . When you have thus gratified the first impulse of curiosity, I shall call you to a table placed in the middle of the Hall, spread with embroidered linnen that trails on the ground, and loaded with choice viands in dishes of embossed plate. Our servants stand silently around; I read in your eyes that you wish them to depart. They understand my signs and, setting down on the pavement the massy vases of wine which they bore, will leave us alone."

Their imaginations are fired by their conversation about Odin and King Arthur, aided by their splendid surroundings and by the skilful use of music emanating from a hidden source: "we shall gaze at the objects in our sight, admire the rich imagery of the plate, the tapers flaming with the wind and diffusing so grand a lustre about the Hall and all its barbarous magnificence. Scarce shall we have finished our repast, when our ears will be struck with the sweepings of distant harps . . . The aweful sound will ring among the pillars and the arches of the roof. We shall grow animated, and rising

THE ORIGIN OF FONTHILL

hastily from our repast, walk to and fro across the pavement. Now agitated, now delighted, now fired, our enthusiasm increasing

> Till full before our dauntless eyes
> The portals nine of Hell arise."

One recollects the eeriness of Fonthill Abbey at night as the notes of the organ, alternately swelling and dying away, sounded down the three hundred feet of empty, candle-lit galleries.

Beckford was a past-master at contriving contrasts. So they "grow calm by degrees and, filled with softer sensations, begin to enjoy the perfume of the Tube roses, to notice the stillness of the Hall, the declining lamps, and the moon full behind the painted casements, mixing her light with their vivid hues. The reflection of these paintings on the marble pavement, where they tremble like the undulating shades of water thrown by the sun on the arches of a bridge, will tempt us to imagine we behold such visions as played before Shakespear's fancy—when he makes Clarence relate his dream, when Macbeth sees prophetic apparitions, or when Posthumus is ravished with more gentle tho' not less mystical trances."

Beckford already shows two characteristics which would have led him to shut himself up in Fonthill, at any rate for long periods, even if he had not been disgraced; these were his contempt for his fellow-men and his unwillingness to emerge from his dream into reality. In the imaginary tower he and Cozens awake to find that "we are yet in the Land of Men, and that we are still subjected to their employments, to their duties, to their material subsistence. How unwilling shall we feel to quit the regions of imaginary happiness! How loth to dissapate the soft illusions of the night!" And when he is showing Cozens his secret chambers at the top of the tower, he says "I seem already to behold the joy and animation of your countenance, when you stand freed from the embarrassments of the world in this lofty Tower, exulting . . . in a situation so far above the Race from whose incursions you shrink, with one all [of] whose feelings and sentiments vibrate in unison with your own; one who triumphs in the reflection of imbibing an air uncontaminated with the breath of wretches, the objects of our contempt and detestation". This was one of Vathek's chief characteristics!

In this essay there is no idea of a monastic construction. Indeed, Christianity and Catholicism are not discussed; Beckford's outlook is pantheistic. "In the midst of this vast temple of Nature" formed by the Swiss Alps from which he wrote, he "silently adored the Supreme Power". The reason is that he had not yet seen the Grande Chartreuse, which he visited the following June. Nevertheless, he must have been influenced in childhood by a monastic ruin on one of his properties, Witham Abbey, where his father started to build a mansion. Witham meant much to him, for it was the last of his English properties which he relinquished before selling Fonthill;[4] and we have seen with what feeling he spoke of it when describing his visit to the Grande Chartreuse. So, in accordance with contemporary ideas, he imagines romantic monastic ruins on his estate.

So much for Beckford's Essay of 1777-8. It was easier to dream than to mould the components of the dream (solitary tower, baronial hall and chapel or ruined monastery) into a unity. There were inevitably false starts and frequent changes of plan; at one stage the tower and the hall were being built simultaneously on *different* spots. The evidence is too fragmentary and dateless to give a complete picture of the development of the conception.

Since the tower was the dominant *motif*, it is not surprising to find that the earliest announcement of Beckford's plan concerns tower-building. In January 1790 he wrote to Lady Craven: "One of my new estates in Jamaica brought me home seven thousand

THE ORIGIN OF FONTHILL

pounds last year more than usual.[5] So I am growing rich, and mean to build Towers, and sing hymns to the powers of Heaven on their summits, accompanied by almost as many sacbuts and psalteries as twanged round Nebuchadnezzar's image."

For this purpose, he tried to procure James Wyatt, the most famous contemporary architect. Beckford's earliest recorded letter to him shows how difficult this was. He had to wait, cajole and threaten; even then he may not have succeeded. The letter, dated 23rd October 1791, runs as follows: "Dear Sir, I have been waiting for you the *whole* summer: if my plans would allow me to wait the *whole* winter also, I might perhaps still afford a month or two's patience; but in a fortnight I have agreed to move, and therefore, should you still retain any idea of coming again to Fonthill, let me beg and intreat you to give me an opportunity *within ten days of the present date* of assuring you that, notwithstanding the disappointment it has been your pleasure to afflict me with, I am ever, dear Sir, your faithful and obedient Servant, William Beckford."

By that time it was too late, for in November 1791 Beckford went to the Continent and remained there until May 1793; then he was only back for six months before sailing to Portugal in November. But during this latter short stay at Fonthill he got some designs from Wyatt for improvements at Splendens and for new buildings; these included a "chapel upon Stop's Beacon,"[6] the spot where his father had started to build a tower.

We know that he was in earnest, because before sailing to Portugal he ordered the construction of a Barrier wall to enclose the 519 acres of Enchanted Gardens and Monastic Demesne, from the midst of which his new buildings were to rise. This was essential, so that his privacy would not be disturbed by the curious during operations; he wanted his buildings to rise fully fledged and perfect, as if by enchantment, before being seen by the tourist. Further, he could only enjoy these grounds as long as they were not profaned by 'unbelievers', by those whose incongruity would shatter their 'monastic' charm and Beckford's dream. Also, since his rejection by the world, bitterness had tinged his literary dream; he saw himself like Louis XI, who shut himself up behind Barrier, palisade and pit at Plessis-les-Tours.

Of course, his explanation of the wall to Redding was simpler and more dramatic than this—it deliberately encouraged the idea that he had acted suddenly, extravagantly, whimsically, like an oriental potentate. He hated hunting, and had vainly forbidden the local packs to cross his land. " 'They will take no denial, yet call themselves gentlemen', said he; 'on they go, worrying poor hares to death, in their red jackets. I will build a wall and exclude them'. This determination was hastened by a whole bevy of huntsmen and their dogs coming upon him when riding alone one day in a retired part of his grounds. He turned his horse's head back to the house in a furious passion, sent for his Steward, ordered the map of the estate to be brought to him, declared he would no longer tolerate such insolent trespassers, and had a builder sent for to contract for a wall immediately. The necessary stone was found upon the land. Not a moment was to be lost. From his natural impetuosity of temper he would admit no plea against his design, short of impossibility . . . He had a contract signed that the whole wall, above seven miles in extent, should be completed in twelve months."[7] There must be some truth in this characteristic story; perhaps this incident spurred him on to start what had in fact been carefully planned.

When Beckford returned from Portugal in June 1796, the first building project of which we hear is the favourite plan of an isolated tower for study on Stop's Beacon, for which Wyatt prepared a detailed plan.[8] That winter the local Press announced that Beckford was "collecting the materials" for this work.[9]

THE ORIGIN OF FONTHILL

But already in October 1796 he was hastily running up, like a bit of stage scenery, a mock abbey at the *other* end of the ridge, which was called Hinkley Hill. Beckford wrote to his new Agent, Captain Nicholas Williams, on 12th October 1796: "Wyatt has been doing wonders according to custom, and he has given the great Hall another push 20 feet or so; we shall reach Knoyle before we have done. You will see Wyatt and converse with him upon all subjects, and arrange by all means some plan of getting forwards with the Convent more rapidly. The windows should be put into the painters hands without delay." This is the first mention of the construction of what later became Fonthill Abbey.[10] It was on a less confined and more accessible site than Stop's Beacon, and its rapid progress tended to monopolise Beckford's interest and energies.

The solitary Vathek-like tower on the Beacon was therefore temporarily (as Beckford thought) abandoned. But he meant to return to it, as he explained to Sir William Hamilton that winter[11]: "If I could . . . I would . . . pass a few months with you whilst my *Babels* were growing; for I have more than one Babel in hand— the grand Babel so much paragraphed in the papers is not yet begun. I am staying my stomach with a little pleasure-building in the shape of an abbey, *which is already half-finished*. It contains apartments in the most gorgeous Gothic style with windows of painted glass, a chapel for blessed St. Anthony (66 ft. diameter and 72 high), a gallery 185 in length, and a tower 145 feet high." The "grand Babel so much paragraphed in the papers," and not yet begun, must be the tower on Stop's Beacon; meanwhile, he was merely "staying his stomach" with the mock abbey. In the end, the key idea of an imposing tower became incorporated in the Abbey; it did not re-emerge as a solitary tower until Beckford's old age, when he began to build one in 1826 on Lansdown, above Bath.

ENGLAND'S WEALTHIEST SON

By the summer of 1797 plans for the "Gothic building" just below Hinkley Hill were much enlarged, and Beckford had expensive ideas about its furnishing and decoration; the tower on Stop's Beacon was definitely languishing.[12] That November he already had the ultimate intention of demolishing Splendens and enlarging the mock Abbey as his mansion.[13]

Now at last, in November 1798, the new building was finally given its name 'Fonthill Abbey'.[14] Beckford began to think of himself as the founder of a real Abbey, in which he might be buried (on the second floor, north of the Tower, which was to have a spire and not, as later, a lantern). Farington notes: "The Abbey to be endowed, and Cathedral Service to be performed in the most splendid manner that the Protestant religion will admit. A Gallery leading from the top of the Church to be decorated with paintings, the works of English artists. Beckford's own tomb to be placed at the end of this Gallery, as having been an encourager of Art."

Pilgrims were to walk 125 feet up this gallery and gaze in awe through wire gratings at the coffin of the Founder-Abbot, who, as a rich man, awaited his final doom at the Last Judgement in this "Revelation Chamber".[15] To impress this lesson on founder and onlooker alike and to remind them of the nearness of Death, the Chamber was to be hung with the gruesome pictures in which West illustrated scenes from the sixth chapter of the Book of Revelation. To the end of his life Beckford kept one of them, *The Opening of the Sixth Seal*, and as late as 1828 bought a picture with the same title by Francis Danby,[16] the apocalyptic rival of John Martin.

There was one hitherto unsuspected influence on the conception of Fonthill Abbey. When Beckford was in Lisbon in December 1793 he drew a highly professional sketch of the ground plan of his proposed *Lisbon* house. Many of its features were developed later at Fonthill— each room opened out into the next to allow an uninterrupted vista, which terminated in an apse beyond

THE ORIGIN OF FONTHILL

the Sanctuary steps, in which was to be a statue or picture of St. Anthony of Padua, illumined by candelabra and hanging lamps of gilded bronze; each room corresponds to one at Fonthill on the main floor; the outer wall was pierced at intervals by large windows, and there was a fountain in the courtyard; there was also an octagon, in some ways similar to that at Fonthill. Incidentally, people have always thought that Beckford got his idea for the Octagon at Fonthill from Batalha monastery, which he did not visit until June 1794, and which Murphy delineated in his book in 1795.

Beckford sent his plan to Wyatt for consideration, with a letter which makes it clear that he was discussing his Lisbon house, and not some plans for Fonthill (which had already been agreed—a mere gothic "chapel upon Stop's Beacon".).[17] The Lisbon plan shows that Beckford could make an architectural sketch and develop his own ideas, and that he influenced the conception and plan of the later Fonthill Abbey—"by far the most exciting building of its time", as Sir Kenneth Clark calls it.[18]

Chapter XIII

THE SPLENDOUR OF FONTHILL

Throughout its existence until the Tower fell in December 1825, the Abbey had only one great day; only once was it filled with gay and distinguished company, when the sound of laughter and din of conversation echoed down the great gallery. And strangely enough, this was before it was ever lived in, when even the first stage of the building was not completed. For when Nelson and Emma and Sir William Hamilton dined there in state on 23rd December 1800, only the first (main) floor was finished, and only the south and west wings were standing.

From the Southern Entrance Hall, the guests passed into the Oak or Brown Parlour on the ground floor; here they dined off a refectory table which filled the whole length of the room (52 feet). This was afterwards Beckford's own dining room. We can imagine his sadness as he dined alone in state with his train of servants round him, recollecting the one glorious evening which the room had known; his melancholy was increased by the brown oak wainscoting, the dark damask curtains, the sober-hued tapestries and the low ceiling.

The guests then went upstairs to the south end of St. Michael's Gallery; at that date this end was divided from the rest of the gallery by a large gothic 'screen', and was called the Library. The 'screen' was thrown open. They looked northwards up the gallery, their gaze led on by two long lines of golden candlesticks on ebony stands. There, at the far end, backed by scarlet curtains, was Rossi's statue of St. Anthony with the

THE SPLENDOUR OF FONTHILL

Infant Saviour in his arms. The shrine was loaded with jewelled reliquaries, and lit by many candlesticks and gilt candelabrae. As they gazed, solemn strains of music broke forth, suggesting "the idea of a solemn religious service [for the Dead], and fixing the wandering thoughts upon things unearthly."[1]

But the climax came when the guests turned round, facing south to the great oriel plate-glass window at the far end from the shrine. Here, the lights on the shrine were mirrored back a thousand times, and the long double line of tapers was narrowed into an endlessly receding perspective, producing a magical effect. Beckford was re-creating his unforgettable experience in York Minster during his English tour in 1779.

In those days the apertures between the eight arches of the altar-screen in York Minster were glazed with plate glass. Beyond is the magnificent painted East window, rising almost from floor to roof, a mass of tracery and colour. Young Beckford had been admiring this window from close to; he then turned round, to find it reflected and magnified in the plate-glass of the altar-screen. He described his sensations in his diary: "But what suggested a finer idea of vision and enchantment than anything I ever beheld was—upon my turning round—its reflection on the glazed work of the screen which, as I advanced (all the way communicating my own motion), spread wider and wider and rose every step I took, till the whole in all its varied hues and splendid colouring hung suspended in the air. This apparition held me in astonishment till the sun disappeared and, the twilight increasing, it faded away. I now retreated, as yet scarcely crediting what I had seen, and moving slowly along, reached my old station beneath the tower."

So Beckford was not just a clever theatrical producer, intent on impressing his guests. He was always creating a dream-world and, above all, reviving youthful memories of his happier past. In a way, he was like a magician, with power over Time: for a fleeting moment he could summon back the Past, as if it had never disappeared for ever down the corridors of Time.

The visit of the Hero of the Nile and the celebrated Hamiltons, supported by the King's favourite, West, who was President of the Royal Academy, was a social climax for the man upon whom no neighbour would call. So he now took the great decision, long delayed, to make the Abbey habitable and obtain building material by demolishing the colonnade and wings of Splendens. Accordingly, the latter's surplus furniture and fittings unsuitable for a Gothic abbey, were auctioned there in August 1801; pictures, similarly unsuitable, or of which Beckford had tired, were auctioned in February and March 1802. Now that he was going to live in the Abbey, the vista (a mere 112 feet), provided by St. Michael's Gallery was insufficient; in any case, he wanted another gallery for pictures and books, and rooms for guests, well away from his own. So King Edward's Gallery was planned, to continue the vista to the north of the Octagon; a second floor was to run above these galleries.

It was fantastic that he should ever have made such plans, and pursued them so perseveringly. For, as we shall see later, he was reeling under a series of financial losses. As Lettice observed, they all stood on "rotten ground", and yet "the humour of Abbey building" grew.[2] This shows that Beckford was incurably seized by building mania—common enough then and in other periods, and a disease which feeds upon itself. We need not therefore find any special explanation in his case, but can easily see contributory factors.

Building was an outlet for his frustrated energy, a compensation for his social disgrace, a distraction from his underlying pessimism and despair—"some people drink to forget their unhappiness; I do not drink, I build," he said.[3] It gave him a sense of consequence to mingle freely amongst his workmen, amongst whom he was that 'sovereign master' he had always longed to be. It gave him a sense of power to gloat over the Abbey rising at night by torchlight, as if by magic. But these explanations are less than fair to Beckford. If there had been no such reasons, still he would have built. For he had a strong creative urge to make things beautiful, enchanting and sublime.

Because of his financial difficulties and a long absence in France, building proceeded "gently, and oh! so slowly, and with all the economy of a Father Guardian of the poorest of monasteries."[4] Lady Ann Hamilton, in her account of her visit to the Abbey in September 1803, makes no mention of the second floor or of the North Wing (beyond giving its proposed length). But there was another reason for delay, responsibility for which lies with the architect Wyatt. The Abbey had been cased in a new material, compo-cement, which was supposed to be 'everlasting'. In less than seven years the English climate had caused it to crumble! The result was that from the summer of 1806 the Tower, if not the wings to the south and west, had to be dismantled and rebuilt in stone.[5] Beckford's temperament and sense of the theatrical are usually blamed for the running-up of the Abbey in timber and cement. But Wyatt's work elsewhere (for example, on the new Parliamentary buildings) was equally shoddy and insubstantial, and of the same materials. The use of compo-cement was a craze of the day, but not shared by all architects. Decision on the use of it was the responsibility of the architect, not of his patron.

We do not know how long this work took; it was sufficiently far advanced for Beckford to move into the South Wing in the summer of 1807. But the Tower was often a web of scaffolding and vibrated with hammering until at least the autumn of 1809.[6] The Octagon was a mere shell, undecorated and unfurnished, until September 1808, when Beckford completed its interior stuccoing.

ENGLAND'S WEALTHIEST SON

As the work proceeded by torchlight, Beckford stood in the Nunnery arcade of the Tower, ninety feet up, in the dampness of September nights, gloating over the scene as the great buckets of plaster swished past him, to disappear into the web of scaffolding far above his head: "It's really stupendous, the spectacle here at night—the number of people at work, lit up by lads; the innumerable torches suspended everywhere, the immense and endless spaces, the gulph below; above, the gigantic spider's web of scaffolding—especially when, standing under the finished and numberless arches of the galleries, I listen to the reverberating voices in the stillness of the night, and see immense buckets of plaster and water ascending, as if they were drawn up from the bowels of a mine, amid shouts from subterranean depths, oaths from Hell itself, and chanting from Pandemonium or the synagogue".[7]

He was not only an onlooker. He was "busy from morning to night shouting, supervising and singing out of tune in the cursèd and interminable Octagon"[8], engaged in long arguments on the spot with Dixon the architect and George Hayter, his Clerk of the Works, uncle of Queen Victoria's Painter-in-Ordinary. In the middle of a letter to his friend Franchi he would have to break off, saying "Farewell. The Octagon is calling me—*j'entends sa voix.*"

Beckford could not begin one of the most ambitious of all his building schemes, the Eastern Transept, until the summer of 1812, when the price of sugar began its fantastic but short-lived rise to the all-time high of 1814, in anticipation of the French collapse and the opening of European markets. The story of the building of this Wing, which continued by fits and starts until 1818, is told in Beckford's letters in *Life at Fonthill*. There we find numerous examples of Wyatt's faulty methods and work. Even in 1821 it was said "the tower is acknowledged to be a weak and dangerous structure, and so tottering are the eight surmounting pinnacles that they

THE RUINS OF FONTHILL, 1825, by John Buckler

are held on their bases by strong iron bars, to the no less disparagement of the building than of the builder".[9] The architect C. F. Porden, during his visits in 1823, exclaimed "Would to God it had been more substantially built! But as it is, its ruins will tell a tale of wonder." Porden was merely anticipating by two years the final fall of the Tower in December 1825!

A contemporary said, "The great Abbey . . . rose like an exhalation and passed away like a summer cloud."[10] This phrase echoes Milton's description of the building of the Palace of Pandemonium by Satan, Beckford's favourite literary Hero. Indeed, there was something Satanic about the Abbey. As Durazzo was conducted round by Tom Moore the poet, he exclaimed at every step, *Un homme doit avoir le Diable au corps pour bâtir une maison comme ça.*[11] This reaction was partly inspired by the melancholy atmosphere of the interior at night and on sunless days. William Hamilton, the artist, found it unsupportable and described "the extraordinary effect which that species of building when suitably furnished, as is here the case, has on the mind. It fills the mind with a sentiment which is almost too much to support, certainly of too melancholy a cast to be long dwelt upon".[12] Beckford deliberately created this impression in order to reflect his religious outlook and sombre spirit.[13]

This spirit was also revealed in the situation of the Abbey and its relationship to its surroundings. In Turner's sketches in the Print Room of the British Museum, the remote and solitary tower of the Abbey broods over the sheep-folds, lakes and farms from its dominating ridge. Whether Turner was sketching the penned sheep, the lovely beeches or the rural scenes, he could not escape from that thin finger pointing menacingly upwards on the skyline. Constable felt the same: "We passed Fonthill Gate; it is strange that such a place, so fairy-like and so filling by every standard a role of taste and elegance, should be standing alone in these melancholy regions of the Wiltshire Downs."[14] The Abbé Macquin also conveys this impression in his poem on the Abbey:[15]

"the splendid mansion, where
Above the puny jarrings of the world,
Above the strife for glory and for power,
Wrapt in his cloak of learning and of wit,
A mind of fire, a deeply feeling heart,
The founder stands aloft—a stranger to our sphere."

Since the Abbey expressed the personality of the most isolated man of his day, and one of the most imaginative and un-English, it was bound to be "an altogether exceptional house"[16], "something apart from the main stream of the Gothic movement, an unexpected piece of treasure-trove carried in on the tide of romanticism, and crumbling as it struck the shore."[17] Like its creator, it did not fit in with society and current conceptions. "Men marvelled at Fonthill, but did not imitate it. They stared at it, invented wild tales of what went on inside it, and when it fell down, forgot it." Like most bons mots, this is an exaggeration. Sir John Summerson suggests that its plan gave Barry his idea for the new Houses of Parliament and influenced Sir George Beaumont's architect at Coleorton.[18]

Nor was James Wyatt the only architect to get professional experience at Fonthill. His sons Philip and Benjamin and his assistant Dixon worked there,[19] and Jeffry Wyatt used to stay. Those who made topographical drawings of it would have got ideas and learnt various lessons. They included Charles Wild,[20] George Cattermole, J. F. Porden, J. C. Buckler and John Le Keux; the first three were young men at the beginning of their careers. Wild was later author of books on our Cathedrals and on mediaeval architecture abroad. Cattermole came to be regarded as an important artist, and wanted to bring the Past to life in his art, with all its architecture and costume and religion. J. F. Porden became a Church architect, and Buckler well-known in the Gothic Revival of Domestic architecture. Le Keux was a fine engraver of plates for Britton and Pugin. Britton himself was the leading publicist of the Gothic Revival in the generation between John Carter and Pugin. He visited Fonthill, corresponded with Beckford and published *Illustrations, Graphic and Literary, of Fonthill*, for which he employed most of the topographical artists just mentioned.

All these professional men had access to Beckford's important library on art and art history.[21] There they might find unique items for study, such as an unpublished royal folio volume of 57 watercolours with manuscript descriptions by John Carter himself, entitled *Antiquities from Coventry . . Tewksbury . . etc.* (1788-1803). The catalogue of Beckford's library (more conveniently studied in the Hamilton Palace Sale catalogue than in the ill-arranged catalogue of the 1823 sale by Phillips) shows him to be a serious, life-long student of mediaeval and modern Gothic, as do some of the subjects in his stained-glass windows. These were commissioned as early as 1799 at a reputed cost of £12,000[22] from Eginton, the reviver of stained-glass manufacture in England. Some of the windows at Fonthill had drawings from mediaeval tombs, including that of Edmund Crouchback in Westminster Abbey (the finest tomb of its period).[23] Even the pictures at Fonthill were an aid to Gothic scholarship—the minutiae of architecture, costume and the goldsmith's work attracted Beckford in his mid-fifteenth century Flemish *Exhumation of St. Hubert* (now in the National Gallery). Fonthill must have been a Mecca for gothicisers; as such, it had more influence than can be directly proved.

His contemporaries described it as 'this fairy palace',[24] 'raised more by magick . . . than by the labour of the human hand.'[25] Constable's reaction is typical: "The entrance and when within is truly beautifull. Imagine the inside of the Cathedral at Salisbury, or indeed any beautifull Gothick building, magnificently fitted up with crimson and gold, antient pictures, in almost every nitch statues, large massive gold boxes for relicks, etc., etc., beautifull and rich carpets, curtains and glasses . . . all this makes it on the whole a strange, ideal, romantic place, quite fairy land."[26]

This contemporary appreciation by well-qualified persons needs emphasising, because nowadays Fonthill is contemptuously dismissed as a 'folly'; and Hazlitt's vitriolic attack on the art treasures which it housed and the taste which it displayed has left an uneasy memory of triviality and meretriciousness. It is therefore worth having the opinion of Dr. Waagen, Director of the Royal Gallery at Berlin, the foremost European art critic of his day. Although he had not visited Fonthill, he had just seen Beckford's rooms and collections in Bath, and talked with connoisseurs who had seen the place. He writes: "On the whole, I came away with the conviction that Mr. Beckford unites, in a very rare degree, an immense fortune with a general and refined love of art and a highly-cultivated taste. Such a man alone could have produced a creation like Fonthill Abbey, which, from the picture that I am now able to form of it, must have realised the impression of a fairy tale. The extensive Gothic building, with a lofty, very elegant tower, from the views which I have seen of it, must have had, in the highest degree, the grandly fantastic character by which this style of architecture exercises so wonderful a charm. Conceive the interior adorned with . . . important works of art, with the most elegant and costly furniture; conceive it surrounded by all that the art of gardening in England can effect by the aid of a picturesquely-varied ground, luxuriant vegetation, and a great mass of natural running water; and you will have a general idea of this magic spot, which so far maintained this character that for a long time no strange foot was permitted to intrude. Accordingly, when Mr. Beckford . . . resolved . . . to sell it with all its contents, the fashionable and the unfashionable world flocked from all parts of England to wonder at this 'lion', the greatest that had long been exhibited ... Unhappily, Fonthill Abbey has resembled also in its transitory existence the frail creations of the world of enchantment."[27]

"The frail creations of the world of enchantment"! This was Beckford's aim. The whole *mis-en-scène* was designed to produce an illusion. He knew perfectly well that, when expressed in perishable media, such creations do not outlast the will that has evoked them. He cannot have expected Fonthill to endure. The fact that it vanished without a trace is therefore no criticism of his work, and no indication of superficiality or failure. He must be judged by a different yardstick. The accounts of his contemporaries indicate that he did succeed in what he planned.

Inside the Abbey were two focal points calculated to astonish and entrance—the vista leading 312 feet up the galleries to the Oratory; and the Octagon—the centre of the building from which each of its four arms radiated, and from which every part could be taken in at a glance. As Sir John Summerson says, "Some of the interiors must have been, at the lowest estimate, sensational; especially the central octagon."[28] Even before King Edward's Gallery was added, the vista was impressive: "the beauty of this Gallery [St. Michael's] must be seen to be conceived. When lit up, the gradation of light is very fine—the sombre hue of the Gallery, lit only by two dozen candles, till it meets that immense blaze of light at the further end, which casts an inconceivable glow over the ceiling and all the near objects. At daylight, the scene, tho' very different, is very fine. If the sun is powerful, its reflection thro' the crimson serge is almost equal to torch-light; and at all times you seem elevated above the world, looking over the finest woods, doubly reflected in water . . ."[29] Then, at the far end of the galleries there was the set-piece of the great theatrical producer. From the light and colour of King

Edward's Gallery, the visitor passed into the gloom and simplicity of the Vaulted Corridor. A curtain fell behind him: "It is but the drawing of a curtain, and not only all the glitter of the adjoining splendour, but all the pomps and vanities of the world seem . . . to be shut out for ever."[30]

The visitor was now in a suitable frame of mind to enter the Oratory itself—goal of his pilgrimage down three hundred feet of crimson carpet. "The perfect simplicity which reigned in such an apartment, in which he [Beckford] was careful to introduce nothing that could distract attention; the simple dim shining lamp; the darkly-tinted light from the windows, deepening the shadows of the recesses around the Statue, and but faintly illuminating the gilt mouldings; the windows nearly veiled in rich purple, crimson and gold draperies; the organ sending its deep prolonged music along the perspective of the immense galleries, while now and then the odour of the incense used in Catholic worship was employed to heighten the effect"—all was intended to produce "illusions that carried the mind into a pleasing captivity".[31]

As Beckford gazed at this solemn spectacle in the evening, in the heart of Protestant England, he re-lived the sensations of 1778 when he first described a Catholic shrine, the chapel of the Grande Chartreuse.

*　　*　　*　　*

Beckford told Redding that his greatest achievement was the creation of the flowering wilderness round the Abbey (within the Barrier wall): "Mr. Beckford was to the highest degree proud of that on which he had lavished years of personal attention, in which his taste and knowledge was more conspicuous than in anything he had ever done besides."[32] He claimed no credit for features outside the Barrier—the grotto by Josiah Lane in imitation of one he had made at Pain's Hill for Beckford's maternal great-uncle, Charles Hamilton[33];

the Alpine Garden formed from a stone quarry under Lettice's supervision[34]; the Great Terrace, the hermitage, the caverns, the old lake in front of Splendens, and similar 'picturesque' features. They had been formed round Splendens and had not been "constructed upon one pervading principle of art". What Beckford had in mind in making this claim, and the sources of his inspiration, are described in Chapter IV of Rutter's *Delineations of Fonthill* (material which comes direct from Beckford).[35]

The pervading principle of design was that everything should appear to be natural, that the art which had gone to the creation of this scenery should be concealed. "We almost despair", says Rutter, "of producing any very distinct impressions upon the mind of the reader. The ornamented grounds of Fonthill, though unequalled in extent, contain very few objects that will admit of individual description. The great principle upon which this labyrinth of groves has been constructed, is that of exhibiting an union of the wildest and the most ornamented scenery, the picturesque and the beautiful, in close society. The utmost profusion of expense has been bestowed, not to amaze the senses by some rich and magical effect of art, but to keep the mind in a perpetual enjoyment of the most striking beauties and richest decorations of nature; they go far to realize the description of the gardens of Armida . . ."

Nature abhors "the horror of straight lines". These were banished from the Abbey grounds; and yet Beckford managed to plant three great intersecting avenues—such was his skill as a landscapist. The most important of the three, The Great Western Avenue, a hundred feet broad, ran for nearly a mile to the Great West Entrance of the Abbey. Half-way along was a depression, of which Beckford took advantage and which he probably deepened. This gave variety to the avenue and helped its 'natural' appearance. The ordinary planner would have filled this up to make a broad stately avenue on level ground, along the full length of which the building at the end would have been seen. Avenues of this familiar type are formed by trees of the same species planted at regular intervals; not so Beckford's. They were bounded by a variety of trees and shrubs, with undergrowth, forming an irregular line, "just as we may suppose they would have been if the avenue had been cut out of a natural wood".[36] He also achieved a natural effect and avoided the appearance of the offending straight line by having these avenues turfed instead of gravelled. Indeed, everywhere he swept away gravel paths, made-up roads and fences, which formalised and broke up the landscape. As the avenue approached the Abbey it widened "so as to leave a broad area in front; and this area is so admirably broken by scattered native trees and wild bushes, so as to leave no doubt in the mind of the spectator of its having been cleared by the founders of the abbey from the native forest".

So much for his avenues. There were other ways in which he created beautiful effects which *seemed* to be natural. Tree-planting was planned to get the right landscape effects and take advantage of different shades of foliage. For example, the Abbey was set off by dark masses of Scotch fir and oak, which also contrasted with their undergrowth of hazel, holly, thorn and furze and with a few larch and birch. This was done on such a large scale and in such a free manner that no idea of planning was conveyed. He also obtained apparently natural effects by planting exotic trees and shrubs, newly introduced into Britain, "in secluded places only; and these he disposed in what may be called by-scenes in the woods, in such a manner as that a person who knew nothing of trees could never suspect that they were not natives. There was an American ground . . ., consisting of many of the trees and shrubs of that country, disposed in groups and thickets, as if they had sprung up naturally . . . There was a rose-ground, a thornery, and a pinetum treated in the same manner." It was

THE SPLENDOUR OF FONTHILL

impossible to say where garden ended and glade began; there were no hard-and-fast lines or divisions of any sort.

His greatest *tour de force* was to create the illusion of a monastic demesne of 500 acres, surrounding the Abbey and in harmony with it. "This place," Loudon wrote, "deserves to be visited by every person . . desirous of improving himself in landscape gardening; because it is the only one in England in which he will find the most perfect unity of character belonging to an age long since past in this country, and only now to be found in certain mountainous regions of Catholic countries on the Continent. The chief object of Mr. Beckford seems to have been to impress this character on all the leading features of Fonthill." As Loudon approached from the Downs on the Hindon side, "the occasional glimpses caught of Fonthill from the high parts of the open downs, surrounded by woods, and without a single human habitation, a fence or a made road appearing in the landscape, convey to a stranger a correct impression of the character of the place . . . On arriving at the miserable little town of Hindon, its appearance served rather to heighten than to lessen this impression." As Loudon walked up the Great Western Avenue, he was struck by "the solemn solitary grandeur of the scene" and reminded of Alpine monasteries by the ground falling away sharply to right and left, the steep sides covered with woods, through which peeped the water of lakes, and the spiry-topped alpine trees.[37] Immediately round the Abbey were no exotic trees or flowers, "save an apricot and a fig tree, planted against the south side of the grand entrance, as we may suppose, by some monk who had brought the seeds of these fruits from some Italian or Swiss monastery". Not far off was a herb garden, "containing such plants as we may suppose the monks might have cultivated to use in medicine". "At the distance of a few yards, there was a range of humble sheds, in which workmen of different kinds were employed, hewing and carving for continuous additions of improvements; and this was also quite in character with the scene, as such was often the case with ancient monastic establishments."

This illusion of living in another age was also created when the Abbey was seen by moonlight. It was like reading a page from Uvedale Price's *Essay on the Picturesque* : "All the characteristic beauties of the avenue, its solemn stillness, the religious awe it inspires, are greatly heightened by moonlight. This I once very strongly experienced in approaching a venerable castle-like mansion, built in the beginning of the 15th century; a few gleams had pierced the deep gloom of the avenue; a large massive tower at the end of it, seen through a long perspective, and half lit by the uncertain beams of the moon, had a grand mysterious effect. Suddenly, a light appeared in the tower, then as suddenly its twinkling vanished, and only the silvery rays of the moon prevailed; again more lights quickly shifted to different parts of the building, and the whole scene most forcibly brought to my fancy the times of fairies and chivalry."

After quoting Price's description of moonlight, Rutter continues: "Such a scene at Fonthill brings to mind the times of devotional seclusion; and when we behold above its turrets some dim light glimmering at a prodigious elevation, we forget the common inhabitants of a modern dwelling, and fancy that *there* is the cell of the pale votary whose
    Lamp at midnight hour
  Is seen in some high lonely tower."

Curious how Beckford's conversation with Rutter on his gardening principles has brought us back to that persistent image of him as a solitary being looking *down* on our sphere of puny worldlings! This was how he saw himself as the young Caliph Vathek, who "cast his eyes below and beheld men not larger than pismires".

One of the beauty spots was Bitham Lake, which Beckford excavated and dammed up in a deep hollow south of the Abbey. Boughs hung over its glassy surface, in which the Abbey with its surrounding precipices and woods were reflected. Herons fished along its edge, and flocks of wildfowl graced its waters. Everything seemed so natural, as if it had always been there. "Here everything is gradually lapsing into antiquity—grass up to the very doors, etc. The lake looks as if God had made it, it is so natural, without the least trace of art; I don't say it is marvellous, for its banks are too flat, but it spreads itself grandiosely, and the swans look as if they are in Paradise."[38]

Beckford often remarked that he looked at things "with the eye of a painter". Thus, like Uvedale Price and many of his contemporaries, some of his landscapes reproduced scenes from Claude, Poussin, Salvator Rosa, Cuyp, Ruysdael, Wilson and Turner. Another important inspiration was literary. One of the classical themes of special interest to him as a boy was that of the Fortunate Isles and other paradaisical gardens. He collected Latin and Greek references to them, which he incorporated in an imaginative essay, *The Dome of the Setting Sun*.[39] The dome was an imaginary 'temple' erected by him in the grounds of Fonthill. The sunset gleamed on its "ivory columns, golden cornices, statues of bronze and amber vases". In the twilight Beckford seemed "like one left desolate behind"; so, to console him, at a sign "a silken pavillion is raised in the center beneath, whose yellow transparent veil sheds a mellow light and by the sweetest deception prolongs the lost, the interesting glow of sunset". Here he made a vow, as it were, which was the basis of his later gardening and life at Fonthill:

> "*Elysium shall be mine*, the blissful plains
> Of utmost Earth where Rhadamanthus reigns.
> Joys ever young, unmixed with pain or fear
> Fill the wide circle of th' eternal year."[40]

In this mood he contemplated the Fortunate Isles "to which the souls of Heroes were transported after death":

ENGLAND'S WEALTHIEST SON

"These freed from grief and every mortal care,
And wafted far to th' ocean's verge extreme,
Rove uncontrouled amid the happy Isles,
Illustrious Heroes".[41]

Overshadowed by his father and harried by an ambitious family, he wanted to be of heroic stature and enjoy the reward without enduring the dust of battle. His hero was the Roman Republican general Sertorius, who, disgusted with civil war, considered retirement to the Canary Islands (one of the reputed sites of the Fortunate Isles). "No wonder", says Beckford, " that Sertorius, . . . disgusted with the iniquity of Rome, [should] be desirous of flying . . . to a country where her wiles and her tyranny were equally unknown, where he might be solaced by the affection of this artless people, and taste . . . the charms of a lasting tranquility. How enviable is the idea of devining the aweful moment of public ruin, when an Empire seems hastening to its fall, and of retiring from the storm of civil dissention to countries so peaceful and serene. Circumstanced as I am in the tumult of an unnatural contest, . . . I shall fancy my pavillion transported far beyond the bound of commerce and navigation to those happy Isles!"

Beckford wrote this during the American War of Independence, when France also was fighting us. He disapproved of our campaign against the colonists, as his Whig father would have done, and hated adult talk about the war, money and trade. He was always against wars, was never deceived by jingoism, and was apt to be a defeatist.

His interest in literary descriptions of legendary gardens was not confined to the Classics. He read about Paradise in Milton and in Ariosto's *Orlando Furioso*, and about enchanted gardens and palaces in Ariosto, Tasso, Spencer and Camoens. This literature echoed his own preoccupation with the idyll of childhood and with the vein of 'indolence' in him (in all the enchanted gardens the heroes were ensnared by indolence and voluptuousness); it also suited his early disillusion with the world. For these reasons, the gardens at Fonthill became an embodiment of the gardens of Paradise and Enchantment. The final touch of Paradise was given by the seclusion of the grounds behind the unscaleable barrier, and the tameness of wild life where no shot was ever fired—the profusion of hares and rabbits, the 'clouds of pheasants', the peacocks displaying themselves on the lawn.

What was most intriguing about Beckford's Paradise was its unexpectedness—in a bleak spot on the edge of the Wiltshire Downs. The conversion of this terrain was a challenge to his wealth and creative imagination. As Rutter says: "we feel the presence of the creative power of unbounded means and exquisite taste in rendering these woods what poetry might depict of the woods of Arcadia; where the kindliest soil and the most genial climate should strew the earth with every sweet, and a garden should bloom in every wilderness. The luxuriant imagination of Milton has painted a part of that scene, which has been almost realized, *under the greatest natural disadvantages*, by the enterprising spirit of unlimited wealth."

And yet, paradoxically, the grounds were economical to run, as Loudon said after revisiting them in 1833: "the greater part of the abbey is now in ruins, and all the interesting parts of the grounds (unless we except the grand avenue and drive, and the American grounds) are in such a state of neglect, as hardly to be recognised for what they were in 1807 . . . The expense would have been very trifling of thinning out the native trees and shrubs in those places where they crowded upon the exotics in such a manner as to injure many of them, and to destroy a still greater number. In addition to this expense, there would have been little more than that of mowing the walks and drives; for the thinning and pruning of the plantations generally, we may reasonably suppose would pay itself. It is a fact worthy of notice, that scarcely any place of the same extent was ever formed that could be kept up at so little expense as Fonthill. The saving by having no gravel walks is very great."

Cobbett was as impressed as Loudon by Beckford's grounds: "Well, we saw Fonthill, but, even if I had the talent to do justice to it in a written description, ten such sheets as this would not suffice for the purpose. When I see you I will at times give you an hour's account of it. After that sight, all sights become mean until that be out of the mind. We both thought Wardour the first place we had ever seen, but Wardour makes but a single glade in Beckford's immense grounds and plantations."[42]

Chapter XIV

PERSECUTION

The splendours of Fonthill contrasted sadly with the solitariness of its owner. For the most striking feature of Beckford's life there, or anywhere, was his ostracism by Englishmen. After 1784 all his friends dropped him, except Sir William Hamilton and the young Marquis of Douglas (later Duke of Hamilton).

A sad example is the diplomat Sir Arthur Paget, who was one of the "pygmy players" in Beckford's opera in London in 1782, and overlapped William Courtenay at Westminster School. As a boy there he wrote to Beckford, just before the Powderham scandal: "My dear William, . . . what would make me wish to leave school now would be to go abroad now with you and Lady Margaret. You mentioned in your last letter you would not trouble me with more of your letters. I beg you will write as often as you please, for I am always happier with your's than anybody's. Pray give my most affectionate love to Lady M; also believe me, yours ever most affectionately, Arthur Paget."[1]

His later career in the Diplomatic gave him several points of contact with Beckford; but whenever he wanted to arrange a party in the neighbourhood to see Fonthill Abbey, he tried to avoid communicating with his old friend; instead, he made the arrangements through somebody else, sometimes anonymously.[2] When once mischance forced him to write direct to Beckford with his request, it was the coldest imaginable letter written to an apparent stranger.[3] Curiously enough, his own life was not blameless, for Lord Boringdon's wife had run away from her husband to live with him. The other members of Arthur Paget's party were the Duke and Duchess of Argyll and Lady Uxbridge; the latter had been divorced by her first husband after he had brought an action for *crim. con.* against the co-respondent, Lord Uxbridge, and obtained damages from him of £24,000.[4] Uxbridge's wife then obtained a divorce and married the Duke of Argyll. So wife and ex-wife were staying under the same roof with their brother-in-law, Arthur Paget! Such complications were rare in those days, when divorce needed a private Act of Parliament. These people moved in a fast set, 'cut' by the County society which so resolutely boycotted Beckford; this was why they dared to visit Fonthill.

Not only did Beckford's friends drop him. It was made impossible for him to find new ones. Lord Cloncurry's account of his meeting with Beckford at Neufchatel on the Lake of Geneva is typical: Beckford's "travelling ménage consisted of about 30 horses, with four carriages and a corresponding train of servants. Immediately upon his arrival, Mr. Beckford set up a fine yacht upon the lake, and by his munificent hospitality soon *ingratiated* himself with the young Englishmen of rank whose names I have mentioned. The friendship, however, was not of long endurance: in the course of a few weeks, letters came from England . . . as a result of which our visits to Beckford ceased."[5]

This was abroad, during war and revolution. For nowhere was Beckford safe from persecution. Shortly after Beckford left Paris, in 1789, Dr. Verdeil wrote: "Some devil or other is persecuting me. No less than three people have called at my house to enquire where you are, who you have with you, whether the 'Italian Abbé' is always in your household, etc., etc. I thoroughy trounced the last messenger, who was a tall, good-looking *garçon* with a military air. I asked him who he was, and on whose behalf he came. He replied that he came from England, where he normally resided, and that he had been charged by certain highly respectable personages to obtain information about you. 'I have no information to give anyone', I replied, 'and if that's why you've come here, you'd better leave off interrogating me any more and, above all, remaining here any longer'. On that, I seized my hat and said 'Allow me, Sir, to leave; a pressing engagement calls me.' Who the devil are these people who hope to find me a spy? There's something sinister behind it."[6]

The supposed Italian Abbé was Franchi, a Portuguese.[7] Anything was regarded as proof of Beckford's guilt—the residence of this Portuguese something-or-other at Fonthill; the keeping of a dwarf—and a *French* one at that, in war-time! Beckford lashed out at this malevolent tittle-tattle, these suggestions that he must demonstrate his respectability by dismissing these 'suspicious' employees:[8]

"I am sick of hearing nonsense about Mr. Franchi, and if possible sicker of the egregious absurdity about the poor helpless Dwarf . . . I care not a farthing for the buzz and gossip of the world. Paragraphs in the newspapers amuse, instead of alarming me; libels I recommend to Lord Kenyon; letters from unknown correspondents I throw into the fire, unopened; visits I wish to repulse, not allure . . .

"The Dwarf, from his unwearied attention (watching like a house-dog continually before my door), merits my countenance. To send him back, as a sacrifice to absurdity . . . would probably break his heart and answer no purpose, except depriving me of a useful servant, and the Abbey of an ornament as appropriate as its painted windows, imaged corbells or ebony stands.

"As to Mr. Franchi, I can neither hear him reflected on, or myself traduced upon his account, with any patience—so perfectly pure is my own conscience upon this particular. Surely it is madness to be for ever probing and probing the wounds I have received; it can only end in driving me from England. Dr. Lettice's eloquence would be more generously and more profitably employed in defending Mr. Franchi than in swelling a chorus of idle and spiteful gossips, which, supposing them to succeed in rousing my indignation to frenzy might occasion . . . my own sudden and desperate departure, without leaving any instructions behind me for paying Dr. Lettice the salary he at present enjoys."

Even artists, to whom he was so generous a patron and whom he entertained so lavishly at Fonthill for weeks on end, could not summon the courage to invite him to the annual Academy Dinner; the other guests might decline the invitation or walk out, as happened once at a Salisbury banquet. Some of the Academicians thought that he should be asked as a matter of form, and that he would have the good sense to decline. But there was a risk . . .! "Wyatt then . . . proposed Beckford of Fonthill. A dead silence. West then spoke of the intention of Beckford to patronize the Arts, and that should an invitation be sent it would *not be accepted* but [merely taken] *as a compliment*. No remarks, till Westall observed that if Mr. Beckford was not to come, why send the invitation? If he were to come, would it not be improper? Wyatt then said, if any opposition he would not press the matter. Hoppner and Rigaud then expressed some disapprobation, and the subject dropped."[9]

Society was not content that Beckford should be excluded from the world. The world must not come to Fonthill either. If ever a neighbour had things in common with Beckford, it was Sir Richard Colt Hoare of Stourhead; for he also was a gardener, author, bibliophile and genealogist, and had certain personal links with Beckford. When he was writing his *History of Modern Wiltshire*, he wanted permission to see the Abbey and get material. He tried every means, but in the end was reluctantly obliged to write to Beckford himself. He received a delighted reply, but took care to come

PERSECUTION

when he supposed Beckford was in London. So the latter had to trick him into a meeting: as Hoare was about to leave after several hours, congratulating himself on having eluded his host, a servant lured him into a room he had not yet seen. There stood Beckford and a table laid for supper! "You never", said Beckford, "saw a poor man so much astonished as when I thus suddenly pounced upon him. Had I been a whole monstrous Gorgon, he could not have been more petrified."[10] It was very late, Hoare could not decently refuse, and they spent an agreeable evening together.

But both soon regretted Beckford's "exuberant civility". For when the local gentry got wind of it, they wrote to Sir Richard "to demand of him an explanation . . . as they meant to regulate themselves towards him accordingly. Sir Richard applied to his friend the Marquis of Bath upon it, and represented that he had no further desire but to see the Abbey; and the meeting with Mr. Beckford was accidental, and to him unexpected. Such is the determination of the Wiltshire gentlemen, with respect to excluding Mr. B. from all gentlemanly intercourse." Beckford heard this and burst out at the breakfast table to Jeffry Wyatt that "he wondered how he could be such a d—d fool as to allow Sir Richard to see the Abbey", and added tartly "Sir Richard had no taste".[11]

If important people insisted on viewing the Abbey, Beckford was obliged to absent himself in order to save them embarrassment and social risk. This happened when the Tory Whip and four other M.P.s were lavishly entertained at Fonthill in 1819[12]—obviously in connection with the use of Beckford's seat at Hindon. Because Beckford did not welcome such humiliation, he refused to allow the visit of the Grand Duke Nicholas (later Nicholas I) in 1816 and is said even to have turned away the Regent.[13]

All this made Beckford very touchy. The Margravine of Anspach and her husband brought some emigrés down to Fonthill and asked Beckford to help them financially. This he did handsomely. The ungrateful wretches then wrote to the Margravine that only necessity obliged them to accept a gift from a man whose character they despised, etc. etc. She was so furious that she showed Beckford the letter. Now along comes Ozias Humphrey, the artist, and asks Beckford to subscribe a guinea for an emigré! "Beckford flew into a passion, and speaking superciliously of Mr. Goddard, Member for Wiltshire, whose sisters are promoting the subscription, asked 'Who is he?'. Humphrey replied 'He is a gentleman of 3 or 4,000 a year and of *spotless character*'." Beckford could not tell Humphrey the real reason for his anger, and away goes Humphrey with a good story about his meanness, adding that "Beckford is at times insolent in the greatest degree". Who should be there during this gossip but William Beckford of Somerley, our man's illegitimate first cousin. He shakes his head knowingly and adds his little say: "Beckford of Fonthill has no heart, no feeling." This was the man who had once written to our Beckford thanking him profusely for "the very generous manner" in which he hoped to save him from his creditors: "I trust that you will find the favour acknowledged with a becoming sense of gratitude, and which I shall always have a pride to testify."[14]

Beckford's position had curious ramifications. It made him envious of his daughters and sundered their lives from his. As good-looking heiresses with distinguished relatives on their mother's side, they were received in the great houses of England, staying at Bowood, Wilton and Wardour, a stone's throw from Fonthill. But even so, if they were to have a chance socially they could not be brought up under their father's roof. After they had 'come out', he was not allowed to call at the London houses where they were living with the Dowager-dragons who acted as their guardians.[15] So much for the reports of his 'singularity' in not having his daughters to live with him! He was

PERSECUTION

never allowed to stay at Hamilton Palace with his son-in-law, although his secretary Franchi could do so, being a mere agent.

Despite all they suffered on his account, his daughters were devoted to him. When his eldest refused to give up penniless Lieutenant-Colonel Orde, there was a furious scene, which she described to her lover: "yesterday my Father took leave of me *for ever:* you will therefore easily conceive (what do I say—Ah! no you cannot) the scene I was witness to; . . . such anger, such violence, *never* but once did I see before; and as I have said before, he, in language TOO *horrible* for me to repeat, left me *for ever.*"[16] Beckford was not reconciled to her until her illness in 1818; he could not bear the idea of a love match, which presented to him all the horrors of sex.[17] But her letter to him after their reconciliation shows her undying affection.

Her younger sister Susan was the same. Beckford wronged her grievously in trying to force her to marry his homosexual friend,[18] the Count of Egmont, and harried her in the most tyrannical way for over two years from October 1803. Nevertheless, her letters to her husband, the Duke of Hamilton, are filled with touching references to her father. During the illness of some *interessante amie,* she wrote: "the tender sympathy that Papa shews me at this terrible time *touches* me to the bottom of my heart. He has never been so dear to me"; she enclosed Beckford's letters, adding "Keep Papa's letters carefully for me; they are too dear for me to *want them to be lost*".[19]

On another occasion Susan wrote from Bath, "He's *unique,* this dear Caliph. Yesterday he made me cry with tenderness, the way he spoke of his affection for me: just to know that I was in the house (even if he could not have the pleasure of my society) was Happiness to him. *C'est comme un avare qui sait que son trésor est dans sa casette* [said he]. I cannot express how much his sweet words have touched me".

ENGLAND'S WEALTHIEST SON

We must emphasise that only Englishmen persecuted him. The difference in attitude of the Englishman and the foreigner is amusingly brought out in conversation between a future Bishop of Bristol (Robert Gray) and a "second-rate" Calvinist-Republican Swiss ("very typical of the kind"). They discuss "the infamous Mr. —", whom the Swiss knew well. This nameless Swiss says of Beckford: "Oh, he was a good fellow, he spent a great deal in our country. The Swiss liked him exceedingly, but one must admit that the English thought otherwise—there was talk of a little *affaire*, but really it was only a *bagatelle*, perhaps a Passing Mistake. But *Messieurs* the English are always so punctilious—certainly they are rather too fastidious in their outlook." At this the good Bishop becomes indignant, begins talking of "the most detestable of crimes", and accuses Mr. Swiss of being "biassed to admiration of a worthless character by the splendor which surrounded him and the expence which he entered into."[20]

Beckford had the pleasure of reading this "snug little passage" in Gray's book.[21] Indeed, the scandal of 1784 was often raked up in print in his lifetime, reviving public memories of forty and fifty years before. The worst example was Murray's publication in 1832 of Byron's Ode *Dives*, written as far back as 1811 and surely passed round by word-of-mouth and hand between then and 1832. No wonder that Beckford never forgave Byron and refused to meet him or shew him the *Episodes of Vathek*, which he so ardently wanted to read!

"Unhappy Dives! in an evil hour
'Gainst Nature's voice seduced to deeds accurst!
Once Fortune's minion now thou feel'st her power;
Wrath's vial on thy lofty head hath burst.
In Wit, in Genius, as in Wealth the first
How wondrous bright thy blooming morn arose!
But thou wast smitten with th' unhallow'd thirst
Of Crime unnamed, and thy sad noon must close
In scorn and solitude unsought, the worst of woes."

Chapter XV

THE SALE OF FONTHILL, 1822

By 1822, England's wealthiest son faced financial disaster. His debts amounted to £125,000,[1] even after the sale for £62,000 of two of his Jamaican estates,[2] which included (ill omen!) a plantation called Fonthill.

Against this, his assets were calculated at £212,500, which would leave him a credit balance of £87,500. His realisable assets (upon which a value could be put) consisted of his one remaining group of Jamaican plantations, known collectively as the Clarendon Estates, valued at £70,000; his Parliamentary seat for Hindon, together with houses there which it was necessary to own in order to control the voters, valued at £12,500; the Fonthill Abbey estate of 5,575 acres, valued at £100,000 on the basis of 27 years' purchase; and its standing timber, valued at £30,000 (but this could not be clear-felled if the estate was to retain its value).[3]

There were other assets which were not available for sale, or which it was difficult to value—his library and collections; the nearby manors of Milford and Woodford, leased from the Bishop of Salisbury, and Fonthill Bishop Farm, leased from the Bishop of Winchester; and the white elephant of the Abbey, which Lord Hertford said was too large for any subject to inhabit.[4]

Mr. Brown, the Duke of Hamilton's Scottish factor, summed up the value of the Abbey as "not a matter of consideration with any of us. Indeed, from the size and character of the Abbey, it must be wholly a matter of opinion whether it should be valued at a large sum or, if stript of the furniture etc, merely at what the materials of it would fetch in the market".[5]

The annual interest due on Beckford's debts swallowed up his Jamaican income; his West Indian merchants had to meet some of his annual expenses from their own pockets; and he could barely live at Fonthill on his modest rent-roll.[6] In 1822 Jamaican sugar was being marketed in England below the cost of production, and plantation values were falling catastrophically. The merchants had no alternative but to insist on being repaid the large sum owing to them and to refuse to finance Beckford's deficits any more. Fonthill must go.

This had long been foreseen. As early as February 1819 Beckford had written of being forced "to a sacrifice which, now that it is at hand, I hardly like even to name."[7] Throughout 1821 and until the Duke's final refusal in 1822, Beckford tried to stave off the sale by inducing his son-in-law to liquidate the bulk of his debts, pay the interest on the Fonthill mortgages, underwrite his liabilities and pay him an annuity, in return for the reversion of Fonthill and the parliamentary seat at Hindon on his death! Colossal demands! The first proposal was that he should immediately find £80,000 to pay the West India merchants' most pressing claims.[8]

Even the last proposal, submitted by the lawyers on 8th August 1822, was alarming enough. The Duke was to pay Beckford a life-annuity of £4,000 a year; take over Beckford's life annuities to dependants of £1,000 a year; pay off two bonds totalling £6,000; discharge Campbell's claim at law, 'as yet unascertained' but estimated to amount to anything from £25,000 to £30,000; and pay Beckford's two Orde grandchildren £3,000 each on Beckford's death. In return, it was *hoped* that the Clarendon estates would, sooner or later, be bought by some crazy optimist for £80,000. This would pay off the Fonthill mortgages of £70,000 and the remaining debt to the West India merchants, which was dishonestly put at £10,000.[9] But supposing the annual interest on these two debts of £80,000 (pending the proposed sale of Clarendon) could not be met by the net revenue from Clarendon? The Duke should pay the deficiency! And supposing Clarendon did not fetch £80,000? The Duke should pay the interest on the balance of the mortgages! As a matter of fact, it was made quite clear to the Duke that both these contingencies would arise; but Fownes' outline of the real position was a masterly understatement. Meanwhile, Beckford was to have full control of the estate, timber and seat until his death.[10]

To this extraordinary proposal the Duke replied: "I wish to assist Mr. Beckford, but I must say that the present proposition appears to me to create insurmountable difficulties. To enter into an obligation to discharge the interest of Mortgages, without knowing the amount of the same. To answer for any deficiency that may remain of the debts upon the Fonthill estates beyond the produce of the sales in Jamaica, without knowing what those sales may produce; and to engage to meet the result of a lawsuit, without the amount being ascertained, or any sum being fixed as the ultimatum to which it may lead, are proposals that I know not how to meet. My affection for Mr. Beckford would lead me to make any specified and limited sacrifice that was within my power. But to engage in obligations without knowing their extent, as a man of business you must feel would be exposing myself and family, in transactions of so extensive a nature, to difficulties that no man can or ought to encounter."[11]

Even after this, Fownes still hoped to make a further modified proposal. Beckford, in a sensible letter, realized the force of the Duke's arguments and the folly of the proposals from his point of view. For the moment, at any rate, he was resigned to the inevitable: "We have been too long drowning and catching at straws. Nothing remains in the shape of solid planks but to bring on the great Sale."[12]

These embarrassing and one-sided demands, and the protracted negotiations, might have severed the friendship of a lifetime. They do not seem to reflect much credit on Beckford and his solicitors. To us, they appear unreasonable. But in those days the upper classes thought that the world in general, and their relations in particular, owed them a living. The Duke's own family was a notable example. His estate, despite its falling rental, was burdened with colossal annual allowances to his relatives:[13] £6,500 each to his brother and three sisters; £2,000 to the divorced wife of his first cousin, the eighth Duke of Hamilton; £11,500 to his illegitimate daughter, Mrs. Westenra; and annual advances to his brother to keep him in his parliamentary seat. These annual burdens made the Duke cautious about adding Beckford to his long list of pensioners.

In those days, too, the family was everything; its chief glory and symbol was the family seat. Fonthill was world-famous and legendary; the Duke was expected to make some effort to save it for his heir, Beckford's grandson. Further, a safe family parliamentary seat was of the greatest value, particularly to a Whig groaning under years of unbroken Tory rule and patronage. In fact, all parties to these negotiations, except the hated Brown, were obsessed by the hope of saving Fonthill—even after Christie's auction catalogue had been published, even after the View had begun, even after negotiations had opened with possible purchasers.

Lastly, when judging Beckford's negotiations with the Duke, we must remember the latter's protracted and cold-blooded haggling over his marriage to Susan.[14] But supposing the Duke had accepted Beckford's last proposition? Franchi said to him, "You would have been irritated afterwards, and M. de Beckford would never have been content; to you it would have seemed too much, and to him too little".

Beckford now embarked on his last piece of stage-management, with Fonthill as "the great theatre". The planning and execution were magnificent; it was the greatest *coup* he ever pulled off. After being closed to practically everyone since the wall was built round it in 1794, the Abbey and its grounds were suddenly thrown open. In order to advertise the contents, an auction catalogue listing the treasures was prepared by Christie and sold, with tickets of admission, at a guinea a copy. There was thus a double appeal, to curiosity and acquisitiveness.

The King's brother-in-law, the Duke of Gloucester, came. He was followed by the Dukes of Beaufort, Buckingham and Wellington, who pronounced it to be "the finest place in Europe". The visiting Marquises were too numerous to name. The 'View' became a major social event, a national 'rage' which developed into 'the Fonthill Fever'. Every week the numbers increased—400 a day, 600 a day, 700 a day—"they must come from the Moon", there are so many, said Franchi. The catalogues were producing thousands of pounds. In order to give ample scope for their sale and time for certain backstair negotiations, Christie's auction was postponed from 17th September 1822 until Tuesday 8th October. The 'view' closed on Saturday 5th. Everyone was agog for Tuesday's auction; many commissions to purchase had been received. Then, on Sunday, a hand-bill suddenly appeared, announcing that the auction was off, and that negotiations were on foot for the sale of the whole estate by private treaty.[15]

This must have been Beckford's object all along. The 'view' and much advertised auction were intended to interest a private buyer for the whole. Several came forward—the Duke of Somerset, Lord Normanton, and perhaps Harriot Mellon the actress, widow of Thomas Coutts, the richest man in London.[16] But they were all put off by Beckford's price, £300,000. His own advisers, Franchi and Fownes, were dismayed at it; "we feel confident that you will never reach £3,000,000" said Fownes, adding an extra nought in his agitation.

But well before 17th September, the date first arranged with the unfortunate Christie for his auction, Beckford was intriguing with Harry Phillips, a rival auctioneer, who had found a most unlikely candidate for the Abbey. This was the eccentric millionaire John Farquhar. He was a Scot who had, in the modern manner, made his money out of gunpowder, depression in the Funds, and real estate. His personal appearance and table manners, and the filth of his bachelor lodgings in Baker Street, led Beckford to nickname him 'Old Filthyman'. He had one weakness, which led to his downfall in the greatest speculation of his life; as his obituary notice put it, "he was a great frequenter of sales, and the eye of the auctioneer was always observed to glisten whenever he made his appearance, and we have reason to believe that his fortune suffered much from this *penchant*, and an unlimited confidence he placed in others."[17]

Phillips played his fish well. "He says", wrote Beckford's agent on 17th September, "the Old Gentleman ought to have a property of importance to elevate him, and people must not talk of rentals; that looks well, and I think now it is even betting. He [Phillips] is prompting another in case the first should prove an abortion; his name is Mr. Barnett."[18] This idea of social elevation and of suddenly acquiring everything in the Abbey beneath the noses of the aristocracy made a strong appeal to Farquhar. He proposed to put down "a sum of money and take the keys [of the place], becoming at one stroke King of Fonthill". The final Agreement was drawn up on Saturday 5th October, the last day of Christie's 'View', and Farquhar deposited £10,000. On the following Tuesday, when Christie's auction was to have begun, the Agreement was signed.[19] Phillips' head was already full of plans for making a nice profit for himself and 'the Old Gent' by exhibiting the place for a couple of years and then auctioning everything.

The whole operation was executed with the utmost secrecy. Even Franchi, who was in charge at the Abbey

THE SALE OF FONTHILL, 1822

(since Beckford was in Bath), did not know that anything was afoot until late one afternoon, when a person "of the lower orders, but very rich (his name is a mystery to me)" came down incognito to view on 27th September.[20] As Franchi said to the Duke, "if ever I see M. de Beckford on a path that is *not tortuous*, I shall be astonished; and still more so if I ever see him on what could be called a straight one".

The estate, with the Abbey fixtures, was sold for £275,000; the treasures and fittings fetched another £25,000. Franchi thought that this total of £300,000 was "at least £60,000 more than the whole lot was worth".[21] Beckford probably made a good profit on the deal, that is to say, more than recouped himself for his capital expenditure at Fonthill since 1796. As far as his library, pictures and treasures were concerned, we can be certain of this from all that we know about him as a collector.

For his keenness and acquisitiveness were countered by meanness, anxiety about money, and astuteness increased by long experience. Whenever he could, he remained incognito, so that his name would not raise the price against him. His taste in books was different from that of other English collectors,[22] so that he avoided bidding fiercely against them. It was typical of him not to enter the ring at the Duke of Roxburghe's 'Bedlamite' sale in 1812, when record prices were fetched and leading aristocratic collectors vied with each other. Instead, he bided his time until 1819 when the Duke of Marlborough went bankrupt and had to sell his Roxburghe prizes at enormous loss. This enabled Beckford, for example, to buy a Froissart for £32, which fetched £63 in 1812; his agent snapped it up when everybody else in the sale-room rushed to the doors and windows to see the passing of the lion of the day, the resplendant and exotic Persian Ambassador—a typically Beckfordian incident![23] Beckford was equally successful in his deals over pictures and treasures, sometimes selling his finest pictures for at least double what they cost him.[24]

He probably also made a good bargain with Farquhar over the Abbey and its grounds. Brown valued the estate, its timber and Hindon at £142,500; but, as we have seen, Beckford received £275,000 for them, with the Abbey thrown in, which Brown had quite rightly refused to value; its material was so poor that it would have fetched little if demolished. In other words, Beckford got £132,500 more than had been calculated. This excess over Brown's valuation went a great way towards recouping him for what he had spent on building the Abbey, which his lawyers estimated to be "not less than £150,000".[25]

We have no idea what he spent on embellishing the 519 acres within the Barrier wall. But their beauty materially increased the value of the property, so he may have got his money back on this outlay. In any case, much of the cost may have been covered by the profitability of his plantations. For, whenever he could, he planted fir, and was a ruthless feller. Writing in 1794, the agriculturalist Davis said that fir had proved far more profitable than any other timber: during the last forty years the price of oak had risen 50%, of ash and elm 30%, but the best yellow deal 300%.[26] Four fir thrived on the space occupied by one oak, and they quickly reached maturity. Davis remarked that during the last thirty years all pines had entirely gone out of fashion because they make monotonous and unpicturesque plantations. Beckford was the last man one would have expected to plant them on a large scale, or indeed at all!

The Sale Agreement with Farquhar specified items in the Abbey (not all in Christie's catalogue) which were to be retained by Beckford. The most important exclusion from the sale was one third of his books, manuscripts, prints and drawings, of which Beckford himself was to have first choice. About 4,000 printed books and 22 manuscripts were sold by Farquhar in 1823; if these were all Beckford's, his library must in 1822 have contained about 6,000 printed books and 33 manuscripts.[27]

Also excluded were some of the Lots in Christie's catalogue, chiefly pictures. The latter are an odd assortment, with only a few items of note; this is probably because Beckford could not afford to retain many of the best, and because the speculative buyer could not take over the Abbey denuded of its most famous pictures and *objets d'art;* also, Beckford only had room at Bath for the smaller pictures. But the few objects of *vertu* were of a high order, and included the Rubens Vase and several mediaeval illuminations.

The transformation in Beckford's affairs was miraculous. All his debts were paid, totalling about £99,500. After investing £25,000 in the Funds to meet Campbell's claim, Beckford had a clear £175,500 of capital from the sale. Some of this was invested in a Government Life Annuity yielding $10\frac{1}{2}$%, and some in the French Funds at 6%; some was to be laid out on a residence and land near London, to yield $3\frac{1}{2}$%.[28] The only claims on him now were the annuities to Franchi and others, which totalled £1,000, and the legal and other expenses of about the same amount.[29]

No wonder that he wrote jubilantly on the day that Fonthill was sold: "Let me announce a great piece of news: Fonthill is sold very advantageously. I am rid of the Holy Sepulchre, which no longer interested me since its profanation; I am delivered of a burden, and of a long string of insupportable expenses. At present I have only to distribute my funds prudently and await the outcome of events. For twenty years I have not found myself so rich, so independent or so tranquil ... Now that I am more solidly than ever able to follow my whims, you only have to make the shores of the Lake of Geneva agreeable, and we will come. I have ample means and not a sou of debts."[30]

Now at last he should have been content, freed from that gnawing anxiety which had become his second nature. But no! The spirit of discontent, vain regrets and conflicting desires followed each other in quick succession. In a letter to his lawyer he complained about the slowness of the legal arrangements for handing over Fonthill to the new buyer, whilst urging him to induce the latter to cancel the contract, so that his beloved Library might remain intact! "I should feel like a person who had received a free pardon at the foot of the gallows . . . I am doomed to exile from a place I can never forget, nor consequently forgive the wretched set who by their imbecility, mismanagement, neglect and petty interestedness, have driven me to this odious measure . . . All the collective importance of the Library is destroyed; the gaps in every class are so wide that the repurchase of 10,000 volumes would hardly fill them. Oh that the galling contract was dissolved and my books restored! . . . How cheerfully would I pay all incurred expenses, and square matters so as to exist upon capital, till the sale of effects, gutting of the Abbey, [and] disposal of Hatch and of Jamaica at the first favourable moment, came to my assistance. God send the miserly old man [Farquhar] one ray of intelligence. What a dreadful load would he take off his own shoulders and what a burthen of eternal regret from mine."[31]

Like his characters in *Vathek* and the *Episodes*, Beckford was always carrying "a burthen of eternal regret". Had he known it, his coup at Farquhar's expense was even more brilliant than could have been supposed. At the speculative auction of the contents of the Abbey, which Farquhar and Phillips held a year later in the autumn of 1823, Beckford may have bought back some items below the valuation for which he had sold them to Farquhar.[32] And Farquhar's whole speculation was seen to be rotten when in December 1825 the main tower collapsed whilst he was in residence, and ruined the finest part of the building! Alderman Beckford's statue stood intact in its niche in the now roofless Great Western Hall "as if it remained to point to the ruins of his son's ambition."[33]

THE SALE OF FONTHILL, 1822

Farquhar died of apoplexy a few months later, after dividing the estate into lots and selling portions of it in disgust;[34] it has never been re-united. What was left of the Abbey (still a great part) was later demolished as building material, except for the northern end which still stands.[35]

Chapter XVI

THE BECKFORD FORTUNE

People always thought that Beckford lost Fonthill through extravagance. How else was it possible for England's wealthiest son to have been forced to sell it? But had he ever been as rich as that? Here we come to one of the quaintest of the Beckford myths—Beckford the millionaire, the boy of ten who was left a million in cash and an income of a hundred thousand a year.

This fable of unlimited wealth was started by his great-grandfather Governor Peter Beckford. When his "strong-box was opened, the larger part of a million of money was discovered hoarded up, and it ever remained a mystery to his family how it had been accumulated."[1] It has remained a mystery to this day. For he never had such a sum! The myth was extended by his son, Speaker Peter Beckford; in 1740 a history book announced that he "lived to be the richest Subject in Europe. He has twenty-two plantations in this Island, and upwards of 1,200 slaves. His money in the banks and on mortgages is reckoned at a million and a half."[2] The family set the seal on this statement by inscribing under their portrait of the Governor that his son "at his death was in possession of the largest property, real and personal, of any subject in Europe." Who could doubt such testimony?

The myth was also embroidered by Beckford's father, the Alderman. He let it be known that, as the Speaker's eldest surviving son, he had been left the bulk of the plantations[3], and that his next surviving brother, Alder-

THE BECKFORD FORTUNE

man Richard, left him his fortune at his death in 1756.[4] Neither of these claims were correct. Whereas William owned 22,000 acres in Jamaica in 1754, his brothers Richard, Julines and Francis and his first cousin Ballard Beckford owned over 26,000 acres between them;[5] none of this ever returned to the eldest branch. Richard left all his estates to his bastard, William Beckford of Somerley, the historian of Jamaica. But the Alderman did inherit all the English property,[6] and probably most of the mortgages.

Planters in Jamaica measured each other by their wealth, which they consequently magnified. A fresh reason for this boasting came when they sent their sons to the most exclusive public school in England, and when these young men settled down in England as landed proprietors and married into aristocratic families. To their new and snobbish connections by marriage and geography, they had little but their wealth to commend them.

The reputation of being so unusually wealthy was useful to an ambitious man like the Alderman. It enabled him to get a nice share of financial pickings in the City. The most prominent people in this circle were allowed to subscribe to new Government loans; they only had to put down a 10% instalment and then sold their allotment of the stock at a profit to the public; today we call this 'stagging'. In 1759 the Government floated a large loan, and Beckford was sixteenth on the list of the "principal and most responsible men in the City" who subscribed;[7] his share was £100,000 of stock, for which he would have had to put down £10,000 or less; a nice operation!

Another form of investment was the great political dinners which, as Lord Mayor, he had to give at his own expense. His last and most opulent one was on 22nd March 1770, "the splendour of which eclipsed anything of the kind prepared in the City within human memory, and never since approached".[8] There were

600 dishes served upon gold plate at a cost to Beckford of £10,000, so we are told. But it netted him six dukes, two marquises, twenty-three earls, four viscounts, fourteen barons and eighteen baronets. Not bad for a Radical mayor who professed strong contempt for the Court *and* "empty titles",[9] and who regarded the nobility as "the scum"!

This ostentation in certain directions for specified purposes indicates a certain cold-bloodedness and calculatingness, which young Beckford inherited as part of his outlook and character. When ostentation does not accord with a man's real situation, it places him in a false position and forces him to be mean. To be considered a millionaire, to be obliged to behave like one— to be, in short, a millionaire *manqué*—what a painful rôle in life! This alone is enough to account for Beckford's anxiety about money and his dislike of disbursing. He was daily in an equivocal position, daily subject to terrors and extortions. Long before his time the family had become prisoners of their own myth, which powerfully affected their dispositions.

The bigger the myth, the more severe the strain. With their touch of megalomania and their love of the dramatic, the Beckfords had to make the biggest possible claim. Now the wealthiest and most famous of all the Nabobs was Clive of India, who returned to England in 1760, worth £40,000 a year. He was sixteen years younger than Alderman Beckford and had started life with none of his advantages. He had arrived in India, to take up a hated clerkship, in debt to his ship's captain and without a single introduction. In despair he attempted suicide. Yet within eight years he was world-famous, redeemed his family estate and extricated his father from debt.

Alderman Beckford could not be outdone! He therefore boasted, just before his death in 1770, that he would leave his son £40,000 a year *"besides many thousands in cash"*.[10] In the Press it was said at his death that he had an annual income of £30,000 from Jamaica and £18,000 from his English estates, besides money in the Funds and mortgages;[11] this was much more than Clive or any other recorded English income of the period.

These claims have been repeated and magnified ever since. But the real truth is recorded in the various lawsuits with the bastards and executors, which followed the Alderman's death. They make it clear that, taking the good years with the bad, young Beckford had been left £20,000 a year 'clear' from Jamaica and another £7,000 a year from his English estates.[12] Moreover, in the attached schedules of accounts of the deceased estate, there is no mention of large amounts of cash held by the Alderman at his death, and no indication of any money in the Funds.[13]

Many years later young Beckford still had a similar income. The Income Tax returns show that his income for the year ending April 1801 was about £29,000.[14] In 1798 and 1799 his Jamaican income was apparently about £22,800 before deduction of the sugar duty and agents' fees and expenses; and *if none of his English estates were yet sold*, they would have earned at least £7,000 a year.

But an income largely derived from a commodity (in this case sugar, rum and logwood, used for dyes) was bound to fluctuate; the Income Tax returns for the year ending April 1800 show Beckford's income as about £45,000. This great increase over the two previous years and the next year reflects the boom prices for sugar in 1799, when British planter prosperity reached its peak before the great depression. Even a temporary increase of this size does not justify the boasts which Beckford made; in 1794, for example, he spoke of an annual Jamaican income of not less than £120,000 for the last three years!

We would have expected anyone to jog along comfortably on £27,000 a year. But for two reasons outside Beckford's control, his income diminished rapidly after about 1800. Firstly, from the close of the century he lost several plantations through lawsuits. The case *Campbell v. Beckford* shows what could happen to the innocent proprietor of a plantation, through the sins of omission or commission of his father and grandfather.

Campbell claimed four plantations named Bogue or Bogie (which had originally been uncultivated), Strathbogie, Ackendown and Retrieve.[15] They had been mortgaged to Speaker Peter Beckford in 1733 for £16,000 currency, on which Peter earned interest at the usual rate of 10%. In 1743 Alderman Beckford took possession of them on the ground that the interest had not been regularly paid. The Beckfords then enjoyed the rents and profits until the plantations were first taken away from them by the Jamaican courts in 1792. The heirs of the original owners tried unsuccessfully to recover them at law in 1756, and Alderman Beckford's counter-petitions to foreclose in 1759 and 1767 also failed. Campbell bought the interest in them cheaply from the heirs for £5,000 in 1778, as a speculation. He did not bring his case in Jamaica against Beckford until 1784, so it must have been as difficult for him to collect evidence of fraud and ruthlessness going back fifty years as it was for Beckford to rebut his charges (which were not substantiated by the impartial English courts in 1801).[16]

Beckford first appealed in July 1787 from the Jamaican Chancery to the highest relevant English court; this was called 'the Lords of the Committee of the Council for hearing Appeals from the Plantations' and was later replaced by the Judicial Committee of the Privy Council. Even at this level the process was endless. The London Court examined the Appeal before it in the form of a number of 'Exceptions' tabled by each side against the most recent Order in the Jamaican Chancery. Some of these Exceptions were allowed and some over-ruled; this meant that one Exception was referred to an English Master in Chancery for investigation and another Exception to his opposite number in Jamaica. The Masters sometimes died before they could make their Report! So Beckford appealed to London in 1787, 1793, 1801, 1816, 1819 and apparently 1824.

Meanwhile, the plantations changed hands whenever the Courts made a new decision. In May 1792 the Jamaican Chancery put them in the hands of a Receiver, whilst a Master investigated what each side owed the other and endeavoured to test the accounts, transactions and damages of three generations of Beckfords since 1733. London reversed this Order at the end of 1793; the plantations were handed back to Beckford in February 1794, until his counter-claims could be settled and whilst a Master in Chancery in Jamaica re-investigated the accounts. Beckford again lost them under a Jamaican Chancery order of September 1799. His appeal to London in 1801 failed. The plantations were now irrecoverable. The annual value of the crops on them was in 1798 and 1799 estimated at £5,700 sterling;[17] the estates themselves were "equal in value to one fourth part of all" his plantations.[18]

Beckford now had to wait (25 years, as it turned out) to see how much of the revenue received between 1792 (when the plantations were first taken from him) and 1799 inclusive had to be disgorged, after allowing for the agreed legitimate expenses of estate management, etc. As late as 1822 his advisers estimated that he might be required to find £27,589,[19] and possibly interest on this sum, over a period, at about $6\frac{5}{8}\%$. Thus, from 1801 Beckford was compelled to set aside £30,000 to meet the final settlement. This eventually took place, apparently out of Court, at some date after May 1826, when the parties compromised at £20,000 or £25,000 in cash, Campbell prudently refusing to take a Jamaican estate in settlement.[20]

There was also the legal cost at every stage during the forty-two years that the case ran against Beckford. After the Appeal of 1801, his lawyer wrote, "This business has been attended with considerable expence, for agreeable to your suggestions I was not sparing in fees to Counsel, etc. My former advances of near £4,000 on your account put me under the necessity of applying to Mr. Foxhall to assist me from your funds on the occasion, which he declined, but very liberally accommodated me from his own. May I beg the favour of you to give directions to Messrs Ransom & Co., to pay me £1000 on your Account to enable me to reimburse Mr. Foxhall and for my other occasions."[21] We recollect what Beckford said in *Azemia* about the cost of Chancery suits!

Catherine Hall, another rich plantation, near Montego Bay, was taken from Beckford in 1807 by Lord Eldon, who placed it under a consignee. It had been mortgaged to Peter Beckford in 1732 for £2,432 currency at 10% interest. Alderman Beckford attempted to foreclose on the mortgage in 1769, but died before he could succeed. His petition was revived during his son's minority; finally in 1784 the Jamaican Chancery awarded the plantation to Beckford, provided that the original owners were unable to pay up the principal and the arrears of interest due. Since they were unable to do this, Beckford 'fairly' (as Eldon admitted later) considered it his absolute property, and spent £10,000 currency on fresh negroes and another £1,000 on buying 'provision grounds'. Meanwhile, a pair of speculators (London merchants) who later went bankrupt, and one of whom was a brewer, bought the right to it cheaply from the original heirs, and then revived the case against Beckford, who suffered the same protracted legal processes as in the Campbell case, from 1790 until 1810 or later. After he had finally lost the plantation, his final adversary Quarrell claimed £20,000 as still due to him.[22]

There seems, indeed, to have been a concerted attack on the Beckford title-deeds to plantations (sometimes by property-speculators), once the family's grip was loosened by the death of the capable and experienced Alderman. But these attacks were not always justified, since in two traceable cases the Privy Council finally refused to take away the plantation concerned from Beckford: in *Beckford v. Wade* (1805), the Beckfords had enjoyed legal possession for over fifty years before proceedings were begun, and the respondent had known the facts (which she had sought out) of her case twenty years before bringing it![23] And in *Cargill v. Beckford* (1784), the latter retained a plantation which had been mortgaged to Peter in 1729 for £7,200 currency and awarded to his family by the Jamaican Chancery in 1736.[24] But whatever the result of these numerous lawsuits, their effect on somebody of Beckford's temperament, riddled by impatience and anxiety, was considerable: it gave his existence a background of instability and irritation, and necessitated his constant attention to business affairs and papers, which he so detested.

An equally important cause of Beckford's loss of capital and income, through no fault of his own, was the steady deterioration of Jamaica's prosperity as a sugar producer. This process set in from 1770 (whilst Beckford was still a boy), when it was noted by Edward Long, the Jamaican historian. There were various causes. For example, the amount of virgin soil was rapidly shrinking and the older plantations were becoming exhausted; at the same time, virgin soil was becoming available at low prices in the former French colonies ceded to us in 1763 (and now therefore in competition on the home market with hitherto protected Jamaica). The price of negroes and of stores from England was increasing; the latter had doubled by the close of the American War of Independence in 1783. The price of a male negro had risen from £25 in 1755 to £60 by 1770; planters were discouraged from replacing old slaves, so that the labour force dwindled and plantations were abandoned; this process was increased by the abolition of the slave trade in 1807, which meant that no more labour could be imported.

Meanwhile, the English duty on imported Jamaican muscovado steadily rose from the outbreak of the

American War in 1775, when it stood at 6s. 3d. per cwt; by 1782 it had almost doubled to 12s. 3d. This war-rate was never reduced, and rose throughout the seventeen-nineties and the next decade, until in 1814 it stood at 30/-. It was not even abated when Jamaica suffered an unprecedented series of natural disasters: in 1780 there were two great hurricanes, an earthquake and a tidal wave; in 1781, 1784, 1785 and 1786 there were almost equally bad hurricanes, causing millions of pounds worth of damage and the loss of 15,000 slaves.

All this produced a twenty-year depression from 1770; it was only temporarily broken by the rising of the slaves and mulattoes on French S. Domingo in 1791. The consequent cessation of sugar production there produced a great price-rise, increased by speculative Continental demand between 1796 and 1799. The ensuing planter-prosperity was soon ended by overproduction and a new adverse factor—the competition from fresh areas with unexhausted soil and cheap labour, namely Brazil, Cuba, the Orient, and Demerara and other colonies captured from the Dutch and French. After 1804 the price-trend of sugar was permanently downward, except for the short-lived boom of 1813-14 (anticipating Napoleon's fall and the re-opening of Europe's markets). In 1807 it touched its lowest point to date; sugar was being sold on the English market below the cost of production. And yet the duties were raised to finance the War.

The deterioration in Jamaica's economy was reflected in shrinking yields on plantations, the growth of indebtedness, and a catastrophic fall in property values. As an example of shrinking returns from Jamaican investments, in the boom years 1795-8 one of the best plantations gave a return of 12% to its owner; in the fluctuating but still prosperous years 1801-04 the return was halved at 6%; in 1805 it was again halved at 3%, and in 1807 operating costs were barely met. As for indebtedness, from 1772 an increasing number of plantations were in creditors' hands or sold to meet debts. When the slave trade was abolished in 1807, the Jamaican Assembly reported that "the sugar-estates lately thrown up, brought to sale and now in the Court of Chancery, amount to about one-fourth of the whole number of the colony; and the Assembly anticipates very shortly the bankruptcy of a much larger part of the community, and in the course of a few years of the whole class of sugar planters". This forecast was proved correct by 1822, when Beckford sold Fonthill and sugar was again marketed below the cost of production. The prolonged depreciation in property values made it difficult for owners and their advisers to decide to cut their losses by selling out, or to find a buyer at a reasonable (*or even any*) price.

Another cause of Jamaica's decline was absenteeism. The whole of the third generation of Beckfords, including the Alderman, were educated at English public schools, and some at Oxford. Only the eldest son Peter, who died in 1737, returned to Jamaica to settle down. His next brother, the Alderman, spent a few years there after his Oxford days in order to learn about sugar; but he never returned. Instead, he bought Fonthill about 1736,[25] in order to become a County figure and a local M.P.

The plantations of absentees were usually managed by attorneys at a commission of 6% of the annual yield, which was a first charge against the season's crop; these agents also had various free living privileges, and could trade dishonestly in the surplus of expensive stores which they ordered from England at the estate's expense. It was often worth more to have such a post than to be the owner of the land! It was in the agent's interest to keep down costs (which might reduce his commission) and force up production. Improvements were therefore put off because they temporarily reduced net returns; buildings fell into ruin; fields were tilled until they were exhausted, and then reverted to weeds. The agent then left or was sacked, a wealthy man in either case.

Beckford cannot be blamed for the successful rapacity of his agents in Jamaica and England, which also greatly reduced his fortune. It was part of the prevailing system. The disadvantages of an absentee landlord owning plantations were summarised by the Duke of Hamilton's factor, when dissuading him from making any sacrifice in order to preserve the Beckford patrimony for his son. "These Jamaica estates would be of less value to your family than to almost every other description of proprietors. Your Grace and your successors must naturally delegate the charge of your estates to agents; at home you can have some check over your people, but you will have none over the West India factors, who might do what they pleased with your property. West India estates should, in order to be turned into proper account, be the exclusive property of Mercantile men or residenters on the spot. These people can manage these estates infinitely better; besides being their own Agents and Merchants, they have it in their power to save commission and to retain the profits on the goods sent home, together with all the profits on the annual supplies sent from England to their estates. To that description of proprietors everything is very favorable, but to others it is quite the reverse; of the truth of this both Mr. Beckford and Mr. Fownes gave me, in conversation, convincing proofs."[26]

The most successful of Beckford's fleecers were the three Wildman brothers, who controlled his affairs for twenty years from 1782.[27] Thomas, the eldest, was called in by Mrs. Beckford shortly after her husband's death in 1770, to advise on the Chancery suit she was bringing against the executors of his Will. He soon gained an ascendancy over mother and son, becoming solicitor, law agent, general adviser and 'banker'.

When Beckford came of age in September 1781, Chancery supervision of his affairs ceased, and Wildman was able to introduce his brothers: James became

Agent in Jamaica, and Henry was West India merchant in London. Until Thomas' death in December 1795, there was no one in a position to check them; even then, there was no effective independent investigation until after the death in December 1801 of Nicholas Williams, who succeeded Thomas Wildman as general agent. Beckford's many absences abroad helped the Wildmans, since Thomas was given a power of attorney.

The Wildmans also gained the whip hand through Beckford's indebtedness to them. In 1795, for example, John Curtis' mortgage for £12,000 on one of Beckford's English estates was transferred, at Beckford's expense, into Thomas Wildman's name;[28] and, as we shall see, from 1797 Beckford owed them enormous sums on his West India account. Their power over him is reflected in the relinquishing of his own seat at Hindon to Thomas in January 1795; the latter was replaced on his death in December by James, who retained the seat until his dismissal from Beckford's affairs in 1802. This happened to Beckford over and over again; for his next West India agent, John Pedley, replaced James Wildman at Hindon in 1802, and Pedley's successor, John Plummer, replaced Beckford there in 1820![29] The argument was "You are heavily in my debt. I must therefore have the use of your parliamentary seat. Otherwise I shall foreclose on your mortgages, plantations and estates, and reduce or stop your quarterly allowance as well".

One can see how well the Wildmans did out of Beckford by the properties they bought. Thomas' eldest son, an officer in the Hussars, bought Newstead Abbey from Byron for 90,000 guineas, and his widow Sarah and her other four children were well provided for (her fourth son had enough money to marry an Earl's daughter). James, whose letters and handwriting indicate an almost illiterate man unable to express himself on paper, bought Chilham Castle in Kent, of which he became High Sheriff.

The Wildmans' unscrupulousness is recorded in the

ENGLAND'S WEALTHIEST SON

Chancery suit which Beckford brought against the widow Sarah Wildman in 1810 in order to recover Quebec Plantation near Port Maria,[30] which Thomas persuaded Beckford to give him in 1790 as a reward for faithful service.

The affair began when James landed in Jamaica in 1782 as Beckford's agent. He soon reported back to brother Thomas that "there was a fine run of land in St. Mary's [Parish] not far from Esher; the same might be settled into a good sugar work at an easy expence". Beckford was never told that it was near a wharf, from which its produce could be shipped direct to England; the Wildmans consistently described it to him as "a piece of waste land in the corner of the Island"![31] When Beckford was abroad in December 1788, Thomas (as usual beginning his letter "My dear Friend") sent him a Deed of Conveyance of "some of your waste lands in Jamaica", with instructions on how to execute it. However, the conveyance was delayed, much to the Wildmans' advantage.

Now that they were assured of the plantation, James hastened to settle and develop it, without telling Beckford, from the beginning of 1789. He transferred gangs of skilled slaves from one of Beckford's plantations, and bought more slaves, stores and breeding sheep at a cost of £8,322 currency. This was in flat contradiction to the policy which Beckford had laid down, that there was to be no new settlement on his Jamaican land; *he was already drawing in his horns* (so early—interesting!), and had instructed James to sell Harbourhead Plantation, for which James had not managed to get a single offer.

Beckford only partially learnt of what was happening after he returned from Switzerland in October 1789 and started to examine his affairs. He wrote an indignant letter to James in December, asking what exactly had been done on Quebec and what its original value was, and calling for accounts. In March 1790 James wrote an evasive reply,[32] full of half-truths, pretending that

Beckford had not really been involved in any unnecessary expense, and that anything which had been done had been to his general advantage. Beckford was definitely not told what had been spent, and the accounts and vouchers which James sent stopped short of the critical period when the settlement of Quebec began. The last sentence of James' letter casually mentioned that he thought Quebec might be sold for from eight to £10,000 currency; but it was not clear from his vague phrase whether he meant before or after its development.

Beckford may not yet have received this letter when on 1st June 1790 he conveyed Quebec to Thomas Wildman, who was still describing it as "a piece of waste land". Wildman saw to it that in the Deed Beckford promised to finance, up to a limit of £5,000 sterling, the full development of the property, including the erection of mills, houses and sugar works, and its stocking with slaves, cattle and implements; he was even to lend his own skilled negroes for building, etc. By March 1791 this had been done, and all but £453 had been spent out of the covenanted £5,000; Wildman then got Beckford to sign a chit that the unused £453 should be paid over by Beckford in fulfilment of the Deed!

This expense was undertaken despite the fact that James refused to enrol the Deed in the Jamaican archives, which rendered it null and void. His main reason for refusing officially to record Beckford's gift was the rumours circulating in Jamaica and England about the brothers' rapacity. Out there it was being said that Beckford owed Thomas a hundred thousand pounds and that "the estates would all belong to the Wildmans in four years, particularly if I [James] was continued in the management". James came over to England on business, and was dining with Beckford's cousin Lord Effingham; the latter was well informed because he often had under his roof William Beckford of Somerley, the Jamaican historian who owned several Beckford plantations. These rumours were hinted at the Earl's table in James' hearing; it was this that made him, so he said, refuse to enrol the Deed of June 1790.

But James was quite willing to enrol a second Deed drawn up instead on 10th November 1791; for in this Deed it was no longer necessary for Beckford to undertake the full development of Quebec, since it had by then been completed: the Wildmans' full enormity was thus not officially recorded and open to inspection! Incidentally, this second Deed conveyed 1,700 acres: the earlier one had only conveyed 1,200 acres "by mistake".

This treatment of Beckford by "his dear Friend" is all the more inexcusable because it was only made possible by the "strong sense of gratitude" which Beckford felt towards the man who claimed to have looked after all his affairs so brilliantly ever since his childhood and whose "ffriendship and affection for me" Beckford thought was "unparalleled". And the conveyance was made at a time when Beckford "was distressed for money to defend" the two big lawsuits instituted against him to take away some of his plantations;[33] besides which, his English properties were by then mortgaged for £25,000.

Nor were the Wildmans fleecing a mean employer. James had, besides all his usual expenses and fees, an unusual and "immense allowance" annually in order to induce him to devote his whole time to Beckford's plantations and not have other clients (an undertaking which he broke). Thomas also had a special annual allowance of £500 between 1781 and 1792; in the next year this was increased to £1,000, and from September 1793 until his death it was £800 a year. Since this allowance was charged to Beckford's annual account, Wildman gave himself 5% interest on it! In the Jamaican Record Office there are also Land Conveyances by Beckford to James Wildman in 1798 and to Henry in 1800, which suggests further plunderings.

The same process was repeated with the next West India agent, John Pedley. He had replaced James Wildman as agent in Jamaica, where he lent Beckford

THE BECKFORD FORTUNE

a large sum, said to be £40,000, to fight and settle lawsuits.[34] So when he arrived in England in 1802 to replace Henry Wildman, Beckford was already in his debt. Within three years all Beckford's remaining English properties, except Fonthill and Witham, fell into his net, sometimes because Beckford could not pay off the mortgages on them and sometimes to meet his loans. He is said to have taken the St. Pancras estate for £12,000,[35] Eaton Bray for £62,000,[36] and all the Hertfordshire property. His worthless and eccentric brother Robert (who changed his name to Deverell) occupied Beckford's Saltash seat from 1802 to 1806, whilst Pedley occupied Hindon; Pedley then sat for Saltash from 1808 until Beckford sold his interest there in 1809, when he departed for ever from Beckford's life.

But what is curious is that Beckford wrote to Pedley as "your warmest Friend",[37] even after he had lost three English estates to him! The rich man's need to trust and love was insatiable. Then, sooner or later, his dream was shattered as he emerged from it a poorer man. His affection turned to hatred, his trust to suspicion, and his bitterness increased. And so the cycle continued, one of the circles in the Rich Man's Hell.

This constant disillusion bred cynicism and inertia, expressed in a letter to his son-in-law at the time of his Quebec lawsuit against the widow of his former friend: "'Tis in vain to do anything, my dear Douglas, . . . Despite all the care we take, we will be duped. Calculations, cogitations, scribbleations are useless. 'Tis in vain to worry: our lot is to be mercilessly robbed and pillaged. . . . Let us amuse ourselves whilst we can and, like the other insects, enjoy the ray of sunshine which precedes the great darkness."[38]

One constant financial drain on Beckford, hitherto quite overlooked, was his election expenses in rotten boroughs and contested elections—expenses which ruined many wealthy men in those days. The control of parliamentary seats by a landed family was an immense asset, being the chief way of exerting pressure upon government in order to get a lucrative sinecure or peerage and to protect one's interests; and one of the privileges of a Member was freedom from arrest for debt. At George III's accession the top grandees only controlled three or four boroughs, and some Dukes had none at all. Yet in April 1784 Beckford sat for Wells, controlled Hindon, and was making his influence felt in Saltash.

Consequently, when he asked the Chancellor Thurlow for a peerage, his whim was at once attended to although he had only just been elected for Wells, his request was very late, he was disliked by the Prime Minister and his Attorney-General (Loughborough), there was an unusually large list of candidates, and George III was jealous of the honour of the peerage and liked restricting their numbers.[39] Despite these formidable obstacles, a patent was made out for "Lord Beckford of Fonthill".

Beckford's expenses at Hindon alone, until he sold it in 1822, must have been enormous. At the General Election of June 1818, when there was no rival candidate, the 'festivities' cost him £1,200, and he had to find another £1,800 "for regaling certain friends" of his agent,[40] nor do we know whether there were additional expenses. Even in the seventeen-eighties, when money went much further, £3,000 a year in a constituency was not unusual, besides an expensive annual 'blow-out' for 'friends'.

There were also the large legal costs of the many disputed elections at Hindon. As we have already seen, Richard Beckford intervened twice-running in 1774 and 1776, and petitioned against the results. Beckford's candidate, Lloyd Kenyon, was returned at the next two elections of 1780 and 1782, thanks to Beckford's lavish expenditure;[41] but both results were disputed by the defeated candidates or their representatives, who alleged gross corruption. This was Kenyon's first seat in Parliament, where he quickly made his mark as a follower of the Chancellor Thurlow: he was Attorney-General twice whilst sitting for Hindon; later, he was much consulted by Pitt and the King, and became Master of the Rolls and Lord Chief Justice. Beckford consulted him about libels in the newspapers. This is a good example of how the control of a borough was worth a fortune. The next Member for Hindon at the disputed election of 1784 and in 1788 was also a useful protégé, the lawyer Edward Bearcroft, later Chief Justice of Chester. In a fulsome letter of thanks to Beckford he reveals the position of these rising toadies vis-à-vis the great: "To say that so humble a being as myself will ever rejoice in an opportunity of serving a person in your situation of life is, I confess, saying very little."[42] When Beckford wanted the seat himself, he gave Bearcroft his other seat at Saltash in the elections of 1790 and 1796.

Disputed elections may have cost Beckford even more at Saltash, where originally he had no interest or influence. Its two seats had been safely controlled by the Government for a generation, until an aspiring local politician, John Buller of Morval, started to intervene in the election of 1780. He lost the contest and his subsequent election petition in 1782. He again lost at the bye-election of April 1783, but could no longer afford the expense of an election petition, so called on Beckford for financial help. They made an illegal secret agreement, which allotted Beckford one of the seats for life in return for the financing of the election petitions, etc. By 1787 Beckford and Buller together had fought two elections and contested the results of three by petition! Their third petition, against the bye-election of 1786, was successful. Beckford said that this struggle cost him "many a thousand".[43]

Beckford and Buller were left in full and unopposed control of the two seats until the general election of 1806. Lord Grenville, who was to become head of 'the Ministry of All the Talents', and his brother the Marquis of Buckingham intervened through their own candidates.

The latter were beaten, but won their petition and so replaced the Buller-Beckford interest: Saltash was once more a Government borough. Within a few months, in April 1807, there was another general election, and the two Grenville candidates won. But this time Beckford and Buller won the petition, and Beckford's nominee, Pedley, was declared one of the rightful Members in 1808. But a year later, in April 1809, financial stringency obliged Beckford to sell his rights in the seat to his partner James Buller for £8,500, after he had held or contested it for a quarter of a century.[44]

The legal fees for the election petitions over the two elections of 1806 and 1807 are said to have cost about £30,000, and those for all the petitions over Saltash from 1782 to 1808 about £100,000.[45] Each side paid its own costs, but perhaps at least half this sum was paid by Beckford's side. Since Beckford had no influence or interest at Saltash, but was brought in from outside in order to finance Buller in return for a seat for life, we may suppose that Beckford paid at least the lion's share of his side's costs; this seems to be implied by the wording of his *Journal* in 1787, and we know that the counter-petition after the 1806 election was drawn up by his agent Pedley. One of Beckford's candidates at Saltash was John Curtis, whom Beckford at the same time replaced at Wells in 1784, presumably by a secret arrangement. The mortgaging to him of one of Beckford's English estates for £12,000 in 1793[46] suggests that already the cost of financing the Saltash seat had become too much.

Beckford was thus involved in a costly system which was part of his inheritance as a landed gentleman. In particular, as a West India proprietor he had to oppose the anti-slavery campaign and the constant tendency to increase the sugar duties. This was one of his chief reasons for wanting Robert Deverell and his brother John Pedley (fresh from Jamaica) in Parliament.[47] For Beckford was not one of those idle men who are almost ignorant of the source of their wealth and ignore attacks on it. On the contrary, he followed the fluctuations in the price of sugar; and even when abroad he scanned the newspapers for the Division Lists of a Commons debate, in order to see who had failed to vote against Wilberforce's Abolition Bill:[48] it was thrown out on its third Reading by a majority of four votes, because some of Wilberforce's supporters were absent, enjoying the first night of a new comic opera!

Beckford's position as a resident landowner in an agricultural area with considerable unemployment, also involved him in large expenditure, as we have seen. There is only one reference to the annual cost of his staff and of keeping the local people fed and employed. In an undated draft of about September 1801, Beckford writes "I see plain enough by the List Mr. White transmitted to me that I am still giving bread to above 100 persons at the expence of about [£]4896 a year."[49] The rents from Fonthill and the two local farms leased from the Bishops totalled £5,000 a year before the deduction of heavy poor rates (which in 1821 amounted to £740 a year); in other words, at times he was paying out more annually to keep people fed and employed than he was receiving from his local net rents. Even at the end, when he was no longer building and planting, and had a greatly reduced establishment, the mere upkeep of the Abbey and estate, with staff wages, equalled the whole of his Fonthill net revenue of £4,000 a year.[50]

As a rich man, Beckford was bound to lose money through the advice or dishonesty of others, or ill-luck. We happen to have four different examples, but there may have been others. In 1798 Benjamin West and his fellow American artist, John Trumbull, after a good deal of persuasion, in the course of which Beckford was suspicious, 'induced' him to buy some estates in America, for which "it is thought Beckford has paid too dear" —"a monstrous price". West's incompetent son Raphael was sent out in August 1798 to act as Beckford's agent. He could see no promise in the vast uninhabited tracts of forest, found that the title-deeds were doubtful and came back in May 1800, just in time to prevent Beckford paying over the money, "having discovered that a set of swindlers were endeavouring to impose on Mr. Beckford".[51] On this occasion Beckford was lucky because Benjamin West, as President of the Royal Academy and favourite of the King, could not afford to make mistakes which might lead to a scandal or lawsuit. One of the estates was in Pennsylvania on the River Susquehannah, and another in New York State on the River Genesee.[52]

Private banks often failed, in which case the client would probably lose, without compensation, any cash deposited in the bank and any shares invested in it. In March 1832 Beckford's bankers failed. One of the partners, Sir George Duckett, had speculated heavily in River shares of canals and inland navigation; the railway came along and the traffic was diverted! Beckford's solicitor White heard from another source the news, which came all unexpected, like a bolt from the blue. He hurried round to the Bank; there was the terrible notice nailed up on the door—suspension of payments. Luckily they only owed Beckford £1,678; as White put it, "the loss might have occurred at a less fortunate time for you". He hastily instructed the Provident Life Office not to pay its annuity into the bank as authorised; indeed, was it safe to trust any bank with these monies, he wondered.[53] Beckford also alludes to "the Pall Mall disaster" around 1810-11 and in 1814.[54]

The great West India merchant houses, or sugar-factors as they were called, also crashed periodically, causing much distress and loss. One of these famous crashes was that of Beckford's West India agents, Messrs. Plummer & Wilson. They had to contemplate stopping payments in November 1830, blaming in their letter which announced this disaster "the extreme pressure on its [our] resources which the long continued and unceasing depression of West India property has occasioned."[55] The firm was reconstituted as Hankey, Plummer & Wilson, indicating that it was absorbed by another West India Firm, that of Thomson Hankey & Co. Messrs. Plummer had been Beckford's agents since 1807. Periodically they sold one of his plantations in order to reduce his overdraft, when they themselves were embarrassed by a depressed sugar market; this meant that Beckford's plantations were sold disadvantageously at the wrong time. For example, Draxhall was sold for £42,000 in November 1821, on the verge of sugar's worst year in history (up to then); only the previous June, the cautious Brown had agreed with a valuation made in March by 'competent judges' that Draxhall, with its stock, was worth £50,000.[56]

A much more common occurrence was the loss of ships with their cargoes. In July 1824 the *Eclipse* was declared a total loss with 150 hogsheads of sugar and 50 puncheons of rum from Beckford's plantations.[57] In order to save money Beckford, as so often, had not insured the cargo; even after this shipwreck he refused to insure the rest of the crop in transit. He owned, in partnership with Henry Wildman, the *Julius Caesar*, in which he sailed to Lisbon in 1787. She was lost about 1798, and in 1818 he was still trying to get the accounts settled and his claims against the now deceased Wildman agreed, in a Chancery suit which he had instituted in 1815.[58]

Beckford was also part-owner, with the three Wildmans and John Cundale, of the *William Beckford*. She ran aground near Margate and was damaged, together with her cargo. In 1799 Cundale began a Chancery suit against the consignee Henry Wildman, who had received several thousand pounds on account of the cargo and on the sale of the ship. Cundale wanted his share and made Beckford a defendant with the Wildmans. Judgement with costs for a fairly large sum was given against Wildman in 1815; but he died in 1816 before he had finished payment of costs, and Beckford tried to get the balance out of his sons, the Executors of his Will.[59] So much for the ways in which a rich man could lose money and the examples known to us from Beckford's life.

But making all these allowances, one cannot deny that Beckford was extravagant. However, his was not the thoughtless extravagance of the young heir who throws everything to the winds in wine, gaming and dissipation, and who spends for the love of it; he hated disbursing anything! He always spent for a purpose—to win social prestige and to fulfil his Caliphian dream. This was why, despite his simple and abstemious habits and rigid regime at Fonthill, he ate innumerable dishes in solitary state off gold plate, surrounded by a train of servants. By his calculated ostentation, in the West Indian tradition, he sought the respect of all ranks, as on his precipitate return from Paris, where he imagined himself slighted by his old friends, the Portuguese Ambassador Marialva and the famous Count of Palmela. Back in London, in his lawyer's dingy office in Lincoln's Inn, he wrote "I came like a thunderbolt, having electrified by sheer weight of money the passporteers, Customs-ites, inn and post-house keepers, in short *everybody* along the *whole* route; of me alone do they talk and think, to me only do they drink."[60]

His desire for social rehabilitation and the promised peerage was one reason for his younger daughter's marriage to the future Duke of Hamilton, which, it was rumoured, might cost Beckford £100,000.[61] This speculation turned out to be a failure; but Beckford could hardly have foreseen the long spell of Tory supremacy which excluded his Whig son-in-law from office and influence! Incidentally, there was another typically Beckfordian reason for the marriage, indicating a certain low cunning, self-regard and lack of patriotism. Beckford's contemptuous hatred for the English ruling classes and their generals induced in him a belief that England could not long hold out against Napoleon. The Marquis of Douglas (as he then was) was an ardent Bonapartist, and laid claim to the English throne and a French Dukedom. It was possible that if Napoleon won, Douglas might become his Quisling Viceroy. So the marriage was an insurance policy against the uncertain future: "I was personally aware of the importance of this alliance—looking into the future and seeing among clouds and constellations the great shadow of the Cuckoo-Philosopher [Napoleon]. God knows what portents may show themselves on the horizon!"[62]

There was only one field in which Beckford's expenditure was *apparently* boundless and in which he was intermittently apt to throw caution to the winds. He really was gripped by building mania. As soon as cash was available, he restarted his lapsed projects, which became more expensive because of his impatience and his love of wizardry: everything had to be done at once; the men worked on Sundays for double pay; the building grew visibly by torchlight. But even so, as soon as shortage of money threatened or ugly rumours came from Jamaica, he stopped dead in a panic and abandoned everything for the time being, or economised disastrously on the materials.

Our ideas of his extravagant building are really inherited from his own deliberate propaganda, passed on to us through Wyatt, West, Farington and Redding. In 1801 he let it be known that the building and furnishing of the Abbey had already cost £242,000 and that "it will cost him near as much to complete it".[63] He told Redding "to a shilling" that the total cost of building alone was "two hundred and seventy-three thousand [and] *some odd hundreds*". What apparent exactness! But the lawyer Fownes, who must have known, stated that "The buildings . . . have cost Mr. Beckford not less than £150,000 on the most moderate calculation".[64]

As a perfectionist, Beckford was bound to be extravagant in building and decorating: everything must be just so. But the constant bungling and negligence of Wyatt and the Clerk of Works (Hayter) greatly added to the cost, and also Wyatt's inability to arrive on time when great numbers of skilled craftsmen were gathered from far and wide, awaiting his "magic wand". By 1807 Beckford alleged that Wyatt's negligence had cost him an unnecessary £30,000.[65]

The extent to which the building of the Abbey contributed to his financial difficulties can be seen from the growth of his overdraft with Henry Wildman. Significantly, "the first Account on which any material balance seemed due to Henry Wildman" was for the year ending 1st June 1797, which covered the first winter's building at the Abbey; this produced an overdraft of a mere £724.[66] But then he continually needed "large sums" for his "expensive building", and the unsettled overdraft rose accordingly for three consecutive years. By 1st June 1798 it was £24,626, then £58,296, and finally £89,976 on 1st June 1800. Meanwhile, Beckford was paying interest at 5% (included in these sums).

This was a particularly expensive form of borrowing: for Henry Wildman claimed that he had to sell his own Government stock at a large loss between 1797 and 1799 in order to find the cash for Beckford, and that therefore the latter should at any time be ready to finance its repurchase at Wildman's request. Wildman took 8th June 1802 as the date of this *theoretical* operation, because he alleged that this was the date he received a copy of the conveyance of Esher plantation (see below), which had been drawn up in Jamaica six months earlier. Accordingly he debited Beckford with £14,820, which was the difference in the price of the stock on the dates he sold it in war-time and 8th June 1802. This was a favourable date to choose, peace with France having been concluded at the end of March! In any case, no money was changing hands or being found for Esher.

If running up this debt of £89,976 was expensive, paying it off was worse! Beckford thought it easy enough, by apparently liquidating it at one fell swoop with the conveyance of Esher, his richest remaining plantation,

THE BECKFORD FORTUNE

in December 1801 to Henry Wildman at a valuation of £88,256 sterling,[67] agreed by arbitration (Wildman had maintained that it was worth less than £50,000). The arbitrators fixed the price at £123,558 currency in order to give the sterling equivalent of £88,256 "at the usual computation of £140 currency for £100 sterling". This was clearly understood by Beckford's attorney Pedley, who signed the conveyance on his behalf in Jamaica. But because there was at the time a 10% depreciation in the exchange rate against Jamaica, Wildman claimed that Esher was only worth £79,430 sterling. He therefore debited Beckford's account with the difference, i.e. £8,825 sterling. This should surely have been irrelevant, since money was not being remitted to England, and the debt extinguished by the conveyance went back to 1798. Wildman also charged 10% for the valuation, a sum of £8,956. Beckford's overdraft of £89,976 was therefore increased by £32,600 (including the charge for repurchasing Government stock), and 5% interest was being paid on it.

To sum up, there was not a single cause for Beckford's financial ruin. There was a sequence of events against a background which he could not help. This unfavourable background which inexorably undermined his fortune was the economic decline of Jamaica and the dishonesty of his agents. Then came a series of expenditures, some of which coincided. When his English estates were already mortgaged for £25,000 (doubtless to finance his parliamentary expenditure), he began to lose plantations through lawsuits. Then, as a coup de grace, came the building of Fonthill.

Chapter XVII

LAST YEARS, 1823-1844

To have spent so much on Fonthill, his childhood home, and then to part with it at the age of sixty-two might well have broken his spirit. He might have sunk into lassitude and despondency. This had happened to a man of similar character and tastes—Thomas Johnes of Hafod. In 1807, when he was fifty-nine, his beloved Hafod had been burnt down, with most of its contents. During the three years of its reconstruction, he became weary and discouraged; without his wife's support he would never have finished it; he only drove over occasionally to see its progress. How different Beckford was! No sooner had he settled in Bath in 1822 than he began ardently negotiating for a large tract of land to turn into another flowering wilderness. By 1825 he had begun to build another Tower as a studious retreat, this time on the top of Lansdown Hill, overlooking Bath.

As usual with Beckford, his youthful recollections inspired him. As he looked north from the summit of Lansdown, he was reminded of the dreary and historic plain of the Roman Campagna which he had first visited in 1780—that "land of solemn recollections, of perished nations, the memento of an approaching eternity. I shall never forget how I first passed over that land of the Dead, strewed with ruins and covered with green turf; I scarcely spoke for miles—I never thought that the desolations of time could be so complete; we find it difficult to swallow hard truths when life opens to us. God knows I had vivacity enough; but I

LAST YEARS, 1823-1844

was struck with the dreariness of the scene, with the barren heaps and solitary towers, miserable sheep, ruined sepulchres and shattered columns . . .; this scene [Lansdown] reminds me of my dreams and meditations there. The surface is smoother, but it has the same dun color, the same 'deathlike stillness' and 'dread repose'."[1]

When Waagen visited Lansdown Tower and Beckford's house in Lansdown Crescent, he found that once again a great collection of pictures and works of art had been assembled, including Raphael's *St. Catherine* and Velasquez' *Philip IV when Young*, both now in the National Gallery. There were the *Hours of Mary of Burgundy* (already mentioned); a unique fifth-century Greek jug for oil, known as the Beckford Vase,[2] about which scholars are still writing, and an almost equally famous Athenian vase, dug up by Prince Lucien Bonaparte[3]—both now in the British Museum. Waagen also noted an early mediaeval gold vessel, a Chinese bronze "the colour of which is more delicate than I have ever before seen", and mediaeval and Chinese glass vessels "likewise remarkable for the beauty of the colours and the exquisite workmanship".

Yet Beckford's rooms were never museums: "what especially pleased me", said Waagen, "was that all these things bear a due proportion in size to the moderate apartments in which they are, and are likewise so arranged that they serve richly to adorn each, without producing, as often happens, by overloading and confusion, the disagreeable effect of auction-rooms." He added: "I shall never forget the dining-room, which, taken all in all is perhaps one of the most beautiful in the world. Conceive a moderate apartment of agreeable proportions, whose walls are adorned with cabinet pictures, the noblest productions of Italian art of the time of Raphael, from the windows of which you overlook the whole paradaisical valley of the Avon, with the city of Bath, which was now steeped in sunshine."[4]

ENGLAND'S WEALTHIEST SON

Beckford collected pictures and, above all, books with such enthusiasm that he soon had to buy the house next door in order to have more room; he built an archway between the two, which made an extra gallery for books. Even so, they overflowed everywhere—into the maids' rooms, into the attics. Of course, he gave Redding a more amusing and arrogant reason for his purchase of the second house: "Now, had I not bought this house, I should have been perpetually annoyed by the ticking of some cursèd jack, the jingling of some beastly piano, horrid-toned bells tinkling, and so on."[5]

When Death snatched away the old Russian Jew, Julius Angerstein, father of the present insurance concern of Lloyd's, Beckford negotiated for several of his pictures. Still smarting under the lash of Hazlitt's scathing criticism of the contents of Fonthill, he wrote jubilantly to the Duke of Hamilton: "My dear Friend, here is a piece of news tolerably interesting to the Picture World: *the Sebastian del Piombo is mine!!!* As you may well imagine, I've paid a *large* sum for it, sweetened, however, by Hogarth's *Marriage à la mode*, Nicholas Poussin's magnificent *Bacchanalian Triumph*, valued at two or three thousand pounds, and the *delicious* little *Apollo and Silenus* by [Annabale] Carracci. They'll no longer accuse me of a shameful passion for old lacquer or modern gothic. I'm the *exclusive* possessor of several *objets d'art* worth possessing . . . Love me in my lifetime, and after my death respect my devotion for the *terrible via* of Michael Angelo and Sebastian del Piombo."[6]

But this was premature. Angerstein's son decided to sell the collection as a whole, Parliament voted the money, and the nation paid £57,000 for the thirty-eight pictures. This was the start of the National Gallery. By far the highest valuation (£8,000) was put on the huge *Resurrection of Lazarus* by Sebastian del Piombo, which long remained the show-piece of the Gallery and was thought by some to be one of the finest pictures in the world!

LAST YEARS, 1823-1844

The first Keeper of the National Gallery was William Seguier, whose valuation of the collection had been accepted by the Government. One of his lucrative occupations was the restoration of Old Masters. When he was dead, Beckford flayed *him* in the same way that *he* had flayed pictures during his life: "The Powers above have done a handsome thing by me. They have finally removed from the varnishing world (notorious resort of sharks, cormorants and land-gulls) the greatest president of cheats and picture-skinners, the merciless be-dauber of my Raphael, Perugino and Mazzolino di Ferrara—one of the prime objects of my very particular dislike and detestation. Little did I flatter myself (when we last met) that my prayers for the extinction of this nuisance, this obese and pampered toad-eater would have been heard so soon; but so it is, and heartily do I say *Deo-gratias*. Now to the point: can you inform me whether his print-hoards are likely to come to the market? Whenever they do, I shall hurry to town on purpose, with your assistance, to pounce down upon a selection from them."[7]

This is strong language. But in those days, picture-restorers tried to outdo the Old Masters upon which they were working. Northcote relates of Reynolds: "It was a particular pleasure to Sir Joshua when he got into his hands any damaged pictures by some eminent Old Masters; and he . . . has often made them, both in effect and colour, vastly superior to what they had ever been in their original state. For instance, with respect to one picture by Velasquez, a full length picture of Philip the Fourth of Spain as a boy: I well remember, when I entered his painting-room one day and saw this picture, he said to me, 'See, there is a fine picture by Velasquez.' I looked at it and greatly admired it, and with much simplicity said, 'Indeed, it is very fine; and how exactly it is in your own manner, Sir Joshua'; yet it never entered into my mind that he had touched upon it, which was really the fact, and particularly on the face."[8] No wonder Beckford detested picture-restorers; but he was ahead of his times.

Now we come to one of those crises in a man's life, which lay bare his inmost character. Beckford's most faithful friend lay dying, perhaps of consumption and alone in London lodgings, attended only by his manservant Wing and the physician Southey, brother of the poet. For a fortnight none of the family, none of the retainers, visited the Chevalier Franchi until the upholsterer Hume came, to find him on the verge of dissolution. He had been without sleep for fifteen days and nights, existing only on arrowroot.

But it was not his body which troubled him most. It was his mind. Something dreadful lay upon Franchi's conscience. The doctor and Hume thought it was financial worry. "I have no doubt he is without money, from some phrensied ejaculations that escaped him, such as, 'Money for my Doctor', 'Oh Dear, it will kill me', and others somewhat similar; and upon enquiry of his man, he told me he thought he had only a few pounds left, and that several bills had been sent to him that he could not pay."[9]

He seemed to be "lost and sinking"; then he rallied a little and talked for a few minutes. But he had "not the power to give utterance to his thoughts." What were these painful thoughts? Memories of his wife, Madame Bête-Bête, whom he had deserted in Lisbon in order to follow Beckford; "I vow that Madame displeases me as much as I once loved her . . ; she is *bête, bête, bête, à faire trembler*," he wrote.[10] Memories of his daughter, whom he had also abandoned, despite his feelings for her—"the little girl is very charming—*elle seul fait mon bonheur.*" And now he had nothing but debts to leave them, having sold the annuity which Beckford had promised them on their wedding day for their joint lives (and he had not told her).[11] Memories of the Catholic faith which he had abandoned—he who had been educated by the Church in a musical seminary and sung as a

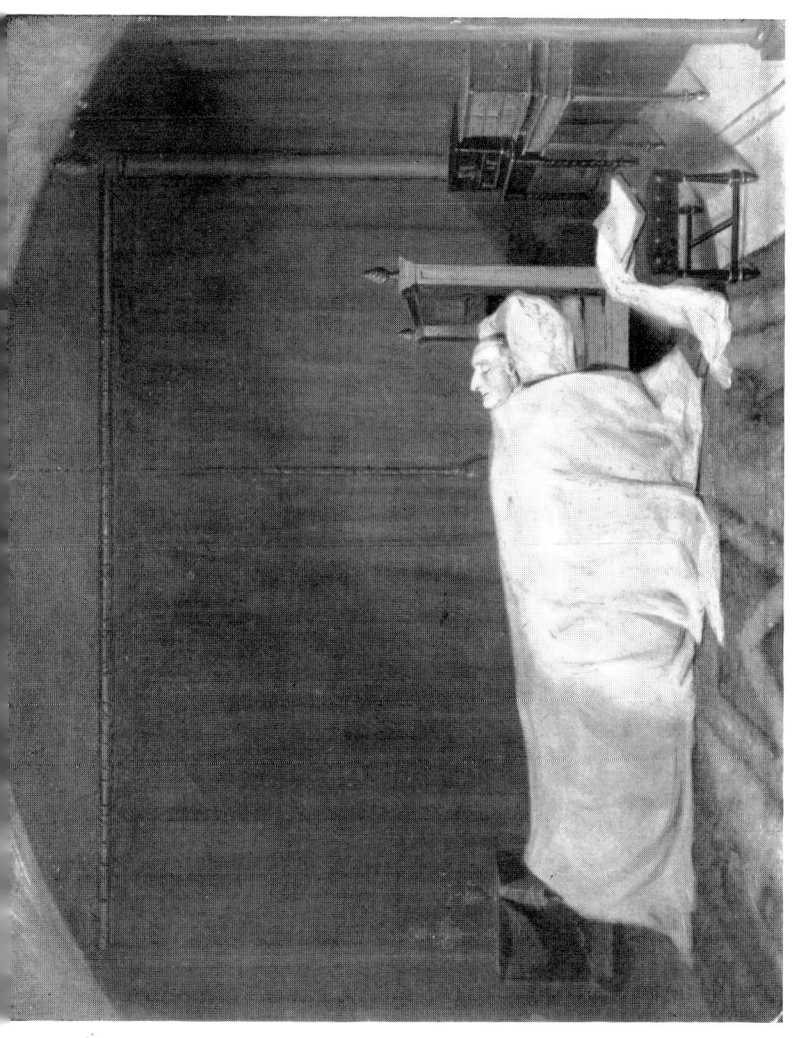

BECKFORD'S DEATHBED, by Willis Maddox

LAST YEARS, 1823-1844

choirboy in the Chapel of the Queen of Portugal. Memories of the blasphemies in his letters to Beckford. Memories of boys . . .

In this mortal sickness of the soul, Franchi was beyond the help of medicine. The Doctor begged Hume to call again that evening "as a little conversation might be of much more service to him than anything else whatever." So it was Hume who stayed by his bedside, "endeavouring to sooth and chear him." No sign of Duchess Susan, his 'dear Sovereign' at whose feet he had so often prostrated himself. No sign of Beckford; not even a line from him. No one to whom he could speak his mother tongue and express his *saudades* of Portugal. Hume could only say that he would write to Beckford to apprise him of his friend's state; "he thanked me and begged I would do so".

His funeral was as lonely and cheerless as his death. "Sir, again to the very mournful affairs of poor Franchi. This morning he was buried at the St. Marylebone ground of St. John's Wood about 10 o'clock in a respectable and becoming manner, followed by his servant and a solicitor (who he had mentioned in his Will), Webster, his Silver Castor and myself."[12]

All this time Beckford was near at hand in Bath. Surely he could have come to the funeral? He was nearly sixty-eight, it is true; but he looked and felt far younger, and lived regularly in London in the season. But he must keep away from anything unpleasant, in case it overtaxed his nerves. He who was solicitous for his own health could not bear another's indisposition.

A steel curtain came down, cutting him off involuntarily from his nearest and dearest. He could not help turning away when his sympathy was called upon. Afterwards, he became a prey to remorse, when it was too late to stretch out a consoling hand to those who had been his dear friends—his wife Lady Margaret; the long-suffering Marquis of Marialva, who had "entreated me not to forget Portugal . . . and to remember he should not die in peace unless I was present to close his eyes;"[13] the Abbé Macquin, and now the Chevalier Franchi, last of those friends except the Duke of Hamilton. Yes, too late, always too late: "That dreadful gulf which now is fixed between us arose before my imagination in all its terrors. I returned home gloomy and comfortless, calling in vain upon her who can hear no more, the companion of my happiest hours, once so lively and blooming, now lying cold and ghastly in the dark vaults at Fonthill".

This regret turned to bitterness, so that he was sundered for ever from his friends: " 'what have they become—friendship—all you read of my friends, dark, cloudy thoughts that accidental circumstances recall with intolerable bitterness', [he said]. Here for a few moments he was silent, talking to himself, as he often did when alone. He seemed for a moment as if he were hardly conscious of the presence of another person."[14]

He had always known that this involuntary loneliness, this iron-clad self-absorption, which leads to bitterness and despair, is the egotist's end. Even as a youth, he had seen himself as the proud and spoiled Caliph Vathek, wandering in his father's Hall at Splendens, inconsolable and lonely amid the crowd of the Damned.

However, an artist gives a more pleasant impression of Beckford when visiting him in November 1843 in Bath. Amongst other things he saw his library in Lansdown Tower "full of unique large-paper copies, with the finest *epreuve d'artistes* of the plates, and in many cases etchings and original drawings were inserted. I remarked in this as well as in every other room in the house . . . that the books appeared to be placed without the slightest regard to order . . . But Mr. Beckford appeared to be able to find anything in a moment, and ran about quite in a state of extasy, pulling out one book after another and exclaiming, 'Good heaven! did you ever see anything like this—look at these delicious impressions—only see the purity of this paper—here's no trick—no retouching—no washing—everything as pure as the day it was printed.' . . . Everything had its history, which he repeated in the most lively manner; for, as was often the case, he was in exuberantly buoyant spirits, and whenever a stool or a chair was in his way, gave himself no trouble to put it out of the way, but leaped over it."

The artist also saw Beckford's library in Lansdown Crescent. " 'There', he [Beckford] said, 'are Vandycks to fall down to and worship.[15] Such glorious impressions can nowhere be found—let's try a volume'. Before I could offer to help him, he had pulled one of them out, and notwithstanding its great weight, had run to the window with it . . . In one of the windows [of the gallery over the road] was a wonderfully fine marble figure of a sleeping child, of which he was very fond, and once said to a friend, with a touch of melancholy, 'It is the only son I ever had'; Lady Margaret, no doubt, coming to his recollection, and his untimely loss of her."

Up to the last Beckford went to London for the season, renting a partly furnished house at £350 a year.[16] Since some of the owner's pictures remained on the wall, "he always apologised as follows when he saw anyone looking at them: 'My dear Sir, don't suppose this vile trash is mine!' To make up for this, he generally sent up to town a few of his own choice works of art, pictures, agate cups, gems and prints in order to be surrounded by things he loved to contemplate", and he also had flowers sent up from his Bath gardens.

He was a familiar figure in Hyde Park on his white Persian mare Deborah, accompanied by two grooms. She ran away with him in the Park when he was in his eighty-third year, but he managed to pull her up unaided.[17] Here Doyle sketched him. Sometimes he rode up the Edgware Road to Hampstead, stopping en route at his mother's house, where he used "to pull up his horse and gaze upon the old family habitation for some time, as if lost in thought or travelling back to byegone times."[18]

ENGLAND'S WEALTHIEST SON

We hardly dare think of his gloomy reveries, as he recollected the tragedies which the house had witnessed half a century before—his Carathis-like mother dying on a July day, unattended by her only son; her many years' residence away from him (she would have been living in the Dower-house at Fonthill, had it not been for the scandal attached to his name, and her intolerable position locally); his daughters brought up without a father—repeating his own fatherless childhood in the seclusion and notoriety which seemed to surround the name of Beckford; their entry against his will into a world "from which I have been so long estranged;"[19] and the terrible quarrels over them with his relatives . . .

His routine in London, even when an octogenarian, was unvaried. He rose between seven and eight, swallowed chicken broth, and rode out to a nursery. Here he trotted round the walks, scissors in hand, and snipped off anything he fancied, regardless of expense; his old servant, nicknamed Poodle, could hardly keep up with him. Loaded with these spoils, he returned for his *toilette des fleurs*, which he arranged himself in vases. Only then did he breakfast, and remained in till half-past two, when he ordered his carriage to take him to exhibitions, views at the auctioneers, Bohn's bookshop in Covent Garden, Smith's printshop in Lisle Street, and Rundell & Bridge, the Court jewellers on Ludgate Hill. On his way back he called for a few minutes at Duchess Susan's in Portman Square. He returned for dinner about half-past six, usually without guests; for conversation at night excited his brain and disturbed his digestion; those who wanted to see him (and they were few) had to call in the morning after eleven o'clock. By ten o'clock he was in bed![20]

This habit of early bed prevented him from going much to the opera. He particularly liked Cimarosa's *Secret Marriage* and Mozart's *Figaro* and *Don Giovanni*. He always followed the score, and was upset for days if singer or orchestra made a mistake. He met Disraeli at the opera; they gossiped for three hours, and Disraeli reported that he was "very bitter and *malin*."[21]

Whilst in London he had a dream "so strange, so melancholy" that he felt "compelled to write it down". It ended up about his dogs Tout (then dead) and Elinor:

"Methought I was sitting in the dusk on a calm summer's evening at the window of the large room on the ground floor at Hartford Bridge, when a distant strain of music struck my ear. It approached, and I saw . . . a vast body of soldiers on horseback descending the hill. Some infantry were mingled with them—young boys with fifes and drums; but the drums were muffled, and the soldiers, whose faces were uniformly pale and ghastly, trailed their pikes on the ground. Two tall figures, mounted on coal-black horses of gigantic size, seemed to pass close to me. They were beating slowly and at intervals upon silver kettle-drums—it was a sort of funeral. It passed on, and the sounds gradually died away.

"I remained motionless. Presently the door opened without any noise, and there stood Demezey, looking the same as when I saw him for the last time before his death above twenty years ago. I thought he said to me with the same low fawning voice, accompanied by the same obsequious bows, 'I hope Your Honour will not be offended, but they are going to Canada.'[22] I answered, 'If so, not one will return; I see death in their countenances'.

"I looked round. He was gone, and I continued to sit on at my window in total silence and solitude . . . The dusk had sunk into darkness when I seemed to hear thrilling, harmonious sounds, and to behold lights gleaming to and fro on the same hill down which the military procession had descended. Suddenly I saw before me a strange vehicle not unlike a hearse. The horses were covered down to their very hoofs with rich mantles, and conducted by beautiful youths, but whose countenances were severe and thoughtful. I saw them by the aid of a broad sheet of bluish light which proceeded God knows from whither!

"They opened a small square door panelled like that of a cabinet, and out sprang the *Tout*, apparently in all the pride of youth and vigour—the *same* bright hues, the *same* white frill, the *same* clear voice, the *same* gestures. But instead of casting the *same* fond, devoted looks at me, as he was wont, he made a frantic rush at Elinor and fixed his teeth in her throat. The floor was floated with her blood, and I awoke in horror."

Our last glimpse of Beckford before his death is on his daily descent from Lansdown Tower with his gardener, Vincent. He was almost as old as Beckford, who treated him with extraordinary freedom, not uncommon between master and man in upper-class families in the eighteenth century, before the chilling formalism of the Victorians put a distance between them. Beckford "used to bend very politely, but rarely looked us full in the face as he passed. He frequently walked . . . with two servants behind leading three horses, and a favourite spaniel of the King Charles sort running along the side. Vincent was his man Friday, who said 'Yes, Y'ur Honour' to every word spoken; but once blundered sadly in making the same response to the question being put to him, 'Do you think me a fool?' Mr. Beckford usually wore a long brown greatcoat with top boots, and to a stranger might seem like a good old Zomerzetzeer farmer . . . He carried his head a little on one side and buried it somewhat in his collar . . . He walked very fast, then he would stop suddenly, as though thinking of Vathek or dreaming in the Halls of Eblis; then bustle on again, and then look back to consult Vincent. Now he would scold him, and then again laugh with a loud haw, haw! Perhaps he might give him a sharp cut with the whip, or reason with him with all the freedom and friendship of a brother."[23]

LAST YEARS, 1823-1844

That amazing vitality and exuberance might have continued for ever. But though unwilling to go to a most uncertain End, in which he had no consolations and no confidence, he was never unmindful of Death. "Beckford contemplated the closing scene of existence very frequently, and wondered he had been spared so long. He never disguised his age . . . exclaiming 'I am almost ashamed of being so old, really death seems to have forgotten me or has unintentionally passed me by; perhaps he means I shall be a centenarian. I have no objection . . . [But] I must submit to go when I am knocked for; still, it is the common doom'."[24]

But he caught a chill out walking in the cold east wind of April 1844. For a fortnight he strove manfully against influenza, fever and growing weakness. Sybarite though he was, he had always been tough, rising at six and bathing in November. He dragged himself about, a tottering wreck. He forced himself, unaided, out of bed. He wrote notes and annotated catalogues in a trembling, daily weakening hand.

Now there was no Ehrhart about him, '*The* Doctor' who had understood him so well and whom he had never forgotten, though he had been dead these forty years. "Up to now Liston has shown that he's no Ehrhart—that's all", he wrote to his daughter.[25] Curious that his last doctor should have been called Robert Liston. Name of ill-omen! For another Robert Liston had been his Walpolian adversary in Madrid in 1788— the Envoy who had refused to recognise him or present him at Court, and who had in the end defeated him.

Franchi had also taken a fortnight to die but without the consolation of The Family at hand. Beckford was luckier, though he deserved it less. Unable to bear his mortal solitude, he summoned his daughter, and she came. "Liston", he wrote, "flattered himself that I was better yesterday. He was deceived, for hardly had he gone when a dreadful shivering shook me from head to foot. Oh, *abregez la distance!* Oh, *abregez la fatale dis-*

tance ... In this and every other business, *avisez pour moi, pensez pour moi, raisonnez pour moi. Ayez quelques soins de moi*—It's my turn now: my feverish, shivering state is so deplorable that I'm worse than you! No letter! Oh, *abregez la distance!* I can no longer bear it."²⁶ In times of crisis he had always expected to have someone to fall back on. It was his oldest cry—*avisez pour moi, pensez pour moi, raisonnez pour moi, ayez quelques soins de moi.*

His devout, conventional daughter was so anxious that he should die in a proper, decent way. Surely he would have a Roman Catholic priest? No. And of course he refused to see the Rector of his parish. He had always hated Anglicanism with its bare churches looking "like a whore clad only in muslin", "without mystery, without ecclesiastical pomp", the altars stripped of candles and relics, the ludicrous psalmody, the total lack of feeling and poetry. "Oh, the disgust and stink of Protestantism (it doesn't deserve the sonorous name of Heresy)," he had written.²⁷

But he was not left alone. His family and dependants gathered in the next room whilst the Most Reverend Mister So-and-So murmured prayers. And the doctor, always the most acceptable person with Beckford, was sent in to harangue him upon what he knew only too well—"our common depravity", our painful position "as guilty sinners".²⁸ Could he believe in the doctor's consolatory sop—the triumphant atonement of the Saviour? Shade of the methodistical Lady Euphemia lecturing the dying Lady Margaret. This positive, hopeful note had always been Beckford's difficulty. He believed in Guilt, Judgement and Damnation. But like Vathek and his companions in Hell, he could not believe that there was Hope for *him*. It was this that had made him desperate and defiant in his pursuit of forbidden pleasures; if he was damned, he might as well be doubly damned. And he had needed to find distraction from the terrible Accusing Voices, but in vain: "the voice which calls us to look into ourselves and prepare for Judgement is too piercing, too powerful, to be resisted; and we attempt, for worldly and sensual considerations, to shut our ears in vain."[29]

And so, with a certain characteristic stubbornness, a certain characteristic constancy, he kept his counsels to the end, "bearing up with uncommon firmness; he spoke to no one about his belief or hope", and told the clergyman that "he [Beckford] could do no more: it was his latest [sic] effort".[30] He was calm and resigned. But like Franchi at the last, he had something on his conscience. "He expressed a wish he had not written some particular thing, but it was not possible to ascertain what he intended."

His strange, complex character peeped out now and then. "There was something peculiar about him almost to the last. His favorite dog slept on a rug in the same room with himself. Just before his death, he ordered it to be taken away and the rug it lay upon to be burned, as if . . . he feared he was to be censured for spending too much of his time upon vain trifles." Was Redding right in this explanation? Or could Beckford not bear to think of that devoted little dog sleeping at another's feet on the same rug? Did he remain a miser, an egotist to the end?

When it was all over, there he lay embalmed, the same evening (2nd May). As always with him, there was curious contrast: the narrow truckle bed; the priceless golden ewers, indicating Midas; and crimson everywhere, signifying his Hamiltonian lineage—crimson curtain, crimson stool, crimson bed-head; the utmost simplicity and economy of furniture, but a pair of little ornamental cabinets, stuffed with intaglios and jewels— those Cat Diamonds given him as a boy. What was the book open at his side, his last and favourite reading? Not the Bible—it is too slim for that!

Chapter XVIII

CHARACTER AND TASTES

On one side of his tomb Beckford had inscribed a phrase adapted from *Vathek*: "Enjoying humbly the most precious gift of Heaven—Hope". But this is the direct opposite of the passage in the book! There, the Voice announces to Vathek and his companions "the awful and irrevocable decree" of their final doom; whereupon "their hearts immediately took fire, and they at once lost the most precious of the gifts of Heaven—Hope". Redding noticed the discrepancy, and could not make out the real meaning of Beckford's epitaph!

Beckford only wrote two poems, and neither show any feeling of hope. One, an adaptation of *Dies Irae*, ran:[1]

"a voice of ire
Proclaims: 'Ye guilty, wait your final doom:
No more the silent refuge of the tomb
Shall screen your crimes, your frailties.
            Conscience reigns;
Earth needs no other sceptre; what remains
Beyond her fated limits, dare not tell:
Eternal Justice! Judgement! Heaven! Hell!' "

Beckford imbibed the sombre tenets of the Evangelicals or Methodists at an early age. Hence his fear of Judgement and Hell, which was reinforced by the Roman Missal with its majestic phrases, appealing to his poetic nature. The Missal came to life for him in the gorgeous services in Lisbon, where the music of Jomelli was like "the cries for mercy of unhappy beings, around whom the shadows of death and the pains of hell were gathering".[2]

His sense of personal unworthiness was in some respects displaced anxiety, partly caused by the disharmony in his family background. This made Mrs. Beckford over-anxious for him to be conventional and successful. Doubtless to cover up the Alderman's notorious character, she impressed his son with his political success and gigantic stature, until he became the Commendatore[3]— an accusing statue at the banquet of life, reproaching his son with trifling and infamy.

No one had more splendid prospects at his Coming-of-Age. But even then his sense of inadequacy gnawed like a worm at his heart: "I begin to think myself good for nothing in this world, and like the flower Narcissus ought to be consecrated to the Manes".[4] Beckford here refers to Bacon's essay on 'Narcissus or Self-love', which (he thought in 1781) described him and his future —showing how perceptive he was, how severe on himself, and how lacking in self-confidence.

Bacon takes the myth of the proud and disdainful youth Narcissus, who pined away in solitude and self-contemplation, as illustrative of the character and fate of men of this type, who are self-destructive. Because they cannot endure the hard knocks of public life, they lead a solitary existence, attended only by flatterers, which increases their disdain and conceit, until they sink into torpor and boredom. Thus, although with their gifts and charm they appear to start life well, later on they deceive the hopes placed in them, producing no fruit and vanishing as if they had never been.

The sense of guilt, natural in adolescence, was increased when Beckford found that his feelings were directed perversely, and that Society and his own conscience threatened to overwhelm him for his 'crime'. This is the burden of nearly all his dreams.

There was a deeper reason for his feeling of inadequacy. Was he heartless? He longed for the affection of others, but was unwilling to commit himself in return. He intrigued with young women and gave way "to the enchanting delirium of a rising passion". But he did not want to get his fingers burned. Of the Princesse de Listenais in Madrid he said, "the young Princess was rather too fond of talking about me. I must take care, or I shall kindle a flame not easily extinguished. I am surrounded with fires; it is delightful to be warmed, but unless I summon up every atom of prudence in my composition I shall be reduced to ashes."[5] This heartlessness is reflected (psychologically) in one of Beckford's constant aversions: he could not bear the thought of fishing, and above all hated the sight of fish expiring on the bank. Fish are cold-blooded creatures! His reactions were abnormally strong, and remind one of Baron Corvo's encounter with the toad.[6]

Beckford was aware of being a genius *manqué*. Swinburne perceived what this meant when he wrote to Mallarmé to thank him for a copy of *Vathek*. "I have always pictured Beckford as a most unhappy man, more deeply consumed by malaise, ennui and melancholia than ever his admirer Byron was. This state is sometimes bottled up and simmering, and sometimes breaks out and explodes everywhere in *Vathek* and in all that is told of him, both true and false. To be a millionaire and to want to be a poet—and only to be half a one! To be conscious of something like genius, but to turn out not to be one after all and nothing more than an *à peu près*! Almost to succeed in finding the path to artistic creation, and then to fall back on one's riches! All this must make the life of the poet *manqué* something much more gloomy than the Hall of Eblis."[7]

This seething of powers which never quite materialised was painful. Beckford describes it in a dissertation on one of his favourite maxims, 'Great talents, great failings': "Great talents are gifts for which often we pay much more dearly than they are worth. They are associated with such great sensibility that it is almost impossible to control. And yet we glory in this divine fire which may at any moment annihilate us and destroy all our happiness! Voltaire died mad, and the derangement of Rousseau's mind in his last years approached insanity. Thus, what we prize most highly when we only know its fine aspect, becomes the object of our aversion when we see its dark side. He whom we despised only yesterday for his cold apathy, we envy when our passions have led us astray! True worth is found between these two extremes. . . . Placed in this world by God's all-powerful hand, what happens to us is His will. We must be resigned, and profit by such insight and wisdom as He vouchsafes us, if we are to be happy. Our bearing is much affected by temperance; we cannot pay this too much attention when vexed. A little bile, a slight difficulty darkens the imagination and stirs the distressing passions of pride, hatred and revenge. I have retained my soul's serenity in stormy times thanks to temperance and exercise."[8] This shows how Beckford was always trying to recover his balance, to exorcise his black demon. But exercise, temperance, an ordered framework of living and varied activity were not enough. He could not escape a "burden of eternal regret" and indefinable melancholy, which found expression in endless complaining and a negative attitude.

His sense of waste and trifling increased with the changing spirit of the Age. Under the impact of the *philosophes* and the Radicals, of the French Revolution and the Evangelical revival, the old aristocratic order, with its tolerance and easy-going ways, broke up. The landowners were in places giving way to the manufacturers. Wealth and position were being called in question; it was felt that they should not protect the privileged from the vengeance of the law which fell so savagely upon the rest. As a sensitive person, Beckford was affected by this changing atmosphere. He endeavoured to *atone* for his wealth and anomalous position: "Mr. B[eckford] is very sensible that great land-holders like himself are prejudicial to a country; he endeavours, therefore, to compensate for the injury fortune forces him to do, by furnishing constant employment for four or five thousand labourers, who are all in his pay."[9]

His misgivings about his life at Fonthill are expressed in his poem *A Prayer*,[10] which opens with the stanza

> "Like the low murmurings of the secret stream,
> Which through dark alders winds its shaded way,
> My suppliant voice is heard; ah, do not seem
> That on vain toys I throw my life away!"

By an extraordinary coincidence this was written a few days before the publication of Hazlitt's denunciation of Fonthill in *The London Magazine* for November 1822. Hazlitt summed up the Abbey and its collections as "a desart of magnificence, a glittering waste of laborious idleness, a cathedral turned into a toy-shop, an immense Museum of all that is most curious and costly, and, at the same time, most worthless, in the productions of art and nature . . . . . Mr. Beckford has undoubtedly shown himself an industrious *bijoutier*, a prodigious virtuoso, an accomplished patron of unproductive labour, an enthusiastic collector of expensive trifles; the only proof of taste (to our thinking) he has shown in this collection is *his getting rid of it*." Hazlitt's article will be discussed later. Naturally Beckford was dissatisfied with his work at Fonthill, being a perfectionist (like every cultivator of Good Taste and Beauty), and at heart an artist and poet. Anyone who is a gardener, interior decorator or collector is particularly vulnerable, knowing that when he is gone his gardens will be neglected or refashioned, his collections dispersed, and the *tout ensemble* vanish.

His sense of failure was increased by his literary misfortunes—the suppression of *Dreams and Waking Thoughts*, the theft of *Vathek*, and the consequent laying aside of the *Episodes of Vathek*. After that, he was never more than a trifler in literature, except for his slender volume *Alcobaça and Batalha* and his distillation of his Spanish

CHARACTER AND TASTES

and Portuguese diaries in the form of travel-letters.

This inferiority-complex and frustration might have led to fearful anti-social conduct, to drinking, gambling and laudanum. But the obsessions which seized Beckford were harmless—a passion for genealogy, the pursuit of a peerage, and calculated ostentation. It was said that "the windows at Fonthill burned and glowed with heraldic lies".[11] They did indeed. And the exasperated tourists, after screwing their necks to decipher the blazoning on the magnificent hammer-beam roof of the Great Western Hall, wrote down in their note-books "fancy arms". But at least this passion was creative. It produced King Edward's Gallery at Fonthill, to commemorate the seventy-two supposed Knightly ancestors of the Jamaican "negro-driver". It inspired the Eastern Transept, whose projected Baronial Hall was to recall the signatories of Magna Carta, from all of whom, by a curious and unique chance, Beckford was descended!

He was not above laughing at all this himself. He wrote to Beltz about his lowly ancestors the Woodwards and Margery Maddock, the Last of the Plantagenets, daughter of a shoemaker and bearer of that famous peaked Beckford nose: "You remember the hearty laugh we enjoyed when the Woodward pedigree slipped out by chance from under one of the grand gartered achievements, with the ingenious portrait of M[argery] Maddock scrawled upon the margin and adorned with a tremendous long and peaked nose. I daresay you recollect my exclamation upon the discovery of this famous nose; and by it, as it peeped forth, I may be said to have pulled forth the pedigree; to be sure it was a rare handle."[12]

Beckford's desire for a peerage of course embarrassed his friends and relations. As soon as he was *en rapport* with anyone with supposed Court influence, the demand was sure to arise. The queer Sir Robert Barclay, that 'Boastful Baronet', was cultivated in 1807 because the Prince Regent was godfather to one of his children. Orde was pressed to use his acquaintance with Sir John

McMahon,[13] the Regent's private secretary, and his second marriage with the daughter of the Duke of Beaufort.

Every time a new reign began, the poor Duke of Hamilton was pestered to approach the Ministry, with a *petit aperçu de ce qu'on pourra dire à ces drôles*.[14] As late as November 1837, Beckford was still chanting his 'Eternal Rondo for the Virtuosi', in which he vehemently urged the Ministry to remember the intentions of George the Third. He pleaded with them: "Gentlemen, you will acknowledge that a man who, by infinitely rare genealogical coincidences, is without exception descended from all the barons—yes, *all*—who signed Magna Carta and whose issue still exists, will not be out of place in the House of Lords." He threatened them with his heavy artillery: its explosions would resound all over England. Surely they would quake at this. "So procure it [my peerage], Gentlemen, procure it—that's what you'd better do!"

The most pathetic thing about Beckford was his inability to rely upon himself. Instead, he leaned upon others—his mother, older women friends, tutors and advisers, upon whom every decision was thrust—"think for me, I cannot very well think for myself". But above all, he relied upon his wealth. The most sober of men, eating sparingly, sleeping on horsehair in an unadorned truckle-bed, careless of his dress, he was at the same time, in the Jamaican tradition, calculatingly ostentatious. This was one of the prime reasons for his lavish hospitality and princely establishments abroad. It was his way of recommending himself to others, of 'ingratiating' himself with them, of causing a sensation—as if his charm and his gifts were not enough!

Hazlitt perceived that one function of Beckford's collecting was to buttress his personality. He said that many of the *objets d'art* at Fonthill were "nothing more than obtrusive proofs of the wealth of the immediate possessor", and that "the specimens exhibited are the

BECKFORD IN MIDDLE-AGE, by Hoppner

CHARACTER AND TASTES

best, the most highly finished, the most costly and curious of that kind of ostentatious magnificence which is calculated to gratify the sense of property in the owner, and to excite the wondering curiosity of the stranger, who is permitted to see or (as a choice privilege and favour) even to touch baubles so dazzling and of such exquisite nicety of execution; and which, if broken or defaced, it would be next to impossible to replace. . . . hardly an article of any consequence that does not seem to be labelled to the following effect—'This is mine'."[15] However, what is wrong with such collecting if it acquires unique items which we would give a fortune to re-assemble? Take, for example, the Meissen dinner service of 363 pieces specially made about 1770 for the Stadholder William V, painted with views of the ports and towns of Holland and her colonies; it is now scattered all over the world—a few pieces treasured by the Rijksmuseum and a few by the Metropolitan . . .[16]

If Beckford relied on his wealth, he was also imprisoned by it. As a reputed millionaire, he did not know whom to trust. From an early age he was surrounded by toadies; he was courted for his political usefulness as the son of his father and as the owner of a rotten borough; he was sought for the literary and artistic commissions and the pensions he could give; and he was fleeced by his agents.

His longing for appreciation, his mistrust of others and continual disappointment with them is shewn in a letter to one of his early pensioners (in which he refers to a letter of hers written nearly two years earlier!): "Had I thought it would give you the least pleasure, I would at once have seized the first opportunity to come to see you. But judging by a certain letter you sent me at Bordeaux, I had every reason to think that your feelings towards me had completely changed. I can never recollect this letter without horror; never in my life will I forget it, and the shock it gave me . . . I see that one can count on nothing in this world, and that only illusion brings happiness. I shall be only too pleased to retreat again into those charming dreams—to persuade myself that you were attached to me for my own sake and not for the help my money gives. Would that I could forget your unjust accusations, and sign myself Your affectionate Friend."[17]

Beckford's isolation was increased by his sense of Fate, which was in part derived from his Oriental reading, homosexual character, un-Englishness and membership of a family which was "ill-starred, persecuted and accursed".[18]

In his autobiographical story *L'Esplendente*, the hero would have liked to be an artist. Beckford was unfortunate in being born into the wrong class, in an age when a gentleman was expected to be a supercilious dilettante in literature and the arts, when he could patronise a Wordsworth, a Coleridge or a Turner, but not be one of them. Even the artists themselves, to whom he was so liberal, criticised him as not being in essence a gentleman[19]—for being too enthusiastic, for not being *borné*, for being in earnest about the wrong things? The prizes which attracted his class did not appeal to him; he cared nothing for political power, administration and extrovert activities. As he noted whilst reading Gibbon, "To use the language of Gibbon— 'Would you have me renounce the temptations of pleasure for the graver follies of fame and dominion?' "[20] There was a perpetual conflict in him between artistic dalliance and duty.

The usual accusation against Beckford is that he had no 'character'—in the English meaning, of which today's example is the business executive—the man who knows his mind and sticks to it, guided by hard-and-fast principles, self-assertive and positive in his dealings with the outside world. Compared to this, Beckford's character may seem pitiful; it was that of an artist or poet; he had what Praz calls 'a feminine mind'.

CHARACTER AND TASTES

There was a proliferation of these 'feminine' characters during the Romantic epoch; a description of one fits all. Benjamin Constant's analysis of his own character in the first chapter of *Adolphe*, and of its effect on his social circle, might have been written by Beckford about himself. This is particularly so when Constant describes his feeling of constraint with others, his boredom, his Romantic concern with death, and above all his destructive and malicious conversation, which turned everybody against him: "A vague uneasiness concerning my character therefore grew in my immediate social circle...; they said I was immoral and untrustworthy", writes Constant.

But despite his artistic temperament, Beckford exerted some self-discipline, as we can see from his early rising, fixed routine and river-bathing in November. And he was persistent. The most hated man in England,[21] he remained at Fonthill. Above all, he was steadfast in the creation and living out of his dream. In the course of its fulfilment, he became one of the great patrons of artists and craftsmen in England and France—silversmiths, sculptors, furniture-makers and designers of stained glass.

We already knew that he gave commissions to the two Cozens, Turner, West, Loutherbourg, 'Warwick' Smith, Vernet and Hubert Robert. But the full scope of his patronage and appreciation of artists, some of whom were still young when he was an octogenarian, only becomes apparent from the examination of the Inventory of his pictures and drawings, made at his death. This and his sale catalogues mention, for example, an album of a hundred sketches by Bonington; views in Tahiti by John Webber, topographical draughtsman to Captain Cook (sale of February 1802); a bound volume of twenty-six drawings of Eastern scenery by Prout, Copley Fielding, Boys, Daniell and others; and works by the neglected Wilson[22], Palmer, Girtin, Ibbetson (sale of February 1802), Etty, Landseer, Stothard,

Roberts, Clennell, Patrick Nasmyth and others. He was enthusiastic about the illuminated books of the despised Blake[23], and was one of the very few who attended Blake's exhibition in 1809.[24]

We can imagine the impression that Beckford, when an enthusiastic and cultured young man, made on old Vernet, who beheld the favourite pupil of his old friend and master Alexander Cozens. When Vernet wrote to Beckford about the commissions he had received from him, he said "I would prefer to work for you than for any other person, because if I am fortunate enough to produce something good, you will perceive it. I only wish I could express the impression that you have made on me."[25] That Beckford understood painting is shown by his remark on Turner's later and more advanced pictures, which he was too old to appreciate; Beckford exclaimed "one must be *born again* to understand his pictures!"[26]

Beckford's comment on the state of Taste and patronage in England in 1834 is relevant now: "Except among a few gentlemen, there is no sound taste for the arts in England. Collections are made from ostentation by people of wealth, who do not know a good from a bad picture. The Government is not sensible, in the true point of view, of the value of art to the nation. A minister picks a committee of taste out of the House of Commons, as he would a committee for any other purpose, and his committee does nothing but blunder. There must be a feeling for art—mere admiration won't do; people admire and affect to be struck with works of art, because others affect the same thing . . . The beauty of art must be inwardly felt; the mind in it must be read, interpreted. Picture shows will not do that. There is Raffaelle: 'he is at the head of painting', everybody says; his pictures it is safe to admire and applaud! Ask why Raffaelle is the prince of painters—they cannot tell you! Now an Italian amateur of the lowest order will explain that and more. A just taste for art is a cultivated taste;

CHARACTER AND TASTES

there is no royal road to it, as too many think there is."[27]

These remarks were made in connection with the threatened dispersal of the finest collection of old-master drawings which has ever been assembled, that of the painter Lawrence, rich in Raphael, Michael Angelo, Titian, Leonardo and Rembrandt, etc. They had cost Lawrence over £60,000, but out of patriotism he offered them in his Will for £18,000 in turn to the King, the British Museum, Lord Dudley and Peel. They all refused. A public subscription, headed by the Royal Academy, petered out. Eastlake vainly tried to persuade the Government to buy them for the National Gallery; the Chancellor of the Exchequer, a Radical and sport-addicted peer, replied that 'if he had his way, he would sell the National Gallery and have nothing of the kind'. Eastlake showed them to one or two Cabinet Ministers and Prince Talleyrand, who exclaimed loudly in their hearing 'If you don't buy them, you are barbarians'. Beckford would have bought them, had he available cash, to "keep them in the country", he said, " . . . they will else be dispersed. I assure you there is nothing like them here, or anywhere else, to be obtained for the money. It is shameful the country does not buy them." In the end, the dealer Woodburn purchased them for £15,000 and dispersed them at enormous profit!

Was Beckford really a man of taste? The satirical and overbearing voice of Hazlitt still echoes down the corridors of Time in vehement denial. "He [Beckford] seems not to be susceptible of the poetry of painting, or else to set his face against it. It is obviously a first principle with him to exclude whatever has feeling or imagination; to polish the surface and suppress the soul of art; to proscribe . . . everything approaching to grace or beauty or grandeur . . . and to reduce all nature and art, as far as possible, to the texture and level of a china dish—smooth, glittering, cold and unfeeling! . . . Is it that his mind is 'a volcano burnt out', and that he likes his senses to repose and be gratified with Persian carpets and enamelled pictures? Or are there not traces of the same infirmity of feeling even in the high-souled Vathek . . .? Alas! Who would have thought that the Caliph Vathek would have dwindled down into an Emperor of China and King of Japan? But so it is."

Let us admit that there was an infirmity of soul and feeling in Beckford, reflected in this way. Nevertheless, the sublime, poetic and romantic in painting did appeal to him. He was the owner of several pictures, now in the National Gallery, which have these very qualities. He loved the sublimities of *chiaroscuro*, with its mystery and drama, as evinced by Rembrandt and his followers (he had at least three Rembrandts, two of which are now in important German museums[28]). Nor could the patron of Cozens (father and son) have been anything but romantic and poetic.

Hazlitt's two venomous articles have been so damaging to Beckford, that the one written whilst he was still owner of Fonthill must be examined more closely. In his list of the pictures in Christie's auction catalogue, Hazlitt confined himself to the occasional items in the first two days[29] (which were almost entirely devoted to china, agate cups and similar objects). But to be fair, he should have examined the Seventh Day, devoted entirely to pictures, including two important Bellini and seven others now in the National Gallery;[30] Rembrandt's *Rabbi*, now in the National Gallery at Berlin; and two Bellini now in New York.[31] Hazlitt, was there really "not one great work by one great name" when you visited Fonthill, full of spleen?

Hazlitt goes on to select four *objects d'art* which he dismisses as 'fooling', but deliberately ignores many treasures too numerous even to list here. They include the Rubens Vase;[32] an exquisite Renaissance vase attributed to Cellini and rich in gold, diamonds and enamel;[33] two silver-gilt Columbine cups from Nuremberg;[34] the late twelfth-century Limoges enamelled reliquary, given to the Metropolitan Museum of New

CHARACTER AND TASTES

York by Pierpont Morgan; and Le Brun's pair of Buhl armoires from the Royal Palace of the Louvre, now back there.[35] It is curious that several other equally distinguished pieces of Beckford's French furniture were not in Christie's catalogue,[36] although they were sold to Farquhar; this may be because, as with Primitives, Beckford's taste was far ahead of his time and such pieces had not yet regained their former popularity. But Hazlitt, like the Roman Procurator, cared for none of these things. "Who cares", he asks arrogantly, "anything about such frippery, time out of mind the stale ornaments of a pawnbroker's shop?"

Like every connoisseur, Beckford made mistakes common to his period—enthusiasm for Martin,[37] qualified admiration for some of West's work,[38] and the purchase of too many minor Flemish and Dutch works of the sixteenth and seventeenth century. His possession of so many of the latter (rightly objected to by Hazlitt) is not easy to understand. For even as a boy he had mocked the finicky realism of the Dutchman Dou, and in 1802 wrote to West: "You know I am no friend to the hard, high finicking Dutch or Flemish style—I must have subject as well as execution, and when the last is not super-excellent neither Gerard Dow, Mieris or Karel du Jardin incline me to break the 10th Commandment".[39] This was his settled judgement to which he rallied periodically, when not overcome by acquisitiveness or the collector's desire to boast the possession of what others coveted. So, he fell for the universally-admired Dou *Poulterer's Shop*, but later was anxious to sell it as "the first Flemish painting in the world according to the gospel of sots, fools and false connoisseurs".[40]

In his best moments he was not swayed by prices and general opinion. This can be seen from his attitude to the Altieri Claudes. He coolly noted "the British rage for this kind of art" and was ready to take full advantage of "their incredible and inexplicable reputation". So he sold them without a pang for record prices. He was enthusiastic about Bellini when nearly everyone despised him as a Primitive. So he wanted 800 guineas for his *Doge Loredan*, which Eastlake and the Trustees of the National Gallery thought an unwarranted price "for so small a picture and a portrait".[41] They only offered 500 guineas. Beckford, now in his last illness, got them up to 600 guineas (having probably only paid half that for it in 1814); but even so, on his deathbed he tried vainly to cancel the sale, as being an unworthy price. Such incidents show that he was a man of discernment and independent judgement.

Beckford's poetic, literary and sentimental mind worked by association, which therefore influenced his taste in pictures. For example, he displayed J. R. Cozens' water-colours, first sketched on their Italian tour together, because "they recalled the most agreeable days of his life", and "he delighted in drawings that reminded him of 'the lively scenes he had visited in his youth, when all was fresh to him and he believed himself an inspired child of Nature' ".[42] His love of the young male form sometimes influenced his choice; were his collection re-assembled, we might be surprised to find how often this motif occurred.[43] For example, when he visited the Empress Josephine's gallery at Malmaison, he longed to buy "a Leonardo da Vinci for the grace and sweetness of its boys; oh, what melting eyes the *putti* have, ah, oh!"[44] The young Cope, later famous for his frescoes in the Houses of Parliament, sold him *The Firstborn*; this picture may have chimed in with Beckford's melancholy recollections of Lady Margaret and his wistful longing for a son.[45]

A theme which always moved him was the Prodigal Son: in his conscience, he was his own father's Prodigal. One of the pictures-of-the-year at the Academy Exhibition of 1838 was Etty's *The Prodigal, in the depth of his misery*, saying "I will arise and go to my Father". Not surprisingly, Beckford bought it and "so highly valued it, it is said, [that] he tied it up as an heirloom".[46]

CHARACTER AND TASTES

He patronised West partly because he had influence with George III and might therefore aid Beckford's social rehabilitation.[47] When judging Beckford's taste, these undercurrents must be remembered.

In reading, he preferred gloomy and severe imagery to beauty for its own sake, and so liked Young and Foscolo's *I Sepolcri*. The only contemporary English poet for whom he really cared was Byron. Like other English Romantics, his favourite poets were Shakespeare, Dante and Milton; in the last two, and in the Spaniard Quevedo, he was specially interested by their differing conceptions of Hell and Satan.[48]

No wonder that Quevedo interested Beckford! In his *Visions* he gives an exact picture of Beckford and his tortured mind: "there was a fellow sitting in a chair, all alone; never a Devil near him . . . or anything else, that I could perceive, to torment him; and yet crying and roaring out the most hideously of anything I had yet heard in Hell; tearing his flesh and beating his body like a Bedlam; and his heart, all the while, bleeding at his eyes. Good Lord, thought I, what ails this wretch, to yell out thus when nobody hurts him! So I went up to him. 'Friend', said I, 'what's the meaning of all this fury and transport, for, so far as I can see, there's nothing to trouble you?' 'No, no', says he with a horrid outcry . . . 'you do not see my tormentors, but the all-searching Eye of the Almighty sees my pains as well as my transgressions, and with a severe and implacable Justice has condemned me to suffer punishments answerable to my crimes . . . My executioners are in my Soul, and all the plagues of Hell in my Conscience: . . . the remembrance of the good I should have done and omitted, and of the ill I should not have done and did; the remembrance of the wholesome counsels I have rejected, and of the ill example I have given. And for the aggravation of my misery, where my memory leaves afflicting me, my understanding begins: shewing me the glories and beatitudes I have lost, which others enjoy, who have gained Heaven with less anxiety and pain than I have endured to compass my damnation. Now I am perpetually meditating on the comforts, beauties, felicities and raptures of Paradise, only to inflame and exasperate my despair in Hell; begging in vain for one moment's interval of ease, without obtaining any, for my will is also as inexorable as either my memory or my understanding . . . And if I chance at any time to have the least remission or respite, the worm of my conscience gnaws my soul' . . . At that word, turning towards me with a hellish yell, 'Mortal', says he, 'learn, and be assured from me that all those that either bury or misemploy their talents, carry a Hell within themselves and are damned even above the ground'."

Beckford's parody of religious terms in his letters and conversation (particularly of phrases from the Mass for the Dead) does not indicate a cynical or scoffing spirit, but means that he was steeped in the Bible and the Mass, and that he was for ever brooding upon the problems of life and death which they present so vividly, majestically and inescapably; it shows, in fact, a naturally religious turn of mind. Roman Catholicism has always recognised that men who are involved in Black Magic, as young Beckford may have been, are likely converts; for, like Gilles de Rais who fascinated him, they are at heart religious—even if the potential love of God is manifested in hatred, even if their faith seems to be puerile and superstitious, like Louis the Eleventh's. Orthodoxy fears indifference, not misdirected feelings.

Vathek was not, of course, written with any religious or moralising intention. But there is no need to accuse the ageing Beckford of hypocrisy when in 1815 and 1838 he drafted Prefaces for fresh editions of the book which definitely point the moral of his tale and its attendant Episodes. Referring to the literary licence of the period (1838) as typefied by Horace Walpole, *Don Juan*, Victor Hugo, George Sand and Edgar Quinet, he thinks that the moral of *his* tales is sufficiently clear to produce

CHARACTER AND TASTES

salutary reflections in his readers, if they will peruse them "*en se pénétrant d'une vérité que la religion même nous démontre, et se disant au fond de sa conscience [que] ceux qui à l'instar du Caliphe Vathek et de ses malheureux compagnons se livrent aux passions criminelles et aux actions atrôces termineront leur carriere par une retribution terrible mais juste dans le sejour de l'eternelle vengeance*".[49] In the 1815 draft the net is thrown even wider, covering those who "*à l'aurore de leur bel age se livrent comme Vathek a l'empire des sens*". Beckford had in mind "the atrocious" de Sade and Casanova and his own early leanings. But this phrase also seems to reveal an innate puritanism which was at tragic variance with his once free-ranging mind.

What Beckford could not bear was the scientific, utilitarian, liberal, scoffing spirit which began by undermining religion and then proceeded, as he perceived, to demolish monarchy and many of the other bases of society. Better ignorance and superstition, he thought, than the levelling process of progress which was to produce a landscape "where all is the same colour, a monotonous plain where one sees neither hills nor mountains! . . . Once you concede that all priests are charlatans and all monarchs tyrants, you can prove, in a mathematical way, what you like; but if you dispute the first step in the argument, you find a labyrinth of the most fatal errors. Oh how right Rome was, and he, infamous vermin, stinking heretic, how wrong!"[50] Beckford is referring to the Introduction to the *History of Charles the Fifth* by William Robertson. As a Presbyterian minister, "an atheist at bottom", Robertson was basically unsympathetic to mediaeval Christianity. Beckford wrote this in 1819, nearly ten years before Catholic Emancipation, when England was still starkly Protestant!

He thought that religion should be given outward form in a historic and majestic institution like the Roman Catholic Church, nurtured upon "supernatural faith and supernatural terror". Then, and only then, was it able to act as a steadying influence, a regulator, in the established order, which otherwise would disintegrate. Beckford jotted down a note to this effect when reading *An Itinerary of Provence and the Rhone* by young John Hughes, father to the author of *Tom Brown's Schooldays*. The passage by Hughes which Beckford castigated is typical of the modern outlook. Hughes was being shown the sights of Tarascon by a shoemaker's son, a civil and intelligent lad, who took the tourists to the Cathedral crypt to see the marble statue of St. Martha, which, "by the light of a single wax candle, had a striking effect". But the statue was chiefly admired for its supposed miraculous powers.

"*Elle devenait invisible pendant la Révolution*", whispered the boy in the crypt.

"*Oui, elle était cachée, voilà ce que tu veux dire, mon petit*", interjected the scandalised Hughes.

"*Eh! non, pardon Messieurs, elle se cacha; mais il y a trois ans qu'elle se montre encore*", replied the boy.

"I trust", comments Hughes, "that this monstrous fiction did not originate in the Ursuline convent which he mentioned; and that the fifty-two good ladies employ their time in more charitable and useful functions than in filling the heads of poor children with stories so hurtful to the real interests of religion. However credulous our young guide was, he was not mercenary, being with difficulty persuaded to accept a franc or two for what he styled the pleasure of having conducted us."[51]

Beckford pounced on this passage, and scribbled in the back of the book as follows: "Favourable mention of a young intelligent guide . . . very credulous but not mercenary—perhaps had he been less credulous he would have been more mercenary. The Ursuline nuns . . . had impressed upon his ingenuous mind a strong belief in miracles, for which the good ladies are set down by Mr. Hughes as acting in a manner very hurtful to the real interests of Religion. It is no easy matter to determine what are the real interests of Religion; but the chief defence of a thousand useful and comfortable establishments plainly arises from what it is fashionable to call supernatural faith and supernatural terror. The desire of chiming in with prevalent opinions and of passing for persons of mind gets the better of . . . many a . . . traveller. Hence, careless of the future and [in order] to acquire a little present applause, they assist . . . in throwing about squibs and crackers which will one day or another set fire to our good old dry institutions and reduce colleges, parsonages and cathedrals to ashes. When they burn and the atmosphere becomes heated, not a mansion, a slated villa or a straw thatch cottage will escape. It is provoking indeed to witness how both priests and sectaries, humanity-mongers and Bible-vendors are at work to produce a general conflagration!"

Beckford's religious attitude was connected with the cult of individualism and chiaroscuro, which he shares with other early Romantics. He apprehended the pitiless pressure of universalism in the coming industrial and socialist society, and in its necessary precursor, conventional and *petit-bourgeois* Victorianism. "We must not oppose received opinion. We must believe all, if we would ourselves be unmarked and not misrepresented . . . People live by each other's example. A universalism rules. Soon no single voice will be listened to, there will be no solitary advocates of new truths in anything. What the many do or dream will be the law. All important truths have been the result of solitary efforts. None have been discovered by masses of people; it is fair to suppose they never will."[52]

Beckford thought that the Iron Man, the Great Organiser of Systems, had already appeared with Pitt and Napoleon: "Both Pitt and Buonaparte were systems, creatures of wheel within wheel . . . set a-going by some invisible agency. Neither of them shared in common with the rest of mankind those feelings which belong to flesh and blood . . . Insensible as brass and iron to tears or remonstrances, on they drove till . . .

sentiments more allied to Nature and humanity arose when the spell was broken; and Europe awoke to another state of things, wondering she had ever submitted to such mechanical enslavement."[53] Beckford was right in suggesting that a whole generation, himself included, had lain under the symbolic spell of Napoleon, the Man of Destiny, the new Satan who rode forth over the face of the Earth, levelling all things in destruction and organisation, like *Death on the Pale Horse* in the Book of Revelation and in West's picture.[54]

So much for Beckford's views. As for his appearance, he was good-looking, with unusual charm; his eyes were expressive and intelligent, and his figure small, slender and well-shaped. As a young man his whole expression was mischievous, but after his first Portuguese trip, when he was in his thirties and beginning to despair of social restoration, melancholy settled upon his features, as upon one who had lost some great opportunity in life. He was attractive to women of all ages. When he was nearly thirty-two "the ladies were very lavish in his praise . . . They all agreed that the woman who could inspire him with love, must be the envy of her sex; while each, perhaps, fancied herself the only one who stood a chance for such a distinction. One lady in particular . . . laid her snares with so little caution and address, that Mr. B—, who was a wary bird, easily escaped being entangled; and he proved to her by his very particular attention and cold civilities that marriage was not [so] attractive a lure as the young lady expected."[55]

Those who came under Beckford's spell were struck by his conversation which, like his character, was uneven and full of surprises. It was in turn humorous, sarcastic and bitter, abounding in sublime and ludicrous images, and strewn with coarse epithets, puns and new combinations of language—something quite original, in fact, and characterised above all by a vivid imagination and a well-stored, literary mind. But like his spirits and

CHARACTER AND TASTES

restless energy, his conversation was often burdensome; his daughter Susan could not stand "hours of Alcobaça on end".[56] And there was a hint of something unpleasant, particularly when he was angry or excited, when his voice became high-pitched and rose to a scream with exclamations like "Gracious Goodness, no" etc.; his lip curled in a sarcastic sneer, his mouth contracted. Even in tranquillity he had a strange expression, "indicating something extraordinary in the man".

This ill-mannered irritability peeps forth in a typical Beckfordian visit to a gallery: "His eagle glance caught at once what was best worth looking at, and a few minutes sufficed to run over even a large assemblage of paintings. When, as sometimes occurred, there was nothing to interest him, he was much out of humour and was certain to run out of the place in a passion. Once, at the rooms of the Society of British Artists, he trotted round the first, stopping occasionally and grunting out an exclamation of contempt, and when he had finished, observed 'Nothing worth a rush here, let's try another'. The same thing took place with regard to the second room; and on entering the third, he ran into the middle, cast a rapid glance around, and then absolutely bawled out, 'Good Heavens! this is the most cursèd of them all! The face of badness can no further go, let's be off'; and he ran hurriedly downstairs to his carriage."[57] Beckford knew very well that everybody was listening and that his reputation for good taste would sway their opinion of the pictures!

The impression which he created in later life is conveyed by Meister, who visited him at Fonthill in the autumn of 1792. Meister perceived that he was not a happy man and that his verve and spirits could not hide a settled melancholy and regret. Spoiled too early by Fortune, he had become *blasé* and discontented, and therefore tried to find satisfaction in the whimsical and strange. The gap between his endowments and his achievements was puzzling: he had, apparently, been able "to advance only halfway towards his goal in fulfilment of his destiny", Meister concluded.[58]

To Meister, an outsider, there still seemed hope for a man of thirty-two. But the answer was already known within; hence the melancholy and regret. And what was his destiny? Perhaps the author of *Vathek* had already perceived it when writing that autobiographical novel at the age of twenty-one.

APPENDIX:

BECKFORD'S CURIOUS LETTER

The caution necessary in assessing Beckford's homosexual guilt from his Papers is nicely illustrated by what at first sight appears to be the most damning and explicit piece of evidence against him. I refer to his unpublished contemporary copy of an unfinished draft in French to an unnamed correspondent—his Venetian confidante, the English-born Countess Rosenberg. The first page is dated Saturday 8th December 1781, and gives a general account of London society, in a rather literary style, ending up about the *theâtre* (i.e. opera). The second page appears to carry straight on, without a break in the sense of time; the draft breaks off unfinished at the end of the third page. The fourth page is dated 24th December 1782 and describes to her one of his striking dreams.

If Beckford thought that this was a damning document, he would not have copied it out a little later in a bold hand and kept it all his life (he did destroy some of his papers). Also, it is written, in fact or fancy, to an Englishwoman, who was "the repository of his most intimate sentiments, as conveyed in his letters"—with which she as good as proposed to blackmail him to the tune of £1,500.[1] Such a composition could therefore have been sent to her.

But it cannot be a copy of a real letter. For its third page refers in the present tense to "the heat of the Dog-star" (i.e. the heat of July or August), and makes it clear that he is at Fonthill then (which could only have been the summer of *1781*, since he was abroad the two following summers). But its first page, which is an integral part of the draft and is dated 8th December 1781, refers (together with page 2) in the present tense to Beckford's activities with Courtenay in London during the 'season', when the opera was on. Fact and fancy are inextricably mixed and cannot be separated (as so often with Beckford); it is really a literary composition, full of self-dramatisation and self-pity. We cannot therefore use it as firm evidence against him in adducing his *conduct*. It is similar to his letters in *Life at Fonthill* about the tight-rope walker Saunders, where he indulges tremendous flights of fancy, involving Death and Judgement. But after one of these flights he explicitly recognises that they are sheer fantasy, and abruptly changes his tone: "I descend and touch ground, and here I am at the door of the china shop. Twenty-four plates at twenty-one a piece is some price . . ." (p. 45). It is, however, of the greatest value in revealing his state of mind. It shews that he has already become a Vathek—the damned Sultan, unable to find the satisfaction for which he risks so much.

Although its start about Courtenay on page 2 seems so dreadful, the imagery with which it continues is harmless and rather childish, and occurs frequently in his writing about the boy. He invites the older woman (who might equally well have been Louisa) to prepare a deadly drink for all three of them so that they can awake in another world and live an insipid, Rousseauesque existence, frolicing about like primaeval children. Sex does not colour this vision at all. Beckford feels that in some respects his affection is harmless and yet doomed to frustration and misunderstanding. This is his fate.

If examined closely, this letter seems to be full of exaggeration. For example, Beckford (who is writing of the summer of 1781) says that he is *accusé de la perte d'un être que j'adore*. If such an accusation had really been made against him, he would not have been allowed to

APPENDIX: BECKFORD'S CURIOUS LETTER

stay at Powderham or Courtenay at Fonthill, nor would they have been permitted to meet in London. In this passage Beckford therefore seems to be suffering from persecution-mania. In fact, as late as the autumn of 1782 Lord Archibald Hamilton (later ninth Duke) was delighted at the 'benefitt' his two boys were reaping during their Fonthill stays.[2]

The reference to Argus in the same part of the letter reminds one of a curious passage quoted by Prof. Chapman (his p. 116), which is Beckford's own extract of a note of his, dated 6th February 1782 but unaddressed and with no indication as to where it was written. The scenery in that note is reminiscent of Fonthill House, where in "The Grand [public] apartment" there was a frieze of Argus lulled asleep by Hermes' pipe.[3] I do not think that it is fair to draw startling (even though tentative) conclusions about Beckford going to bed with Courtenay from an extract so difficult to make sense of. Prof. Chapman connects this extract with an equally curious one from Louisa's letter dated "Saturday" [2nd February 1782]. It is indecipherable at key points: is Louisa speaking of herself or Beckford? If it is he who has had "the complete enjoyment" of Courtenay, would she (in love with Beckford) have been so delighted? As a passionate woman surely she would have drawn the line there! Beckford's Papers are as baffling as his character.

Returning to his letter to Countess Rosenberg, the full text (with grammatical mistakes and lack of accents, but repunctuated where necessary) of the pages which I have discussed (pages 2 and 3) runs as follows:

"Du theatre je le porte dans mon lit. La Nature, la Vertu, la Gloire tout disparoisse—tout s'egare, se confond, s'aneanti. O Ciel, que me puis-je mourrir dans ses embrassements et plonger mon ame avec le sien dans le bonheur ou les peines qui ne doivent jamais finir. Faut-il vivre dans la crainte d'un moment qui doit nous separer encore. Ne soyez pas dont surprise si je desire la mort avec avidité. Accourez, composez quelque doux breuvage qui nous assoupira tout trois, qui fermerà nos yeuxs sans angoisse, qui derobera nos ames et les livreront imperceptiblement aux champs fleuries de quelque autre existance.

"Pale et delicat, les yeuxs languissant,—[i.e. Courtenay] deviendrà le plus gentil des ombres. Courrones des fleurs de Narcisse vous me venez a cotè de lui. Nous habiteront les mêmes bois, le même gazon nous servirà de lit, on nous trouverà etendû sur les bords de la même fontaine. Le murmure des fleuves eternels calmera s'il est possible les elans de nos ame. Nous seront si penetrè des fautes que l'amour nous a fait commettre, si langoureux et si blême qu'on n'aura pas le courage de nous faire des reproches.

"J'etouffe. La chaleur est dans mon ame. Ce n'est pas a notre climat qu'il faut se prendre. Un soleil gazeè, un ciel rient [i.e. *riant*] moins qu'etincellant, preservent une temperature rafraichisante dans les ardeurs de la canicule; mais la Nature me prive de ses bienfaits, elle ne veut pas que je jouis des dons qu'elle a repandû sur l'Angleterre. Je cherche inutilement l'ombre epais des bois qui nous environne. Le gazon seche sur mes pieds, j'etend mes bras, et il n'y a plus de verdure. Mes entrailles sont consumeè et je brule d'un soif mortel que—[Courtenay] seule pourrà eteindre.

"Assurement il n'y a point d'enfer pour moi dans l'autre monde puisqu'on me damne sur la terre. Connoisez-vous un etat plus affreux que celui que j'eprouve—epiè par mille Argus sans coeurs et sans oreilles, contraint d'abbandoner l'unique esperence qui me conciliez a la vie, menacez a chaque instant, accusez de la perte d'un etre que j'adore avec toutes les affection humaines concentrè dans un point. Tel est ma situation actuelle, tels sont les Daemons que le Destin a lachè a mes trousses.

"Que ne puis-je me refugier dans vos bras, ma tendre amie. Il n'y a que vous sur ce planette qui pourrà me consoler. Suis-je coupable—non—La simpatie" [draft breaks off].

SHORT LIST OF ABBREVIATED TITLES IN NOTES

Athenaeum	Review of Redding's *Memoirs* (see below) in *Athenaeum*, 11th December 1858.
Chapman	Guy Chapman *Beckford*, new ed., 1952.
D.N.B.	*Dictionary of National Biography.*
English Journal	B's unpublished English Journal, 1779.
Farington	*The Farington Diary*, abridged by James Greig, 8 vols., 1923-8.
Farington's *Manuscript*	Full MS text of the above, at Windsor Castle.
H.P.S.	Catalogues of Hamilton Palace Sales of B's Library (Sotheby) and pictures and antiques (Christie), 1882.
Inventory	Inventory of B's Collections in Bath, 1844 (in his Papers).
Journal	*Journal of W.B. in Portugal and Spain, 1787-88*, ed. B. Alexander, 1954.
Life at Fonthill	*Life at Fonthill, 1807-22*, trans. and ed. B. Alexander, 1957.
Melville	Lewis Melville *Life and Letters of W.B.*, 1910.
Morrison	*Collection of Autograph Letters . . . formed by Alfred Morrison* (Second Series), privately printed, Vol. I, 1893.
Morrison-Hamilton	Ditto: *Hamilton & Nelson Papers*, 2 vols., 1893-4.
Oliver	J. W. Oliver *Life of W.B.*, 1932.
Phillips	Catalogue of Contents of Fonthill (then owned by Farquhar), auctioned by Phillips, 1823.
P.R.O.	Public Record Office: MSS there quoted (usually followed by ref. number).
Redding *Memoirs*	Anon. *Memoirs of W.B.*, 2 vols., 1859.
Redding's *Manuscript*	MS ditto (different from the above), 2 vols. folio, 1846 (see my Preface).
Yale	Catalogue of Exhibition to mark Bicentenary of B's birth, Yale Library, 1960.
Zinan	B's unpublished Arabian Tale *Histoire de Zinan*, 1815.

NOTES

INTRODUCTION

[1] Wake's answer to B's Bill of Complaint in P.R.O. (C.12/1321/18).
[2] *English Journal*, 25th August 1779.
[3] Redding *Memoirs* i.146; not in *English Journal*, which, however, only covers two days in Plymouth.
[4] *English Journal*, 24th August 1779.
[5] *Journal*, pp. 302, 309.
[6] Letter to Lady Hamilton, 2nd April 1781 (Melville, p. 105).
[7] B. made list of his purchases, with prices.
[8] Letter to Louisa B., Paris, 19th January 1784 (Chapman, p. 172), in which he describes an MS he purchased; this is not the same as another MS he purchased there, which is now called the Rosenwald Hours, after its recent owner, Lessing Rosenwald of Jenkintown, near Philadelphia, who has donated it to Library of Congress. It has belonged to some of the most distinguished book-collectors in the world. It was amongst the 91 Hamilton-Beckford MSS returned by the Prussian Government when their Parliament refused to vote enough purchase-money, and resold at Sotheby's on 23rd May 1889 (see sale catalogue, and de Ricci *English Collectors of Books*, p. 86).
[9] Letter to Lady Hamilton, already quoted.
[10] Mrs. B. to Sir W. Hamilton, 26th December 1780 (Morrison-Hamilton i.65-6).
[11] Letter in French to Countess Rosenberg, 7th October 1781.
[12] B's jotting on letter from Mrs. (later Countess) Harcourt, 4th September 1781.
[13] Title of operetta, location of its performance, and help towards identification of the boy-players are given in *Reading Mercury*, 22nd April 1782. B's bogus letter to Louisa, dated April 5th, 1782 (Oliver, pp. 109-115), pretends that it was held in Queensberry House by permission of "Old Q." (4th Duke). But the newspaper makes it clear that it was in his predecessor's house (later called Uxbridge House) in Burlington Gardens, which may by then have been sold to Lord Paget (later 1st Earl of Uxbridge), whose eleven-year old son Arthur Paget (later the diplomatist) was one of the players. The other boys were John Spencer (born 1767), son of Lord Charles Spencer (brother of 4th Duke of Marlborough), and Henry Fitzroy (1765-94), son of 1st Lord Southampton. The Miss Fawkener who sang as Belinda may possibly be the younger daughter of Sir Everard Fawkener (see *D.N.B.*). Since B. lies about Queensberry House, it is possible that many of those his same 'letter' alleges to have been present at dress-rehearsal were not; the newspaper does not mention them, and Horace Walpole's letter to William Mason (14th April) only names Lord Thurlow and Lady Harcourt.
[14] B's letter to his bookseller G. Clarke (Junior), quoted in Melville, p. 327; and *Life at Fonthill*, pp. 339-40.

NOTES

[15] B. to Thomas Wildman, 9th March 1787; in this letter is his earliest suggestion that he might stop in Madeira instead of going on to Jamaica.
[16] Further details about Franchi are in *Life at Fonthill*, pp. 28-30.
[17] B's draft to Lady Craven, Basle, 11th October 1789.
[18] Verdeil to B, 5th July 1791.
[19] Journal for Thursday 5th June 1794 (*Yale*, p. 96); this extract differs slightly from B's own printed *Excursion*.
[20] *Life at Fonthill*, p. 83.
[21] B. to Franchi in Italian, 27th October 1824.
[22] B's "Ex[tract] to Lord Paget, Rome, June 29, 1782". The ninth Lord Paget was then a man of thirty-eight, whereas it sounds as if B. was writing to a younger contemporary. B. knew Paget's sons well; I suggest this was written to Hon. Henry W. Paget (b. 1768), the great soldier better known as 1st Marquess of Anglesey; he was styled Lord Paget when his father was created Earl of Uxbridge in April 1784. When B. was making this *early* extract from his draft after that, he would have thought of him as Lord Paget.
[23] B. to Franchi in Italian, 20th October 1821.
[24] Farington's *Manuscript*, 2nd August 1799.
[25] Letter to B. from Edward Bearcroft, K.C., M.P. Morrison-Hamilton i. 227 mentions B's letter from Lisbon on 10th June 1796, which shews that his letter from London on pp. 218-19 has been wrongly dated in transcription (The Morrison Catalogues do sometimes have mistakes).
[26] B's authorship is given in *Literary Gazette*, 1826, p. 710. Jerdan was Gazette's editor and knew the late Abbé Macquin, from whom he may have got this information. For B's authorship on general grounds, see my note in *Yale*, p. 48.
[27] Violet Stockley *German Literature as known in England, 1750-1830*, (1929), p. 247.
[28] *European Magazine*, Vol. 19 (1791), pp. 350-2. This review does not mention B's name.
[29] See note 14 above.
[30] Lettice's letter to B., 10th November 1798.
[31] *Journal*, p. 19 n. 2 gives the reference.
[32] During this long French stay, B. came back to England at least once (July 1802). Oliver, p. 259, states that B. again visited Paris in 1806 and 1808; this is based on Melville, pp. 268-9, who prints 2 letters from Pedley to B. "at Paris"; the last phrase is in each case Melville's incorrect addition (the second letter is addressed to B. at Fonthill, and last para. of first letter makes it clear that B. is also there).
[33] B's draft from Paris to Benjamin West, beginning of 1802.
[34] *Literary Correspondence of John Pinkerton*, 1830, ii. 217.
[35] B's draft to Wyatt "from Lausanne, [ ] Sept. 1801". One must also infer from his letter to Sir W. Hamilton from Fonthill, 4th July 1802 (Oliver, p. 244), that he had recently returned from Switzerland.
[36] B. to Franchi in Italian, 27th October 1824. I assume that the castle is Leuk.
[37] Rembrandt's *Christ at the Column*, sold for 58 gns; now in Hessiches Museum, Darmstadt.
[38] Title-page of Catalogue of September 1807 Sale (of Materials). August sale of pictures etc. is reported, with prices, in *Gentleman's Magazine* (1807), Part II, p. 880.
[39] Signed Agreement with Edward Foxhall, upholsterer, dated 31st July 1807. For Foxhall, see *Life at Fonthill*, p. 47n.
[40] *Life at Fonthill*, p. 196, and Christie's catalogue.
[41] B's undated draft to Lady Anne Hamilton, about 26th July 1804; she was Douglas' sister and engineered the match.

ENGLAND'S WEALTHIEST SON

[42] R. S. White to B., 8th August 1809. B's in Italian to Franchi, "Friday" [11th August 1809] states that the Duke of Hamilton's financial demands were delaying the marriage.
[43] Undated press cutting (c.1823) on B. at Bath; now at Brodick Castle, Isle of Arran.
[44] *Life at Fonthill*, p. 267.
[45] End of B's story *Zinan* in French. For its date see *Life at Fonthill*, p. 182.
[46] *Life at Fonthill*, p. 341, where the Latin tag has been misprinted and should read *Fortis super enatat Undis*.
[47] Ditto, p. 193.
[48] Vevey Testimonial (see Chapter IX).
[49] Dated 29th March 1844 (Oliver, p. 325); I have paraphrased as well as quoting.
[50] Duchess of Hamilton labelled the lock "*Precious* hair cut off on the fatal 2nd of May at Bath, 1844".
[51] F. Beckett to William Smith, 2nd May 1844 (partly quoted in *Yale*, p. 70).

NOTES

CHAPTER I

[1] It is sometimes stated that the obscure father was the first Peter Beckford to emigrate. This is incorrect, and is due to the natural desire of the Beckford family to add a generation to their history and lineage. A Peter Beckford of Field Lane, Holborn Bridge, issued between 1648 and 1672, an undated Token, which does not indicate his trade (see *Boyne Trade Tokens,* revised by G. C. Williamson, 1889, i. 598).

[2] In the Jamaican Public Record Office in Spanish Town (*Patent Liber* 3, folio 69). This is the earliest authenticated mention I know of Peter actually in Jamaica. We cannot infer from this patent how long he had already been out there. He is described as having "transported himself together with his servants"; but since a planter was granted so many acres for each servant and member of his family, once he was out there it was customary to get together by devious means as many 'servants' as possible, in order to get the maximum grant of land; therefore this patent does not tell us anything either about Peter's status when he first immigrated.

[3] Jamaican Public Record Office, *Patent Liber* 7, folio 108, and 8, folio 118. If he was the Richard Beckford, late of London, who died in Jamaica on 27th October 1683, he cannot be Sir Thomas' brother, Alderman Richard, a master-Clothworker, who died in 1679. The existence of two contemporary Richard Beckfords of London shows how confusing the early Beckfords are.

[4] The branch headed by Alderman Sir Thomas Beckford of Maidenhead, which later settled at Ashtead, was granted arms in 1685. Governor Peter and his descendants illegally used them; so in August 1791 William Beckford, wanting to regularise matters, asked for this grant to be confirmed in his own line; but, giving a specious reason, he added a 'distinction or augmentation' to their arms (College of Arms, *Grants* XVII. 414). This seems to indicate that he could not bear the same arms as the other branch because he could not prove kinship or descent. Also, a pedigree book in the College of Arms (*Norfolk* I. 104-105), written at the end of the eighteenth century, gives both families but shows no connection between them. The two contemporary genealogical trees in the Beckford Papers only start with Peter of Clerkenwell, and do not mention the other branch.

The claim that Governor Peter was a nephew of Sir Thomas Beckford probably originates in Burke's *Landed Gentry* (1833), from information supplied by Beckford (Melville, p. 279). The only authentic evidence I have found of a connection between Governor Peter and these other Beckfords is in the Deeds of November 1675 and October 1676 (see note 3). When elected Lord Mayor in 1762 Alderman B. referred obliquely to the other branch in his speech, boasting that his "family were citizens, and some of them had borne the highest offices in the City for a century past" (*Public Advertiser,* 30th September 1762); but his reasons for making this claim, true or false, are obvious. The Christian names of the other

ENGLAND'S WEALTHIEST SON

line crop up occasionally in our Beckfords, but it is not safe to deduce anything from this in face of the evidence at the Royal College of Arms.
[5] Cundall *Governors of Jamaica in the Seventeenth Century*, 1936, p. 131.
[6] Redding *Memoirs*, ii. 101.
[7] G. W. Bridges *Annals of Jamaica*, 2nd ed. (1828), i. 339.
[8] The full account is in manuscript in our P.R.O. (*Colonial Office* 137/4, p. 320).
[9] Charles Leslie *New History of Jamaica*, 1740, p. 267.
[10] *Diaries of Mrs. Lybbe Powys*, 1899, p. 166.
[11] The two medals of 1770 are described in *British Numismatic Journal*, xxii. (1934-7), p. 274. The Guildhall speech was also commemorated in a Staffordshire statuette by Ralph Wood (specimen in Brighton Museum); the figure is simply called *Beckford*, showing how well-known he was.
[12] Redding's *Manuscript*, i. 32.
[13] Alderman B's speech in the Commons, quoted in *Essays presented to Sir Lewis Namier*, ed. by Pares and A. J. P. Taylor, 1956, p. 66 (Miss Sutherland's essay).
[14] *Letters of Mrs. Elizabeth Montagu*, 1809, iv. 80.
[15] Cumberland's *Memoirs*, 1806, p. 145. For Dodington, see *D.N.B.*
[16] Richard Beckford (*c.* 1743-1796), M.P. for Bridport, 1780-4; Arundel, 1784-90; and Leominster, 1790-6. Partner successively in the West India merchant houses of Collett & Evans, Beckford & James, and Beckford & Keighley.
[17] Rev. Dr. Charles Wake (*c.* 1722-1796), D.C.L., a doctor's son who graduated from Oriel; B.C.L. from All Souls'; Rector of St. Margaret's, Westminster; Prebendary of Westminster; married Barbara Beckford, 1755.
[18] She is mentioned as the mother of Rose and Thomas Beckford in the Chancery suit *Thomas Beckford v. Pittmann*, 1808 (C.13/488 in P.R.O.).
[19] Alderman Beckford's Will, made in June 1765 and proved in July 1770, lists all his children and gives most of these details.
[20] *Diaries of Mrs. Lybbe Powys*, p. 166.
[21] Undated second letter (after October 1768) from Beckford's tutor Drysdale to Robert Nairne; printed in *Wiltshire Gazette*, January and February 1924.
[22] Richard Warner *Excursions from Bath*, 1801, p. 119.
[23] Redding's *Manuscript*, ii. 109. The "barbarous roll of the eye" occurs frequently in Beckford's first book, *Biographical Memoirs*, written at the age of sixteen.
[24] *Biographical Memoirs*, pp. 114-115.
[25] *Azemia*, ii. 103-104.
[26] R. Gore-Brown *Chancellor Thurlow*, 1953, pp. 41-2.
[27] Lettice to Beckford, 10th March 1800.
[28] Redding's *Manuscript*, ii. 18.
[29] Letter of 7th July 1786; for her earlier letter about Lady Margaret Beckford's death, see Chapter IX.
[30] From Falmouth, 3rd March 1787.
[31] Draft to James Wildman about his son (Beckford's godson), 17th April 1796.

CHAPTER II

[1] B's extract from his letter to Pacchierotti of 16th January 1781 (made on the back of his draft to Lady Hamilton, 29th December 1780).
[2] Jotting on his copy of his letter to Thomas Wildman, Falmouth, 4th March 1787. He labels it as coming from Bailly's *Lettres sur l'Atlantide*, p. 155, but I cannot find it there.

NOTES

[3] Redding's *Manuscript*, ii. 68.
[4] From draft of B's undated letter to Mrs. Hervey. It corresponds to the end of the letter of 3rd October 1777, quoted in Melville, p. 34.
[5] Fully quoted in *Life at Fonthill*, pp. 38-39.
[6] Redding's *Manuscript*, i. 52.
[7] *Biographical Memoirs*, p. 53.
[8] *L'Esplendente*, p. 29. A note at the end of the manuscript shows that B. wrote it before March 1780. On its p. 75 he refers to "the lives of the Christian Saints and the Fathers of the Desert", i.e. *The Lives of the Fathers of the Deserts* which he describes reading "again and again" in letter of 5th June 1778 to Mrs. Hervey (Melville, p. 51). This, and handwriting of B's MS, suggest that *L'Esplendente* could have been written about then. The book was J. F. Bourgoing de Villefore *Les Vies des SS. Peres des Deserts, d'Occident*, Paris, 5 vols. from 1708; ii. 260-272 has St. Bruno's life.
[9] Redding's *Manuscript*, i. 56.
[10] *L'Esplendente*, p. 31.
[11] *Chatham Correspondence*, 1838-40, iv. 313 (letter dated 11th December 1773).
[12] Extract from same letter.
[13] Fragment on a sheet which includes a draft to A. Cozens (dated 23rd December 1779).
[14] *Athenaeum*.
[15] George, 16th Earl of Morton. John Penn, playwright (see *D.N.B.*). B's five drafts to Morton are undated, but the first one can be dated by its reference to the opera *Artaxerxes*, which, according to Genest's *Annals of the English Stage*, was only performed once at Covent Garden whilst these particular boys overlapped at Eton (1775-76), on 25th April 1775 (a Tuesday; Beckford saw it on a Friday). Puppet shows were only just being fashionably revived in England, so this is an early reference.
[16] Ben Jacoup appears in *L'Esplendente* from p. 34.
[17] Redding's *Manuscript*, ii. 3-4. For the sinister side of Cozens, see Chapter VII on B's portrait of him in the third *Episode of Vathek*.
[18] B. indicated this by writing Cozens' initials *A.C.* at the end of some of his compositions, e.g. *Fonthill Foreshadowed, Dome of the Setting Sun* and *English Journal*.
[19] Printed, with many mistakes, in Morrison, i. 198. I have quoted from the original manuscript, now owned by Mr. Babb of Yale, the handwriting of which enables me to date it.
[20] Beckford's tutor Lettice showed the manuscript of *Biographical Memoirs of Extraordinary Painters* in the Senior Common Room of Sidney Sussex College in December 1779. His letter of 12th December (Melville, p. 68), mentioning this, says of the stories "they please me *better than ever*", which shews that he had seen them in draft at an earlier date. In the preface, written by Lettice, great play is made with the youthful precociousness of the author, which suggests that Beckford was younger than nineteen. The article on Beckford, compiled by Lettice, in the *European Magazine* for September 1797 states that it was "written at 16 years of age". The book was partly inspired by J. B. Descamps' *Vie des Peintres Flamands*, even echoing some of its phrases and details; it is significant that each of the four volumes of B's own copy of Descamps has his signature with the date 1777 (*Yale*, Item 187). Finally, in her copy of *Biographical Memoirs* B's half-sister Mrs. Hervey, writing in 1798, notes that he wrote it "in his 18th year" (*Yale*, Item 11), i.e. between 29th September 1777 (his seventeenth birthday) and 29th September 1778; this still makes 1777 possible as the year of composition! So it seems reasonable to accept Redding's statement in his *Manuscript* (i. 65) that Beckford was sixteen when he wrote it, "before his departure for Geneva", which occurred about June 1777.

ENGLAND'S WEALTHIEST SON

CHAPTER III

[1] Thomas Brudenell-Bruce (1729-1814), Lord Bruce of Tottenham (Wilts), cr. Earl of Ailesbury, 1776.
[2] Sir John Gibbons (c. 1717-July 1776), M.P., 2nd Bart. of Stanwell Place, Middlesex. His heir (3rd Bart.) was connected by marriage with the Bullers of Morval; possibly through this link Beckford became involved in struggle for Parliamentary borough of Saltash (see Chapter XVI).
[3] William Matthew Burt, M.P., fourth generation of planters in Nevis; married a Jamaican. Appointed Gov. of Leeward Islands, Oct. 1776; died in office in Antigua, Jan. 1781.
[4] Information about the lawsuits is based on: (i) B's Bill of Complaint against his father's Executors, October 1770. (MS in P.R.O.=C.12/1325/21); (ii) some of the 'answers' are in C.12/1321/8 and C./12/1321/18; (iii) *B. v. Collett* (C.12/1321/8). This represents earlier evidence and accounts, which B. used in his Chancery proceedings of 1781-82 in connection with his coming-of-age. In B's *Journal* we find old Capt. Thomas Collett, formerly of King St., Covent Garden, still in B's service and devoted to him. (iv) Richard B's Appeal in House of Lords, 14 February 1783; (v) John B's ditto, May 1774; these two printed appeals are in House of Lords Library and State-Paper Room of B.M.; (vi) Reports of Master in Chancery (C.38/699), dated 27th June and 4th July 1782, on claims of John and Richard B. arising from B's above Bill of Complaint.
[5] Mrs. B. is probably referring to this in her letter to Sir W. Hamilton of 26th December 1780 (Morrison-Hamilton i. 65-6). She mentions "the many, many thousands" B. might lose if steps weren't taken in time before his majority.
[6] Brigadier-Gen. Richard Smith (d. 1803), M.P., gambler and prominent Foxite; of obscure origin, retired from India 1769. For activities in Hindon 1774 election, was fined £666 in the King's Bench, with six months' imprisonment, June 1776. See Holzman *Nabobs in England*, N.Y., 1926.
[7] *Report from Select Committee appointed to try . . . petition of James Calthorpe and Richard Beckford complaining of an undue election . . . for Hindon, 1775*, on which I have based my account of 1774 election.
[8] For the three Hindon elections and Parliamentary proceedings, see *Journals of House of Commons* under 'Hindon', and constitutional histories quoted in next note. The 1776 election is mentioned in *Westminster Magazine*, (1776), iv. 287; but I was unable to consult it since the B.M. series was blitzed and that at Bodleian is incomplete.
[9] T. H. B. Oldfield *History of Boroughs* (1792), iii. 140; and his *Representative History of Great Britain*, 1816, vol. v; R. H. Peckwell *Controverted Elections* (1804-05), i. 376n.
[10] These voting figures show that the pamphlet refers to 1776 election, since they do not correspond to the figures of all the other Hindon elections given in Henry Stooks Smith *Parliaments of England*, iii. 93-95.
[11] Richard Beckford to W.B., 5th December 1791.
[12] Ditto, 12th A[ugust] 1791.
[13] Richard B. to Sir W. Hamilton, 2nd December 1791; and W.B. to Hamilton, Paris, 15th December 1791 (both in Morrison-Hamilton i. 156-57).

CHAPTER IV

[1] Redding's *Manuscript*, i. 79.
[2] Edward Hamilton is described in Geneva Archives as *"major au ervice d'Angleterre aux Indes Orientales"*. Born in Geneva, 1734. His mother

NOTES

Marguerite Vasserot of Amsterdam was probably sister-in-law of Jacob Huber, father of Jean Huber (1721-86) who painted Voltaire and married cousin of Mme. Necker.

[3] Redding's *Manuscript*, i. 92.
[4] Described in B's letter to Lady Effingham, 22nd August 1777.
[5] Edward Bright, the miller of Malden, died of over-corpulency in 1750, aged 30 and weighing 44 stone.
[6] B's *Excursion to the Grande Chartreuse*, written at the time and published in *Dreams and Waking Thoughts* (1783). For the book on St. Bruno, see Chapter II, n. 8.
[7] Redding's *Manuscript*, i. 84.
[8] Ditto, p. 85.
[9] *Grande Chartreuse*.
[10] Redding's *Manuscript*, i. 87.
[11] Ditto, echoing *Grande Chartreuse*.
[12] Earliest draft fragment of *The Vision* is on back of draft to Mrs. Hervey, to be dated 3rd October 1777 (see Chapter II n. 4).
[13] Similar to phrase in B's reverie at Fonthill, 4th December 1778 (Melville, p. 62); Nouronihar's experience is like B's own dream described there (Melville, pp. 64-5), in which he tries to reach his father.
[14] Dated Cologny, Sept. 1778 ("Feb. 1781" added on folder later, when B. was in Paris after leaving Venice). This is B's earliest account of a personal 'homosexual' affair.
[15] *English Journal*, 24th August 1779.
[16] B's fair copy, dated 22nd May 1778. As late as 1834 he intended to publish it in *Alcobaça and Batalha*, which shows how important it still was to him.
[17] William Courtenay (1768-1835), 3rd Viscount Courtenay and 9th Earl of Devon. Fled to France to escape arrest as homosexual, 1811. Died unmarried in Paris in obscurity. Instrument of B's ruin, 1784.

CHAPTER V

[1] B's original letter, dated 16th April, 1780.
[2] Redding's *Memoirs*, i. 149.
[3] Redding's *Manuscript*, i. 100. This shows that about 1844 Redding saw a Diary by B. now lost.
[4] These and subsequent undated quotations come from *English Journal*.
[5] Jotting dated 23rd December 1779. Next day he incorporated it in letter to Cozens (printed in Melville, p. 77). *Frengui* is B's spelling of one of the variants of Feringhee, which is an Oriental adaptation of Frank (i.e. the white barbarian invaders); this was once the ordinary Indian term for a European, but came to be used contemptuously, especially with reference to their being Christians.
[6] Redding's *Manuscript*, ii. 109.
[7] Redding's *Manuscript*, i. 100 (wording slightly different from *Memoirs*, ii. 221).
[8] Letter in French to Count Benincasa in Venice, 21st October 1780.
[9] Redding's *Manuscript*, i. 117 (my italics). Redding states that this melancholy was caused by "some affair of the heart, some longing after ... the society of the Cornaro Palace". (p. 113).
[10] From letter to Louisa Beckford, 25th February 1782. Aria was *Pur nel sonno almen talora*, from Gluck's *Orfeo*.
[11] Letter in French to Countess Wynne d'Orsini-Rosenberg, 12th March 1781 (B's extract on paper watermarked 1821).

ENGLAND'S WEALTHIEST SON

[12] B's extract from letter in French to 'Duchesse de S.C.', Venice 6th January 1781 (on reverse of draft to Lady Hamilton, 29th December 1780). Gasparo Pacchierotti (1740-1821) was the singer, in opera *Quinto Fabio* by F. G. Bertoni (1725-1813). According to Heriot *Castrati in Opera* (1956), p. 171, Pacchierotti was probably the finest of all the *castrati* singers.
[13] Undated jotting in French on same page as a phrase which appears again in a letter to Lady Hamilton from Paris, 2nd April 1781.
[14] Jotting on same sheet as above.

CHAPTER VI

[1] B. to Lady Hamilton, 14th October 1781 (Melville, p. 122). The celebrations are described there and in Redding's *Memoirs*, i. 202-5.
[2] Note of 9th December 1838 (Oliver, pp. 89-91, but my repunctuation).
[3] This and the next quotation are used in his argument by Chapman, p. 101.
[4] *English Journal*, 27th September 1779.
[5] Dates in H. A. Dobson *At Prior Park*, 1912, pp. 279-80.
[6] W. H. Pyne *Wine and Walnuts*, 2nd ed., 1824, i. 302-3. This description of Satan's Palace of Pandemonium in Hell is similar to B's description of Palace of the Central Fire, ruled over by Moisasour, Prince of Hell (*Vision*, pp. 58-9).
[7] *Dreams*, Letter XXII, October 30th. References to Ki come from de Maillac's book (see next note).
[8] B's unpublished *Chinese Reading Notes*, p. 37, paraphrasing de Moyria de Maillac *Histoire générale de la Chine, ou annales de cet empire* (Paris, 1777-83), i. 236.
[9] *Chinese Reading Notes*, pp. 20-21, commenting on J. F. Bernard *Recueil de Voiages au Nord* (Amsterdam, 1715-27), viii, 142-3.
[10] Ysbrants Ides *Three Years' Travels from Moscow* (London, 1706), p. 75 (not noted by B.).
[11] *Chinese Reading Notes*, pp. 11-12, based on *Recueil* (as above), viii, 425-6, translating J. B. Muller's *Moeurs des Ostiackes*. The unpublished postscript of Lettice's letter of 23rd March 1780 to B. probably refers to this reading: " . . . Poor Kutuchta! Poor Delai Lama!" H.P.S., Fourth Portion, Lot 1071 shows that B. autographed Kircheri's *La Chine* in 1778. In *Fonthill Foreshadowed* (1777), p. 24, B. already complained that "in my early years" he had read too much about China and Japan!
[12] These extracts come from B's Reading Notes on Windus *Journey to Mequinez*, 1725. Mulai Ismail was ancestor of the present King of Morocco, and consolidated the present Dynasty.
[13] Text of B's note (closely following Lobineau, i. 614-16) was twice copied in Redding's *Manuscript*, i. 123 and ii. 60.
[14] Robert Hume to B., Fonthill, 11th October 1823, and London, 20th November.
[15] Praz *Romantic Agony*, 1951, p. 310. Other literary sources for *Vathek* are given in Marcel May *La Jeunesse de William Beckford et la Genèse de son Vathek* (Paris, 1928), and in the *Notes* at the end of *Vathek*.

CHAPTER VII

[1] Redding *Manuscript*, ii. 110.
[2] *Life at Fonthill*, pp. 178, 182.
[3] Redding *Manuscript*, i. 122. This also appears in some of B's letters.

NOTES

[4] Ditto, ii. 34.
[5] Ditto, i. 121.
[6] At least one of *Episodes of Vathek* was being composed in 1783; a second was well under way by May 1784 and was perhaps finished in March 1785, when a third was started; all three were 'nearly finished' by February 1786. Unfortunately, Beckford did not refer to them by name during their composition, so they cannot be more definitely dated. For these dates, see *Bibliography of W.B.* by Guy Chapman and John Hodgkin (1930), p. 70. Written in French, they were not translated and published until 1912 (Stephen Swift & Co.; trans. Sir F. T. Marzials).
[7] B. to Sir George Yonge, 5th February 1784.
[8] *Life at Fonthill*, p. 134.
[9] B's original French is stronger: *C'était toujours un corps mort que j'embrassais* . . . (p. 80 in French section of 1912 ed.).
[10] Preface to Lausanne edition of *Vathek*, reprinted in Melville, p. 141.
[11] Redding's *Manuscript*, i. 124, and Preface to *Al Raoui*. My reasons for assigning it to B. are in *Yale*, pp. 83-5.
[12] Feidah was a singing-girl and the blind man her accompanist. They feature as Al Raoui's companions at the beginning of B's story, before the homosexual young man is introduced to tell his own tale, which is then 'inserted' into the main tale, in Oriental fashion.

CHAPTER VIII

[1] Redding's *Manuscript*, i. 141.
[2] Unpublished Journal of Baron Louis de Prangins for 18th October 1782. B. was returning from Italy through Switzerland en route to Paris.
[3] Draft to Louisa (Chapman, p. 165) on back of letter to B. at Geneva, dated 2nd September 1783, from George Tierney, the statesman; B's wife pined because of her miscarriage. Her mother's sisters married distinguished men—1st Marquess of Stafford, 9th Duke of Hamilton and 4th Earl of Dunmore.
[4] *Green Notebook*, 11th July 1783. The four next quotations are also taken from it, under July. This Notebook is described in *Journal*, p. 23.
[5] Ditto, 12th July. M. T. Bourrit wrote several celebrated Romantic books on the Alps; he followed Rousseau in emphasising their sublimity.
[6] To Lady Gower (later Lady Stafford), Geneva, 20th October 1783 (in Granville Papers, P.R.O.).
[7] *Green Notebook*, 10th August 1783.
[8] Farington, i. 52.
[9] Gore-Brown *Chancellor Thurlow*, 1953, p. 224. Fawkenor may be a mis-spelling for Fawkener (see Introduction, n. 13).
[10] *Morning Herald*, 27th November 1784 (Chapman, p. 185). The suggestion of a frame-up of B. by Loughborough often recurs, and sometimes quite naturally and incidentally in correspondence. For example, in his unpublished letter to Wildman from Falmouth, 5th March 1787, when suggesting that he might go on from Jamaica to the United States, B. says: "If the Americans understood Lord L[oughborough] to be my calumniator and that I was the victim of his machinations . . ."
[11] Farington's *Manuscript*, 8th December 1798; Farington, i. 188 (22nd January 1797).
[12] Dated Fonthill, 22nd November 1784 (Granville Papers, P.R.O.).
[13] Jotting at Dover, 29th October 1784.
[14] W. Beldam to Lord Hardwicke, 24th November 1784 (Hardwicke Papers, B.M. Add. MSS 35, 623). Courtenay was at Westminster School.

ENGLAND'S WEALTHIEST SON

[15] *Letters from Mrs. Carter to Mrs. Montagu . . . upon Literary and Moral Subjects* (1817), iii. 233-4. Published by a clergyman in B's lifetime, raking up a scandal over thirty years old.
[16] Morrison-Hamilton, i. 95.
[17] Undated jotting, referring to Rev. W. Tooke *Russia* (1780), iii. 125-6 (quoted in my text).
[18] Robert Potter *Tragedies of Aeschylus translated* (1779), ii. 11-12 (First Chorus in *Agamemnon*). The 'merciless Powers' are the Fates and Furies, sent by Jupiter to avenge an impious deed. B. comments on this verse in a jotting which can be dated March 1785.
[19] Jean Huber to Mlle. Necker (later. Mme. de Stael), October 1785 (*Revue de Paris*, 1936, vol. 43, p. 819).
[20] Thomas Wildman's letter of 14th April 1789, with B's interpolation (Chapman, p. 229).
[21] *Journal*, pp. 87, 133.
[22] Farington, iv. 243.
[23] Morrison-Hamilton, ii. 193 (letter to Marquis of Douglas, later B's son-in-law, 2nd July 1802).
[24] Listed in Inventory. *Rex v. Passingham*, 20th February 1805, is summarised in *Annual Register*, 1805, pp. 365-6 (B.M. copy of the trial was blitzed). B's French draft to Macquin, 25th November 1806, mentions it being copied out for him.
[25] This takes into account the three most damning pieces of evidence (unpublished and in French) against B. in his Papers, viz. two short jottings in Madrid on 27th and 31st May 1788, and the literary composition about Courtenay, dated 8th December 1781 (printed in my Appendix).
[26] *Journal*, p. 309. Sometimes the boys were the seducers! (e.g. *Journal*, p. 86).
[27] Copy of French draft to Rosenberg, 24th December 1782. B. conceals the child's sex (he would not be referring to her niece Augusta Wynne, who married next year).
[28] Undated letter in Italian, 11th August 1809. For character and talk of Lafões, see *Journal*, p. 172. "Words, words, words" was favourite remark of Abbé Xavier (the Abbade of the *Journal*).
[29] B. to Abbé Macquin, 23rd July 1812. For Saunders, see *Life at Fonthill*.
[30] B. in Italian to Franchi abroad, 27th October 1824. *Patapouf* is English slang for a catamite.

CHAPTER IX

[1] Jotting dated Chambesis (=Chambesy), 29th July 1786.
[2] Draft to Thomas Wildman, 18th January 1786 (also quoted in next paragraph).
[3] Lettice to Miss N-, from B's chateau, 24th May 1786 (given in Redding's *Manuscript*, i. 145, which quotes six of Lettice's letters written in May and June; these were incorporated by Lettice in his private Journal, which Redding used).
[4] Jotting of March 1787. B. refers to Shakespeare's *Richard III*.
[5] Letter to Lady Gower, 29th (should be 27th) May 1786 (Granville Papers, P.R.O.).
[6] Redding's *Manuscript*, i. 146, quoting Lettice's letters.
[7] Letter of 7th July 1786. Margaret, later Mrs. Orde, was B's eldest daughter.
[8] Partly quoted in Oliver, p. 198, and dated 24th July 1786. Signatories included Gibbon's doctor, Scholl (who attended Lady Margaret),

NOTES

a French major-general and other officers, de Blonay, a High Court barrister, Justices and Calvinist ministers.

[9] *Memoirs of 'Buck' Whaley* (1906), p. 298.

[10] Draft to Lady Craven (Oliver, pp. 257-8); undated but must be after building of Barrier wall, which B. ordered just before sailing to Portugal in November 1793 (from which he returned in June 1796).

[11] Jotting on sheet dated 29th July 1786. B. refers to two *colourless* passages in de Lussan's book (1755 ed., vi. 399 and 404) and fuses them in his imagination and bitterness into something quite different.

[12] Presscutting (about October 1822) inherited from B. by his daughter the Duchess of Hamilton, and now (by descent) at Brodick Castle, Arran. This is one of the four accusations against B. "of being steeped in all kinds of Catholic monstrosities" listed in Redding's *Manuscript* ii. 30. Two of them we now know to be true (praying to and swearing by St. Anthony); so this newspaper statement may be correct.

CHAPTER X

[1] B's draft to Thomas Wildman, 11th March 1787 (printed by B., with alterations, as Letter V in *Portugal*), begins: "T'was you, Sir, who . . . would not let me rest until I had consented to this blessed Jamaican expedition."

[2] B. first plaintively and playfully suggests wintering in Portugal in unpublished letter to Wildman, 5th March; but in most of these letters he suggests Madeira.

[3] Undated draft from Lisbon to Mrs. Hervey, April or May 1787.

[4] Unpublished portion of the letter to unnamed correspondent, 8th March, which appears in *Portugal* as Letter III.

[5] Jotting of 13th March. Biographical notes on most persons in this chapter are in *Journal*.

[6] Undated draft to Wildman.

[7] Printed from P.R.O. in Parreaux *Portugal dans l'oeuvre de W.B.* (Paris, 1935), pp. 185-8. B's draft to Wildman from Lisbon, 22nd August 1795, refers to his recent presentation.

[8] Letter in Portuguese, 1st January 1788. Marialva wanted B. to relinquish gaiety of Madrid for wilds of Salvaterra, where Portuguese Royal Family were hunting boar! (Marialva's letter in Portugese, 10th February 1788).

[9] It has been suggested that Beckford began his Journal soon after arriving in Lisbon on March 24th. But we know that he did not begin it until 25th May for four reasons (additional to the general ones given in my text): (1) No other entry has a similar full heading, viz. "Lisbon. May 25, 1787", even when written on scraps of paper (like this opening page). (2) The first *complete* page of the Journal is numbered with the figure '1', after which the numbering of the pages is maintained for a long time. The reason why Beckford did not number his opening page is that it was the last page of a four-leaf sheet, the rest of which was already filled by an older French draft letter (see photo in *Journal*, facing p. 36). He snatched it up as the first available piece of paper on which he could begin his Journal, when the urge seized him after his visit to the Marialva Palace. (3) At a later date he had the Journal copied out by an amanuensis (through a mistake this copy was not made available to me when I edited the Journal, nor was I told of its existence). By this time, the opening page was detached from the rest and mislaid, so that the copyist had to start at Beckford's first *numbered* page, and follow his numbering. If there had been an earlier section of the Journal, Beckford would have had it

T   279

copied then. (4) He preserved many scattered journal jottings (even pencil notes) going back to 1778 and made in several countries; there is no trace of *anything* for the first part of his stay in Portugal before May 25th.

[10] Undated draft to Mrs. Hervey, April or May 1787 (partly reproduced in *Portugal*, Letter VIII).

[11] B. to Sir W. Hamilton, 2nd February 1797 (Morrison-Hamilton, i. 227).

[12] B's French draft to Marialva of 15th July 1796, and M's reply in Portuguese, 15th August.

[13] Marialva's in Portuguese, 18th October 1799.

[14] Ditto, 8th December 1796.

[15] Luis Pinto de Sousa Coutinho to Marialva in Portuguese, London 15th December 1787.

[16] B's draft to Wildman from Paris, July or August 1789.

[17] B. in French to Dr. Schöll, 5th February 1790; also proposed in above letter (n.16).

[18] Horne to Wildman, Lisbon, 6th November 1790.

[19] *Life at Fonthill*, p. 125.

[20] Redding's *Manuscript*, ii. 5. For B. on Marlborough, see *Life at Fonthill*, p. 311.

[21] We can reasonably assume that B's new house in Lisbon was on site of the one he occupied in 1787. For *Journal* shows that latter was in the neighbourhood, near house in which Horne lived. Horne arranged everything for B. in 1787 and is therefore likely to have leased him one of his properties when it was difficult for a traveller at short notice to get accommodation in coveted area near Royal Palace. *Journal* mentions that B's house "is composed of planks, and came ready made from America soon after the earthquake" (p. 122). So it was easy for B. to demolish it, when he bought it in 1794, to make way for his own building. Information about latter comes from B's draft to Thomas Wildman of 22nd August 1795, and contemporary Portuguese documents quoted in article on Beckford in Vol. I of *Lisboa de Outrora* (edited by G. de Matos Sequeira and L. de Macedo, Lisbon, 1938).

[22] Information on Monserrate from well-informed article on it in *Enciclopedia Portuguesa*, which gives no sources but is partly based on article *Beckford e Monserrate* by Luiz de Castro in *Ilustração Portugueza*, Oct.-Nov. 1906. This latter article (not in B.M.) is discussed in Mrs. Inchbold *Lisbon and Cintra*, 1907, p. 157-8. An 1808 watercolour of Monserrate is reproduced in *Archivo Pittoresco* for 1864, Lisbon, p. 245. J. Wells published two Views of it by Noël in 1794 and 1795.

[23] *Works of Lord Byron: with his Journal and Correspondence*, ed. R. E. Prothero and pub. Murray, 1898-1904, ii. 47, quoting Byron's letter of 26th September 1811 to R. C. Dallas. Byron was asking whether he should alter (as offensive to B.) his stanzas on B. which I quote in my next para. and which come from *Childe Harold*, Canto I, stanzas 22-3.

[24] Printed as Appendix in *Yale*, with Introduction by me.

[25] Redding's *Manuscript*, ii. 8.

[26] Ditto, ii. 20, quoting Lettice's letter of 21st July 1799.

CHAPTER XI

[1] This story of Brunet's is supported by two pieces of evidence in B's Papers: (1) For remainder of his long life Chardin received annual pension of £100 from B., who did not give pensions lightly and in 1822 only four others (including to his grandchildren and Franchi: see Chapter XV, n.10). His solicitors would have stopped this one (as they curtailed

NOTES

Lettice's, despite long years of service and friendship) long before Chardin's death in 1826, had it not been given for a very special reason. (2) Letter in English to B. from his Parisian banker Perregaux, written about 16th May 1793, mentions large present of money he had made on B's behalf: "Your acknowledgement is not only magnificent, but never could be better placed, and was most gratefully received by ye person I presented it to in your name; he had not an idea of it". On folder in which he put this letter B. wrote "Merigot, 1793". Chardin is mentioned by name in another part of the letter, so the present was not for him. For Chardin, see *Life at Fonthill*.

² Alger *Englishmen in the Revolution*, 1889, p. 350, based on the Archives Nationales (A.F. ii. 288). Endorsement of his passport is quoted in Chapman, p. 244.

³ Draft to Wildman, 3rd May 1793 (Oliver, p. 216).

⁴ Alger *Napoleon's British Visitors and Captives*, 1904, p. 111.

⁵ Redding's *Manuscript*, ii. 1.

⁶ 1794 Journal: see *Yale*, p. 91, and p. 97.

⁷ *Life at Fonthill*, p. 309.

⁸ B's draft reply in French of 1st September 1789 on letter from de Marnoir, Paris, 29th August. Huitzilopochtli was Mexican God of War, who claimed human sacrifices. B. got his information from Cullen *History of Mexico*, 1787, vol. I, which he read on its publication (*Journal*, pp. 170-1). Church of St. Geneviève was demolished during Revolution.

⁹ Draft to Wildman, July or August 1789.

¹⁰ To Sir W. Hamilton, 15th December 1791 (Morrison-Hamilton, i. 157).

¹¹ All this is in Chardin's reply in the *Rapport par Junius Dupérou* presented to Section de Brutus, Paris, 20 November 1793 (pamphlet in Bibliothèque Nationale). The last sentence in this quotation backs up the phrase about endorsement of his passport, quoted above. For Chardin's re-arrest in connection with B's library, see Oliver, p. 215n. Louis-Grégoire Deschamps (1746-94), *dit* Destournelles, was at the time one of the six Ministers who formed the Government (Conseil exécutif provisoire), each acting in turn as its President, and was himself President in May 1793. He was Finance Minister from June 1793 until the Ministries were suppressed; when later arrested, poisoned himself.

¹² B. to Wildman, 29th November 1791 (Melville, p. 179, with mistakes).

¹³ *The British Critic*, periodical founded in 1793 by Nares and Beloe, both Tory clergymen. B's mock *Address* is reprinted (with slight alterations) in Redding *Memoirs* ii. 210-218, and the dream about Isle of Mum in ditto, pp. 189-190.

¹⁴ For a similar hit, see *Life at Fonthill*, p. 174 and note.

¹⁵ For B's views on prison reform, see his note on Penn's system in his copy of Clarkson's *William Penn* (commented on in my lecture on B., *Yale Gazette*, April 1961).

¹⁶ Redding's *Manuscript* ii. 108-9. These *Hours of the Master of Mary of Burgundy* are world-famous and most important, and were executed between 1477 and 1482, during the marriage of Mary (daughter of Charles the Bold) to Maximilian I of Austria. They were amongst Hamilton-Beckford MSS sold to Prussian Government in 1882, and are still in Berlin Print Room (MS. 78. B.12). See Pächt *The Master of Mary of Burgundy*, 1948, with several Plates of Beckford's MS (No. 15, *Death Triumphant*, is very Beckfordian). B. mentions them because he had probably only recently bought them from Sir John Tobin, who had acquired them at the Hanrott Sale (Dibdin *Literary Life*, 1836, ii. 975-6). They are listed in B's Inventory (MSS section), which I handed to Mr. Anthony Hobson to collate with *The Hamilton Palace Libraries: Hamilton*

ENGLAND'S WEALTHIEST SON

Collection of Manuscripts, Sotheby, 1882, one vol. (suppressed after private sale of MSS to Berlin).

[17] Article by J. C. Loudon, landscape gardener, in *Gardener's Magazine*, September 1835. One reason for local drunkenness, not mentioned by any of B's critics, was existence of rotten borough of Hindon, with its drink-money at elections (see Chapter III).

[18] *Athenaeum*.

[19] To Franchi, Bath, 13th September 1823. Charles Ferdinand Porden (1790-1863), nephew of the better-known William Porden; see Colvin *Dict. of Eng. Architects*.

[20] James Wadsworth (1768-1844) of Durham, Connecticut. Student of science and political economy; applied science to agriculture. Pioneer in public education schemes. Friend of J. J. Astor.

[21] I. Allen *History of Vermont*, 1798. B. made notes in his copy.

[22] B. to James Wadsworth, 7th September 1798 (Melville, pp. 252-5, from B's *Letter-Book*).

[23] Indenture made 20th April 1799, now with New York Historical Society. The land was in Twelve-Mile District on W. side of Genesee R. in Ontario County.

[24] This and following quote from Trumbull are in Prof. Sizer's ed. of *Autobiography of Col. John Trumbull* (Yale, 1953), p. 307.

[25] William Beckford (d. 1799), illegitimate son of Alderman Richard B., younger brother of the Lord Mayor. Inherited father's plantations, spent some years on them, and wrote *Descriptive Account of Jamaica*, etc. On returning, lived at Somerley Hall, Suffolk.

[26] B. to Wyatt, 10th April 1794 (Melville, p. 215, with mistakes). The Haiti slaves massacred the whites in 1793 and 1804.

[27] See my lecture on B., *Yale Gazette*, April 1961.

CHAPTER XII

[1] Redding's *Manuscript*, ii. 19.

[2] *Fonthill Foreshadowed*.

[3] Handwriting of B's draft and its opening enable it to be dated from Switzerland, 1777-8. Initials *A.C.* at end show it was written for Cozens. No title given, but for convenience I have called it *Fonthill Foreshadowed*. I have followed text of 32-page fair copy of 7,000 words, restoring the few deletions in it (which restorations correspond to B's draft).

[4] *Life at Fonthill*, p. 92 note 4, etc.

[5] This is probably Catherine Hall, or Draxhall near St. Ann's Bay. Both plantations, which had been occupied by B. as mortgagor claiming arrears, were adjudicated to him by Jamaica Chancery in 1784 (see Chapter XVI). But in mentioning enormous increase in income from this plantation, he may be overlooking fact that after 1784 his agents had developed it at cost of £11,000 'currency', which would now be increasing its productivity.

[6] Draft to Wyatt, Lisbon 10th April 1794. Printed by Melville, pp. 214-15, which omits most of important last paragraph, which ends " . . . if the West Indies are as well guarded [against slave rising] as the British Isles [against interior discontent and French invasion], we may still live to erect the buildings both grecian and gothic you designed for Fonthill."

[7] Redding's *Manuscript*, ii. 6.

[8] Farington's *Manuscript*, 20th July 1796; his sketch of Wyatt's plan is reproduced in Dale *James Wyatt* (1956 ed.), p. 146.

NOTES

[9] Brockman *Caliph of Fonthill* (1956), p. 96, prints the report from *Salisbury and Winchester Journal*, which is garbled version of what Wyatt told Farington on 20th July.

[10] Rutter *Delineations of Fonthill*, 1823, p. 109 mentions a plan in 1796 for a ruined Convent, i.e. a sham but habitable ruin, but admits that the idea was never executed. One would have supposed that he got this information, together with Wyatt's alleged design which he reproduces, from Beckford. But the fact remains that there is no reference to it in B's Papers or in Farington; Redding's *Manuscript* mentions it, but at this point he is following Rutter. We cannot therefore assume that this was the origin of the Abbey and that B. was merely one amongst the many who liked building sham ruins. From boyhood his dream was much grander than this.

[11] Letter of 2nd February 1797 in Morrison-Hamilton, i. 227.

[12] Farington's *Manuscript*, 6th August 1797. Until November 1798 Farington always vaguely calls it a 'Gothic building', as if it had not yet been given a proper name or purpose.

[13] Ditto, 6th November 1797.

[14] This and next quote are from ditto, 16th November 1798.

[15] Ditto, 22nd December 1798, which also tells us that West was to paint the pictures, for which he would get an allowance of £1,000 a year.

[16] Danby *Opening of the Sixth Seal* (1828) is now in National Gallery of Ireland, and was re-exhibited at R.A. in its *First Hundred Years of the R.A.*, 1951-2 (Item 409).

[17] Letter of 10th April 1794, discussed in note 6 above. B. marked folder in which he kept his Lisbon plan "Plan for Necessidades House. W[illiam] B[eckford]"—meaning drawn by himself (folder was inscribed with and contained other architectural items which were not his).

[18] Kenneth Clark *Gothic Revival*, 1950, p. 110.

CHAPTER XIII

[1] Redding's *Manuscript*, ii. 26. To give idea of effect B. intended, Redding goes on to quote from *Portugal*, Letter 34. J. C. Rossi (1762-1839) was sculptor to Prince-Regent and did monuments in St. Paul's (see *D.N.B.*).

[2] Ditto. ii. 32, quoting Lettice's letter of August 1802; also quotes Lettice's complaints of curtailment of his allowance and that his salary for education of B's daughters was in arrear (summer 1803).

[3] *Life at Fonthill*, p. 116.

[4] Ditto, p. 127. Lady Anne Hamilton (see *D.N.B.*) was sister of 13th Duke of Hamilton (B's son-in-law) and looked after B's daughters. Her diary for September 1803 is in B's Papers.

[5] *Gentleman's Magazine*, 1806, Part II, p. 1128; 1807, Part I, p. 326.

[6] Draft to Lady Craven, 22nd July 1809.

[7] *Life at Fonthill*, p. 81. One can date this 1807-8 building work from *Life at Fonthill*.

[8] Ditto, p. 78; my next quote comes from p. 80. See this also for Dixon and Hayter.

[9] *Gentleman's Magazine*, 1821, Part II, p. 495. Next sentence comes from Porden's letter to Franchi, 13th September 1823 (already quoted).

[10] *Athenaeum*. Building of Pandemonium is described in *Paradise Lost* i. 710-30, which might be a description of Fonthill being built, especially at night; it is no accident that B. mentions Pandemonium in his description of work on the Abbey by torchlight.

[11] Moore *Memoirs* (1853), iv. 235. Durazzo was of a Genoese family, two of whom at this period are in *Enciclopedia Italiana*.
[12] Farington's *Manuscript*, 8th November 1800. For William Hamilton (1751-1801), R.A., see *D.N.B.*
[13] See remarkable parallel to this in *Barkiarokh*, quoted on p. 96.
[14] Letter to his wife, 24th August 1823, in *Correspondence of John Constable*, iv. 215, compiled by R. B. Beckett (typescript in V. & A. Library).
[15] Signed 'A Visitor', in *Literary Gazette*, 1822, p. 603.
[16] Sir John Summerson *Architecture in Britain*, 1953, p. 284.
[17] This and next quote from Steegman *Rule of Taste*, 1936, pp. 85 and 83.
[18] Summerson, pp. 270-1.
[19] see *Life at Fonthill*. The Victoria & Albert has a sketch of a gateway at Fonthill by Benjamin Wyatt.
[20] The Victoria & Albert has a fine watercolour by Charles Wild, shewing the Abbey with its projected spire (therefore an early drawing). For Wild and others mentioned in this section, see *D.N.B.*, dictionaries of artists and architects, Summerson and Sir Kenneth Clark.
[21] Rutter, p. 14; he mentions Jeffrey Wyatt as studying there.
[22] According to article on Eginton in *D.N.B.*; but copy in B's Papers of his account for glass "now finished", which seems to include all his work, dated April 24th 1799 totals £954.
[23] Rutter, p. 12 lists drawings from mediaeval tombs. His mistakes are corrected in B's own MS list of "Portraits in the Windows of the Brown Parlour" (=Rutter's "Oak Parlour"), which shows that 2nd Earl of Oxford's tomb was at Earl's Colne Priory, Essex; the tomb in Malvern Priory is not named.
[24] *Mirror of Literature*, 23rd November 1822.
[25] Benjamin West, 5th January 1801 (Melville, p. 238).
[26] Constable to his wife, 29th August 1823, iv. 218-19 (see note 14).
[27] Waagen *Works of Art and Artists in England* (1838) iii. 129-30.
[28] Summerson, as above, p. 285.
[29] Lady Anne Hamilton's diary (see note 4).
[30] *Mirror of Literature*, 23rd November 1822.
[31] Redding's *Manuscript*, ii. 30.
[32] Ditto, ii. 33b.
[33] Ditto, p. 34. Hon. Charles Hamilton (1704-86), M.P., son of 6th Earl of Abercorn. One of greatest gardeners of century, laid out Pain's Hill, Surrey (still existing), c. 1735. For him and Lane, see Barbara Jones *Follies and Grottoes*, 1953; Tunnard *Gardens in Modern Landscape*, 1938, p. 25.
[34] Redding's *Manuscript*, ii. 33.
[35] The Quaker Rutter, local bookseller, would not himself have known a passage from an Elizabethan translation of Tasso, or have been able to put his finger on the right passage in Chaucer, *Comus* and Uvedale Price. Further, he uses on p. 84 same six lines from *Paradise Lost* which Beckford recited to the French-speaking traveller Meister (*Letters*, London 1799, p. 303 note).
[36] Quotations and information in next few pages taken, unless otherwise indicated, from J. C. Loudon's article in *Gardener's Magazine*, September 1835, pp. 441-9.
[37] The alpine aspect of Fonthill is conveyed in Turner's watercolours illustrated in E. G. Cundall *Fonthill Abbey, a descriptive account of five watercolour drawings*, Tarporley (privately printed), 1915.
[38] *Life at Fonthill*, pp. 97-8.
[39] MS bound with B's letter to Lord Thurlow dated 22nd May 1778 and *Hylas*; all three copied by amanuensis.
[40] Pope *Odyssey*, iv. 563.
[41] Hesiod *Works and Days*, verses 170-3.

NOTES

[42] To Dr. Mitford, 29th August 1808: see *Friendships of Mary R. Mitford*, 1882, i. 42.

CHAPTER XIV

[1] From Beaudesert, 12th August 1784.
[2] Mr. de Starck's letter to B., 19th February 1811.
[3] Dated only "21st August", beginning "Sir" and ending "Sir, your very obedient servant".
[4] All this was in 1810. The offending woman was Charlotte, wife of Henry Wellesley (later Lord Cowley), Wellington's brother. Uxbridge (Henry Paget) was later made Marquis of Anglesey, and Boringdon was created Earl of Morley.
[5] Cloncurry *Personal Recollections*, 1849, p. 11 (October 1792). The young bloods included the royal Duke of Sussex.
[6] Letter in French from Paris, 20th September 1789. For Verdeil, see *Journal*.
[7] For Franchi, see Introduction.
[8] Undated draft to unnamed correspondent on green notepaper B. used at Lausanne, September 1801 (for letter to Wyatt). In any case before death in April 1802 of 1st Lord Kenyon mentioned, then Lord Chief-Justice. For B's French-speaking dwarf, see *Life at Fonthill*.
[9] Farington's *Manuscript*, 13th April 1797. Richard Westall did several illustrations for *Vathek* about 1795, three of which are in Victoria & Albert Museum (Dyce Bequest); one of these is reproduced in A. C. Ward *Illustrated History of English Literature* (1955), iii. 32. Also did frontispiece for 1823 English ed. of *Vathek*. Hoppner painted B's portrait reproduced here. For J. F. Rigaud see *D.N.B.*
[10] Redding's *Manuscript* ii. 36, shewing how vividly he reports an incident in contemporary language. My account is from his *Memoirs* ii. 142-4, supplemented by details in his *Manuscript*.
[11] Farington iv. 33 (16th October 1806).
[12] *Life at Fonthill*, p. 306. The Whip was William Holmes (d. 1851).
[13] For B's refusal of the Regent, see *Morning Chronicle*, 20th September 1823, and undated contemporary press cutting at Brodick Castle, and Redding's *Manuscript*, ii. 34.
[14] W.B. of Somerley's letter of 20th December 1788. For emigrés and Humphrey see Farington's *Manuscript*, 25th February and 24th December 1797. Margravine of Anspach is better known as Lady Craven (see *D.N.B.* for her and the illegitimate W.B.). Ambrose Goddard was the County Member, 1772-1806.
[15] B's Italian letter to Franchi, 13th December 1807.
[16] Margaret B's letter to Orde, 22nd April 1811, in possession of her descendant, Lord Harrowby. For Orde see *Life at Fonthill*.
[17] *Life at Fonthill*, p. 89.
[18] Ditto, p. 270 (and see note on Egmont). Franchi calls him *miseravel hidalgo*.
[19] Susan's letter in French to Hamilton of 4th September 1815. Her letter in French in next paragraph is 10th October [1830].
[20] Rev. Robert Gray *Tour through Germany, Switzerland and Italy in 1791 and 1792*, (1794) pp. 209-210, where he reports the Swiss' words in French. For Gray see *D.N.B.*
[21] B. to Lettice, 5th October 1796 (Melville, p. 243).

ENGLAND'S WEALTHIEST SON

CHAPTER XV

[1] Debts mentioned in Fownes' Memo. of 29th March 1822, which lists them as follows: mortgages on Fonthill, £70,000; debt to W. India merchants (Plummer), £14,000; 'bonds' of £3,000 each to Royal goldsmith Rundell, B's banker Morland, and another (see also "Proposals to Duke of Hamilton", 6th August 1822); "other debts", £7,000; and £25,000 in reserve to meet coming legal claim of J. G. Campbell (see next chapter).
Rev. Sir S. Clarke Jervoise, 1st Bart., had mortgage on Fonthill Estate for £15,000 (Plummer to Fownes & White, 1st March 1820); the other mortgages on it were held by Mr. Grenfield (Fownes to B., 17th August 1822).

[2] Draxhall (with Fonthill) and Harbourhead; see next chapter, note 56.

[3] Valuations given in Brown's to Hamilton, 3rd June 1821, which, however values Clarendon at perhaps £80,000. Since he had also valued Draxhall too high, I have followed Fownes' Memo. of 29th March 1822, fixing it at £70,000. Plantations in Clarendon group included Dank's, Lime Hall, Kay's, Rock River, Moore's, Retreat and Danning's Hays Pen; they were mostly between Rio Minho and Rock River in Clarendon Parish.

[4] *Mirror of Literature*, 23rd November 1822. The 3rd Marquis of Hertford was pilloried by Thackeray and Disraeli.

[5] Brown to Hamilton, 3rd June 1821.

[6] Messrs. Plummer undertook to pay interest at 5% on B's various debts (as well as on the £14,000 owed to them after sale of Draxhall); these debts were mortgages on Fonthill, three bonds and "other debts" (specified in note 1 above); they were therefore debiting B's account with £5,000 interest on debts totalling about £100,000. This neatly cancelled out their allowance to B. of £5,000 p.a. (four-fifths of which was theoretically based on what they were supposed to receive from sale of his Jamaican sugar; the extra £1,000 p.a. was added as a *loan* in return for Plummer's occupation of the Hindon seat). The only Jamaican estate left was Clarendon, 'produce' or 'free returns' (i.e. before deduction of sugar duties, agents' fees, etc.) of which were estimated at £4,640 in 1821 (Brown to Hamilton, 3rd June 1821; since then sugar prices had been falling). Therefore his Jamaican allowance was not actually earned, but put him in debt to Plummer at rate of perhaps £1,000 p.a. As well as paying interest on his debts, Plummer also paid out £1,000 p.a. in pensions (see note 10 below) and up to another £1,000 p.a. on legal and other expenses (see note 29), so that his annual debit with them in 1822 must have been running at something approaching £3,000 p.a. (apart from his capital debt to them)!
B's only other source of income was his Fonthill rent-roll of £4,000 p.a. less 'public burdens' (i.e. poor-rates) of £740 p.a., and £1,000 p.a. from manors of Milford and Woodford (leased from Bishop of Salisbury) and from farm at Fonthill Bishop (leased from Bishop of Winchester). But Brown reckoned that in fact B. only received £4,000 p.a. net from his English lands (letters to Hamilton of 3rd June and 17th September 1821).

[7] *Life at Fonthill*, p. 287.

[8] Ditto, p. 330 (9th February 1821). B's next proposal was that Hamilton should find £30,000 to meet Plummer's most pressing claims (which had been reduced by coming sale of Draxhall for £42,000), and pay annual interest of £3,500 on Fonthill mortgages: see *Life at Fonthill*, pp. 327, 333, and Fownes to Hamilton, 3rd November 1821.

[9] I say 'dishonestly' because in letter to B. few days later (17th August) Fownes estimates debt to Plummer's "above £12,500" and "likely to be

286

NOTES

increased". Nevertheless, Fownes was really an honest man.

[10] "Proposals submitted to Duke of Hamilton", dated 6th August 1822 and sent to Hamilton with Fownes' letter of 8th, lists following 'life annuities': children of Mrs. Orde (B's eldest daughter), £300 (solicitors' memo. of 29th March only allotted them £200); Franchi, £400; Macquin, £100 (only started about 1817); Dr. Verdeil, £100; and Chardin, £100. The two Bonds to Morland and Rundell were secured on certain pictures and valuables at Abbey which B. particularly treasured. Brown consistently valued Clarendon at £80,000, but see note 3 above. For Campbell, see next chapter.

[11] Hamilton's reply to Fownes, 12th August 1822.

[12] B. to Fownes, 17th August 1822.

[13] Listed in Brown's to Hamilton, 3rd June 1821. Mrs. Westenra (d. 1844), née Anne Douglas-Hamilton, married January 1820, as 1st wife, H. R. Westenra, later 3rd Lord Rossmore. *G.E.C.* and 5th Lord Rossmore in his chatty *Things I can Tell*, 1912, pp. 6-7, say she was illegit. dau. of 8th Duke of Hamilton (d. 1799). Rossmore also says she went into Society with her respectable *aunt* Lady Anne Hamilton (after whom she was probably called); but the latter was the devoted sister of *10th* Duke of Hamilton and would have been under no obligation to illegit. dau. of her late cousin, a wastrel drunkard who heavily damaged Hamilton fortunes. Being illegit., young Anne might well have brought a fortune with her in order to marry well, but such a huge annual allowance *after* marriage seems unthinkable unless it was from a father devoted to her (i.e. 10th Duke). All this seems to indicate she was dau. of 10th Duke, whom we know from his Papers had an illegit. dau. (and Farington i. 339 shows him living abroad with an Italian woman).

[14] White to B., 8th August 1809; B's draft to Lady Anne Hamilton, 26th September 1804. Next sentence quotes Franchi in French to Hamilton, 27th September 1822.

[15] *The News*, 13th October 1822.

[16] Fownes to B., 16th August 1822. Somerset (who was Hamilton's brother-in-law and had already bought B's Witham Friary) and Lord Normanton are mentioned in Fownes' of 17th, from which next quotation is also taken. D[uke] of S[omerset]'s ardour is mentioned as early as 2nd August (B's Italian letter to Franchi).

[17] *Morning Chronicle*, 15th July 1826. For Farquhar, see *D.N.B.*

[18] Robert Hume, London, to B. in Bath. His next letter quoted is dated 2nd October 1822.

[19] Hume's second letter of 8th October, from Fonthill, which also informs about Phillips' plans. In *Life at Fonthill*, p. 328 I gave Sale date as Monday 7th, following *The Examiner* of 14th October; this was before I had seen Hume's letter, which is conclusive (without this, Franchi's to Hamilton of 8th October is not conclusive, its French being ambiguous). Sale Agreement copy in B's Papers is dated Saturday 5th October.

[20] Franchi in French to Hamilton, 27th September, as is his next letter quoted, dated 8th September.

[21] Ditto, 8th October. Sums agreed on are given in Sale Agreement.

[22] de Ricci *English Collectors of Books*, 1930, pp. 84-7. For B's library see also W. Y. Fletcher *English Book Collectors*, 1902; Quaritch *Dictionary of English Book-Collectors*, Part IV (1893); William Clarke *Repertorium Bibliographicum*, 1819. I have not discussed quality of B's library because this is being done by my friend, Mr. Anthony Hobson, to whom I have loaned Inventories, Library Catalogues and other relevant material from B's Papers.

[23] *Life at Fonthill*, p. 311.

ENGLAND'S WEALTHIEST SON

[24] He sold Garofalo's *Holy Family* and Mazzolino's for 1,000 guineas to National Gallery although they cost him less than half this (Redding *Memoirs* ii. 256); in the same transaction he sold them Raphael's *St. Catherine* for 6,000 guineas, having paid 2,000 for it (Dibdin *Literary Life*, 1836, i. 410n). They paid 600 guineas for Bellini's *Doge Loredano*, which cost him 300 guineas or less (List of B's reserve prices in Franchi's letter in French to Hamilton, 23rd September 1822). He bought Perugino's *Virgin and Child with St. John* for fifty guineas about 1820, bought it back at Farquhar's 1823 Fonthill sale for the same amount (Redding's *Manuscript* ii. 89), and sold it to National Gallery for £800. In 1799 he bought the Altieri Claudes for 6,500 guineas, selling them in 1808 for 10,000 guineas (*Life at Fonthill*, p. 47n.).

He never seems to have paid much for objects of *vertu* in front rank. He bought the Rubens Vase for £420 (Franchi's account in Portuguese, October 1818). In 1819 he bought Hungarian topaz vase attributed to Cellini for £285 (B's Italian letter to Franchi, 1st November 1819, and Baldock's undated letter); it fetched 600 guineas in the 1823 sale, despite Press campaign of false assertions against its quality; it was recently sold by Lord Rothschild to a Fifth Avenue millionaire. He bought for about 200 guineas (B's reserve list—see above) two columbine cups, one of which fetched £3,244 at H.P.S. (see Chapter XVIII, note 34). See Chapter XVIII note 35 for another striking bargain.

[25] Fownes to Hamilton, 3rd November 1821.

[26] Thomas Davis *General View of Agriculture of Wiltshire*, Board of Agriculture, 1794 (1811 ed. is unaltered).

[27] Not counting Gibbon's library which he bought in 1796 and kept almost intact in Switzerland; and ignoring his earlier book sales, and books he left in Paris when he fled in 1793. At his death he left over 10,000 printed books and 80 manuscripts.

[28] Solicitors' Memo. of 29th March 1822. B. also still had "near £1,000 p.a." from the three local manors and farms leased from Bishops of Winchester and Salisbury (Brown's to Hamilton, 3rd June 1821), and fluctuating income from Clarendon plantations.

[29] Brown estimates legal and allied expenses of Fownes & White at £1,000 p.a. (letters to Hamilton, 3rd June and 17th September 1821). From Plummer's letter to Fownes & White, 1st March 1820, they can be calculated at £700 p.a. (pensions then being £900). Solicitors' Memo. of 29th March 1822 only allows £300 p.a. for 'law charges', as does Franchi's letter of 9th February 1821 to Hamilton (*Life at Fonthill*, p. 330). But Brown's estimate is probably more comprehensive and he is always very cautious and conservative (despite once accepting high valuation of Clarendon plantations), so that it is safest to take his estimate.

[30] Undated letter in French to Dr. Schöll, *Life at Fonthill*, p. 340.

[31] B's fair-copy to [Fownes, November 1822]; its genuineness is confirmed by Fownes' two letters to B., 14th November and 14th December 1822; already on 11th October, Hume writes to B. about his desire to get his Library back. B. had a manor in neighbouring parish of E. Hatch. 'Jamaica' was his Clarendon estates, which had not been sold because of low price of sugar and reluctance of buyers for anything Jamaican.

[32] Fownes to B., 24th October 1823.

[33] Presscut in Bath Municipal Library (Hunt Collection).

[34] *Gentleman's Magazine* (1826), i. 123, and ii. 647. The Abbey and acreage within Barrier Wall were sold to John Bennett of Pyt House, the County Member, who sold it to 1st Marquess of Westminster about 1836, from whom it has passed down in family descent.

[35] That much of the Abbey was left after the fall of the Tower in 1825 is shewn by Buckler's drawing given here, and by Mr. Lansdown's des-

NOTES

cription of his visit in October 1844 (see *Recollections of the late William B.*, ed. by Charlotte Lansdown, Bath 1893, pp. 40-1, 44-6).

CHAPTER XVI

[1] Redding's *Manuscript*, ii. 111.
[2] Charles Leslie *New History of Jamaica*, 1740, p. 267. *Gentleman's Magazine*, 1735, ii. 737 puts him as "worth £300,000"; but this might exclude his mortgages, from which so many plantations were gradually obtained.
[3] Redding's *Manuscript*, i. 7 says that Speaker Peter left most of property to eldest son Peter (whom Alderman William succeeded on latter's premature death in 1737).
[4] Redding *Memoirs* i. 6, 16.
[5] MS *List of Landholders in Jamaica*, 1754, in P.R.O. (C.O. 142/31). Speaker Peter's Will divided Jamaican plantations between his sons.
[6] Speaker Peter's Will left all English lands to his eldest son Peter (from whom Alderman Beckford inherited); they are described as in Counties of Middlesex, Hertford and Bedford.
Alderman B's English properties in 1770, with their rents and charges, are listed in the first two Schedules of *B. v Collett* (C.12/1321/8; for this document see Chapter III note 4). In London he owned a house in Monument Yard (rented), two houses in Air St., Piccadilly, leased by Thomas Pitt (presumably the 1st Lord Camelford), and a house and farm in Kentish Town (bought for £2,200 by Peter Beckford in 1686: see receipt in B's Papers). He only rented the house in Soho Square where our young B. was born. He also owned Skay Farm, Beckford, Glos.; Eaton Bray, Bedfordshire, on which he raised a mortgage costing him £600 p.a. in interest; several houses and a farm in Markyatestreet, Herts.; Caddington Bury Farm, near the Herts-Beds border, was held on long lease from the Dean and Chapter of St. Paul's, and probably near it he owned Gosbill's Farm and South Farm. Most of above property may have been inherited by Alderman B., but he acquired what follows. In Somerset he owned Witham Friary, Nunny and Truddoxhill. Near Fonthill he also owned land in Tisbury, E. Hatch and E. Knoyle; he held Fonthill Bishop Farm on long lease from Bishop of Winchester, and Manors of Milford and Woodford ditto from Bishop of Salisbury.
The total *net* rentals received from all these properties add up to about £8,760, from which must be deducted £646 (interest on mortgage above and rent on Caddington Bury Farm). But some of the lands in Wilts and Somerset were "settled by way of jointure on Mrs. B."; her jointure-income was £1,000 p.a., which brings young B's English income to the approximate £7,000 p.a. which I mention later on.
In *Life at Fonthill*, p. 156, B. also mentions having owned lands in Bucks. This is supported by Sir John Gibbons' 'answer' to B. (for this document, see note 12 below), which unfortunately gives no details.
[7] Namier *Structure of Politics in Reign of George III*, 1957, pp. 53-5.
[8] Redding *Memoirs* i. 61-3.
[9] Redding's *Manuscript* i. 13.
[10] *Historical MSS Commission*, x. 25 (Cathcart).
[11] *London Chronicle*, 23-26th June 1770.
[12] B's Bill of Complaint in P.R.O.: 1771 'answers' of Gibbons (C.12/1321/18) and Charles B. (C.12/1321/8). In Richard B's Appeal to House of Lords (1783), net annual value of B's real estates in England and Jamaica is stated to be £25,000 and upwards. In John B's Appeal (1774), B. is described as "seized of a Real Estate of £25,000 p.a." For these documents, see Chapter III note 4.

ENGLAND'S WEALTHIEST SON

[13] Schedules (especially No. 5) attached to *B. v. Collett* (C.12/1321/8). £4,000 was received from his bankers, Messrs. Hoare, in April 1771 (3rd Schedule), but this is more than balanced by a debt owed to them of £52,000, on which interest was being paid in February 1771 (Schedule attached to Gibbon's answer, as above).

[14] Parish Returns from tax Collectors sent to H.M. Receivers-General, still in their original sacks in P.R.O. Return for Fonthill Gifford (sack E.182/1098) shews £2,992 which, at rate of 2/- in £, indicates income of about £29,000. This was second year of Pitt's new Income Tax, which was then discontinued as result of Peace of Amiens. When renewed in 1803 the system and method of recording were altered, and give no such clues. 1800 Tax Returns shew Fonthill Gifford as £4,569. Calculations in next sentence are based on material mentioned in notes 17-18.

[15] Case *Campbell v. B.* (and vice-versa) is best stated in *Printed Cases in Appeals decided in 1801-2-3*, now in P.C. Office in Whitehall. This gives case for each side, with all relevant printed documents, as it was to be presented to 'Lords of Committee of Council for hearing Appeals from Plantations'. Volumes for years of B's subsequent appeals are missing. *Ackendown* and *Bog* (=Bogie?) are near Westmoreland coast close to Parish border with St. Elizabeth; there is a *Bogue* not far to the east, near Black River in St. Catherine's. *Retrieve* is well to the west, beyond Gabaritta River and Little London.

[16] From the facts I give it is obvious that the information supplied to Prof. Chapman (p. 16 of his 1952 ed.) is much exaggerated. He thought that 'logwood' meant logs; in fact, it is a tree, grown on the plantations, from which a black dye was extracted; B. was accused of felling at one period not £250,000 worth on Strathbogie (which would have been impossible) but £26,000 worth. Campbell's chief accusation of 'wasting' the land was not against Beckford (although this was alleged on Ackendown) but against his father on Strathbogie; but the Alderman's action may have been in connection with estate reorganization, perhaps consequent upon the exhaustion of some sugar areas and their conversion to pen lands for cattle raising.

[17] Memo. 'Campbell v. Beckford' prepared for Duke of Hamilton by B's solicitors, 6th August 1822. Crops estimated at £8,000 Jamaican 'currency' (=£5,714 sterling).

[18] B's amended Quebec Bill (see note 30).

[19] Memo. as note 17. Interest-rate at $6\frac{5}{8}\%$ calculated from figures in Brown's undated *aide-memoire* of about November 1821.

[20] Letter to B. from R. S. White (Junior), his solicitor, 9th May 1826. Appeal was going to be lodged again some time after July 1824, but *all* official records for 1824 are missing, so we do not know result.

[21] White's letter of 9th November 1801. Foxhall is Edward Foxhall, upholsterer (see *Life at Fonthill*). This shews that business-men, etc. and not the gentry had ready money available; this was how they climbed.

[22] Francis Vesey, *Reports of Cases . . in Chancery during time of . . Lord Eldon*, xiii. 577-9; and numerous case-papers in P.R.O.—e.g. William Dawes Quarrell's Complaint v. B. (C.12/2189/1). *Currency* means Jamaican money; Jamaican pound was only worth 14s. 3½d. sterling. The difference in values soon becomes large (e.g. £100 sterling=£140 currency), so that in reading lawsuits it is necessary to note which pound is meant. Conversion tables are sometimes in Jamaican Almanacks.

[23] Vesey, xvii. 87-100 (plantation is not named and papers not in P.R.O.).

[24] *Privy Council Papers* (*Plantations*) in P.R.O. (P.C.1/61/11). It was Ward's Plantation, near Port Morant. Other cases I have seen are *Ross v. B.*, and those involving Lime Hall plantation, and Draxhall in 1798.

NOTES

The latter case is interesting because it involved what is now Jamaica College, the leading educational institution in Jamaica before the coming of the Federal University. Draxhall was acquired by Beckford in 1784, in the case involving Catherine Hall (see text above). It had been one of the securities for the intended foundation and endowment of the Jamaica Free School (now Jamaica College) under the will of Charles Drax in 1721. Possibly through the dishonesty of Alderman Beckford and others, the foundation never materialised and its endowment vanished. Proceedings were eventually brought against young Beckford as the owner of Draxhall; he was only discharged on the payment of a large sum in Jamaican currency, variously estimated as £5,200 and £11,200 (F. C. Cundall *Historic Jamaica*, 1915, pp. 303-4, and in *Journal of Institute of Jamaica*, vol. I (1891-3), p. 354).

I have also seen mention of a lawsuit involving Gordon's plantation.

[25] *Yale*, Item 5, gives a letter from Fonthill in 1736; Redding's *Manuscript* i. 8 says 1737, and that the estate was between 4 and 5,000 acres.

[26] Brown to Hamilton, 7th September 1821. J. S. Fownes, B's solicitor, had become senior partner in firm Fownes & White after *old* White's death in 1817.

[27] Thomas Wildman (1740-1795), M.P.; Henry (d. January 1816); and James (1747-March 1816), M.P., whose son, James Beckford Wildman (b. 1788) was B's godson. Further details of them are in this chapter and *Burke's Landed Gentry*, 1952. Facts about their early connection with B. are mostly taken from his amended Quebec Bill (see note 30). Thomas' name often crops up in W. India deeds; he evidently specialised in such legal businesss.

[28] Sarah Wildman's answer to B's amended Quebec Bill. For Curtis, see note 46.

[29] Plummer's letter to Fownes & White from Fenchurch Street, 1st March 1820, outlines the arrangement, especially its financial side. For Plummer and his firm, see later and *Life at Fonthill*.

[30] Vesey, xvi. 438-43 (3rd ed., 1815), and records in P.R.O. (C.13/113/44); these are B's original Quebec Bill of May 1808 and its amendment of February 1810, with Sarah W's answers to each.

[31] Thomas W. to B., 1st June 1790. Next letter quoted is 16th December 1788.

[32] This letter, minus its beginning and therefore with no date, is in B's Papers; but it is fully dated 14th March 1790 in Sarah W's first answer.

[33] Campbell case, and suit pending over Catherine Hall. A further mortgage of £12,000 on B's English property was obtained from Curtis in 1793 (already mentioned in my text and at note 28).

[34] Redding's *Manuscript* ii. 26b. and p. 32, quoting Lettice's letter of August 1802. John Pedley (1762-1838), M.P.; for his seats see my text.

[35] Farington iv. 242. Note that this was the amount of Curtis' mortgage, which B. was never able to pay off; Pedley had probably therefore taken it up.

[36] Farington, ditto; Redding's *Manuscript* ii. 26b; Pedley's letter to B., 21st February 1805, about arranging Eaton Bray sale. *Victoria County Hist.* for Herts., ii. 189, 191, shews that in 1804 Pedley acquired from the Dean and Chapter of St. Paul's the Caddington Hall estate (which may be the land that the Beckfords had on a long lease: see note 6). For Deverell see *D.N.B.*

[37] B's draft of 23 November 1806. Melville, p. 271 misdates a Pedley letter 1817 instead of 1805.

[38] B. in French to Marquis of Douglas (later Duke of Hamilton), 14th September 1810. For his hatred of Thomas Wildman's memory, see *Life at Fonthill*, pp. 145-6.

ENGLAND'S WEALTHIEST SON

[39] Lord Thurlow to B., 14th April 1784 (Melville, p. 229, with several mistakes). Another letter of about same date (Melville, pp. 185-7) suggests peerage in return for B. letting a Government man (Kenyon) have B's seat and support at Hindon.

[40] *Life at Fonthill*, p. 298.

[41] Kenyon to B., 14th September 1780. See *D.N.B.*

[42] Bearcroft's letter of 27th October 1788; he also thanked B. on 24th April 1784. He died in November 1796.

[43] *Journal*, pp. 58-9. History of Saltash struggle up to 1790 is in Mr. Ian Christie's article in *English Historical Review*, April 1956, in which are a few of the references in B's Papers which I gave him.

[44] White's letter to B., 11th April 1809. Melville, pp. 268-70 prints two letters from Pedley to B. about Saltash; in that of 11th December 1806 Pedley wrote "The Marquis of B." (i.e. Buckingham) and not "Bute" as Melville transcribes.

[45] T. H. B. Oldfield *Representative History of G.B. and Ireland*, 1816, iii. 144-5.

[46] See note 28 for my source. John Curtis (*c.* 1751-1813), M.P., hovers mysteriously in the background of B's life. His father was a business associate of Alderman Beckford (see latter's letter to him, 24/6/1765 in Morrison, First Series, 1883, i. 62).

[47] B's undated drafts to [Deverell] from Paris, 14th February (?) 1802.

[48] B's draft to James Wildman from Lisbon, 17th April 1796.

[49] Draft letter described in Chapter XIV note 8. Fonthill rentals are mentioned in Brown's letter to Hamilton, 3rd June 1821. Sarah Wildman's first Quebec answer states that in her husband's time (d. 1795) "rents and profits of his [B's] estates in England were £6,000 p.a. and annual proceeds of estates in Jamaica were frequently £40,000." The latter figure is a gross exaggeration (except for an occasional boom year), but the English figure seems to be an understatement (before B. sold some of his estates).

[50] Brown to Hamilton, 3rd June and 17th September 1821; Fownes to Brown, 12th June.

[51] Farington's *Manuscript* for 1798 (24th March, 20th May, 16th November and 8th December), 1799 (17th June and 22nd September), and 11th May 1800.

[52] Dunlap *Arts of Design*, ii. 286-9 (quoted by Sizer) shews that one of estates was on River Genesee. This cannot be estate bought there by B. direct from Wadsworth in April 1799 (see Chapter XI), because he had already paid for it, whereas he had not yet paid for these other estates. Sizer, p. 306 (see Chapter XI, note 24) thinks that Farington, 8th December 1798, refers to B's deal with Wadsworth; but that is because this is the only entry about B's land deals printed in Greig's ed. of Farington, and therefore Sizer did not know that there were other deals going on (not having seen Farington's *Manuscript*). Latter's scattered references give impression that West-Trumbull-B. deals were Wadsworth land *resold* to B. by West and Trumbull. West had been buying earlier on the River Susquehannah at three shillings an acre (Farington's *Manuscript*, 17th December 1797); B. came in at ten shillings an acre—for 25,000 acres!

[53] White's letter to B., 20th March 1832. B's bank was then styled Duckett, Morland & Co., having been Ransom, Morland & Hammersley of Pall Mall, 1786-1819. For speculations of Sir George Duckett, 2nd Bart., see his son's *Anecdotal Reminiscences of an Octo-nonagenarian*, Kendal, 1895, pp. 47, 106.

[54] Italian letters to Franchi, e.g. 5th February 1814, and one undated (about end of July 1810). Pall Mall was his banker's address (see note above).

NOTES

[55] Plummer & Wilson's of 24th November 1830 to Fownes & White, who sent on copy to B. Their style periodically changed (see *Life at Fonthill*), but for at least century from 1848 it was Thomson Hankey & Co. For Thomson Hankey see *D.N.B.* under his son of same name. For another sugar crash which nearly affected B. see Melville, p. 267 (where 'Rangoon' should read 'Ransoms'—B's bankers).

[56] Brown's to Hamilton, 3rd June 1821. In Italian letter to Franchi, 15th November 1821, B. thinks Draxhall has been sold for £42,000. About a year or less earlier, B's agents sold for £20,000 (Brown's to Hamilton, 3rd June 1821) Harbourhead Plantation, near Port Morant, which B. had tried to sell as early as 1789.

[57] Fownes & White to Plummer & Wilson, 24th July 1824, and latter's reply of 26th.

[58] Answer of Thomas and James Wildman (sons of Henry Wildman), 29th April 1818, in P.R.O. (C. 13/2880), to B's Bill of Revivor of 29th February 1816 in the case *B. v. Henry Wildman*.

[59] *B. v. Thomas and James Wildman*, and their answer, 1816, in P.R.O. (C. 13/2873); also in Esher case below.

[60] *Life at Fonthill*, pp. 309-10.

[61] Franchi's Portuguese letter to B., 20th September 1804. Farington iii. 95 for 3rd August 1805 suggests Douglas wanted cash sum of £20,000; but this (if correct) might have only been part of larger Settlement. See *Life at Fonthill*, pp. 87-8 for what Douglas got on marrying Susan in 1810.

[62] B. to Franchi in Italian, 13th August 1809.

[63] Farington's *Manuscript*, 26th May 1801. Next quote (my italics) is Redding *Memoirs* ii. 313-14, 146.

[64] Fownes to Hamilton, 3rd November 1821.

[65] Farington iv. 242.

[66] This and rest of material in chapter comes from *B. v. Henry Wildman* (1815) over Esher Plantation, in P.R.O. (C. 12 and 13/2870). Esher is south of Quebec Plantation, which is near Port Maria.

[67] Deed of Conveyance signed in Jamaica on B's behalf by Pedley, who wrote to White on 18th December 1801 that Esher had been conveyed at valuation of £88,200 sterling (White's to B. of 9th February 1802).

CHAPTER XVII

[1] Redding's *Manuscript* ii. 110.

[2] No. E.695 in British Museum: their *Catalogue of Greek Vases* (1896), iii. 343-4. In B's day it was perfect, but was subsequently broken at Hamilton Palace.

[3] No. E.543 in B.M.; see Beazley *Attic red-figure Vase Painters*, 1942, p. 844. These and other treasures are described and drawn in *Illustrated London News*, Nov.-Dec. 1845 (three articles on Bath sale of part of B's collection).

[4] Waagen *Works of Art and Artists in England*, 1838, pp. 6-8 (part of a long and valuable account of B's collections). B's pictures are inadequately noted in Passavant *Tour of a German Artist in England* (1836), i. 314-18.

[5] Melville, p. 322.

[6] Letter in French to Hamilton, 16th May 1823. B's note on folder states that he offered £16,000 for pictures mentioned, which compares with £12,500 for which Government bought them. Angerstein's executors were able to make Government raise their offer considerably partly because of "the large price offered at one time by Mr. Beckford" (Whitley *Art in England, 1821-37*, p. 68).

ENGLAND'S WEALTHIEST SON

[7] B. to Smith of Lisle St., printseller, 14th November 1843. The three pictures mentioned are now in National Gallery (No. 168, 181 and 169 or 641).
[8] Northcote *Reynolds* (1819) ii. 189.
[9] Robert Hume to B. in Bath, 2nd August 1828; my details of Franchi's death are all from Hume's August letters. For Hume, see *Life at Fonthill*. Dr. H. H. Southey is in *D.N.B.*; he published a treatise on consumption in 1814; as a fashionable doctor and physician to George IV, his fees would have been large.
[10] Franchi's Portuguese letter to B., 20th September 1804, from which next quote also comes.
[11] Hume's of 15th August. To raise money Franchi sold to B. for £3,000 his annuity of £400 a year. He left debts of over £900, and Hume estimated his effects not worth £600.
[12] Hume's of 9th August. Franchi was dead by 7th. His silver-caster was Samuel Coulson (see *Life at Fonthill*, p. 323).
[13] *Journal*, p. 281; next quote is from p. 62.
[14] Redding *Memoirs* ii. 323.
[15] H.P.S. I.2742: fetched highest price of any item in sale. Account of artist's visit comes from Redding *Memoirs* ii. 360-71, supplemented by his *Manuscript*. The marble figure is "A Sleeping Cupid, in Parian marble" by Fiammingo (for him see *Life at Fonthill*), which was Lot 69 of Eighth Day of Sale of B's effects at 20 Lansdown Crescent, Bath from 24th July 1848 onwards.
[16] Accounts of W. India merchants, enclosed with White's letter of 13th June 1840 (misdated "May"). B's address was 23 Gloucester Place, Portman Square, and later 127 Park Street, with front on Park Lane. Next quote is from Redding's *Manuscript* ii. 74.
[17] Redding's *Manuscript* ii. 72b. Doyle's sketch is reproduced in Melville, p. 344.
[18] Redding's *Manuscript* ii. 73. This was Old West End House (now demolished), south of West End Green and on west side of West End Lane, on site near Iverson Road now occupied by Midland Region Railway line.
[19] B's undated draft to Lady Anne Hamilton, about 5th April 1806. The quarrels about their education are revealed in Lettice's unpublished letter to B., 10th November 1798.
[20] Redding's *Manuscript* ii. 73; my next para. is based on p. 76. The nursery was Andrew Henderson & Son, Edgware Road.
[21] Monypenny and Buckle *Disraeli* (1929), i. 252.
[22] Must refer to organised emigration to Canada from Wiltshire to reduce population and unemployment, and perhaps to newspaper report of shipload drowned; one such party went from Purton in 1837, aided by local Poor Law Guardians (*Victoria County History for Wiltshire*, 1959, iv. 84). This shews B's concern for the poor. At *Hartford Bridge* (between Bagshot and Basingstoke) there was a posting-house, *The White Hart*, so in his dream B. was on a journey (significant for dream-analysts!). This is the only dream written out *in full* by B. (27th March 1838).
[23] Undated local presscut (*Bath and Cheltenham Gazette?*) in Bath Municipal Library (Hunt Collection Presscuts, p. 171).
[24] Redding's *Manuscript* ii. 48.
[25] Letter in French to Duchess of Hamilton, 20th April 1844 (Oliver, in French, p. 328). For Sir Robert Liston, diplomatist, see *D.N.B.* and *Journal*, and for Dr. Ehrhart see *Life at Fonthill*. *The Medical Directory of Great Britain and Ireland* for 1845 shows that Dr. Liston can only be the Robert Liston (1794-1847) in *D.N.B.* He was probably called in from London because he was Consulting Surgeon to Hospital for Diseases of

NOTES

the Chest, which suggests that B. was suffering from pleurisy.

[26] Ditto, 21st April (in Oliver). I have left a few phrases in French which reproduce B's *spoken* phrases over a lifetime.

[27] *Life at Fonthill*, p. 66.

[28] *Autobiography of Rev. William Jay*, 1854, p. 28 note.

[29] Redding's *Manuscript* ii. 61b, quoting B's note in his copy of Jay *The Christian Contemplated*. Jay's father worked at Fonthill as a mason and apprenticed his son there; Jay became a great Chapel preacher in Bath in B's lifetime!

[30] Rev. Erskine Neale *The Closing Scene*, 2nd Series (1849), pp. 25-6. Next two quotes are from Redding's *Manuscript* ii. 116, which is one of my main sources for B's last illness. B's servant (G. Beckett), in his letter of 29th April 1844 to Mr. Smith (in Mr. Babb's possession), tells us that B. had influenza badly.

CHAPTER XVIII

[1] Britton *Fonthill Abbey*, 1823, p. 60; and in B's Papers.

[2] *Portugal*, Letter XXXIV.

[3] B. calls his father the Commendatore in his Italian letters to Franchi.

[4] Jotting of 24th June 1781, to which B. adds the reference "see Bacon's *Essays*, p. 7—wisdom of the ancients". He was using 1705-6 ed. of Bacon's *Works*, and refers to the Part called *Wisdom of Ancients*, pp. 6-7 (i.e. Essay entitled *Narcissus or Self-Love*).

[5] *Journal*, p. 308.

[6] A. J. Symons *Quest for Corvo* (Penguin ed., 1940), p. 74.

[7] Swinburne's letter in French of 9th June 1876 in Mallarmé *Oeuvres Complètes*, 1951 (Pleiade ed.), p. 1599.

[8] French Memo. dated Monserrat (Portugal), 25th July 1794.

[9] Meister *Letters*, London 1799, p. 312. Original Swiss ed. (Zurich, 1795), p. 255, is much stronger: land-holders *dévorent un pais, au lieu de l'enricher*.

[10] Poem submitted to Macquin in letter from Bath, 30th October 1822, shortly after B. sold Fonthill.

[11] *Athenaeum*.

[12] *Life at Fonthill*, p. 39.

[13] Rt. Hon. Sir John McMahon, 1st Bart. (d. 1817): references to him are in B's Italian letters to Franchi. For Barclay see *Life at Fonthill*.

[14] Letter in French to Hamilton, 24th October 1837. French memo., dated 24th November and quoted next, also sent to him.

[15] Hazlitt's criticisms of Fonthill are reprinted in Centenary Ed. (1934) of his *Works*, x. 55-60, and xviii. 173-80. They originally appeared in *London Magazine* for October 1823 (after B. had sold Fonthill) and November 1822 respectively.

[16] Phillips, 17th Day, Lot 762. See Metropolitan *Bulletin*, mentioned in my note 31.

[17] French draft to Mme de Starck, 10th December 1789.

[18] *Zinan*. This story contains, in death of the general Abraha, remarkable picture of Fate and echo of death of B's great-grandfather, Governor Peter B.

[19] Farington ii. 118.

[20] Jotting on back of receipt dated April 1790. B. gives ref. as "p. 94, vol. 6, 2nd Ed.", but I cannot find it at this page in the various confused editions of the period. Immediately below this jotting is one on Gilles de Rais!

²¹ "There is scarcely an Englishman . . . who would not give a quarter of his goods to see you ruined" wrote Franchi in Portuguese, 20th September 1804.
²² For his purchase of two Wilsons, one of which is now in National Gallery, see *Life at Fonthill*, p. 305 and note; he treasured one of them enough to reserve it from Christie (Seventh Day, Lot 76) in his Sale Agreement with Farquhar (see Chapter XV). Unless otherwise mentioned, the artists' names in this section of my paragraph are taken from B's Inventory.
²³ H.P.S. (First and Fourth Portions) lists B's copies of the very fine and rare books and engravings by Blake; the former, with their whereabouts in America (e.g. at Harvard), are listed in Sir G. Keynes and Wolf *William Blake's Illuminated Books, a Census*, New York, 1953.
²⁴ H.P.S. I.957 is the *Catalogue* of this Exhibition; and see Keynes *Blake Studies*, 1949, p. 81.
²⁵ Letter in French from Joseph Vernet (1714-89), Paris, 2nd April 1783.
²⁶ Redding's anon. article in *New Monthly Magazine* (1844), Vol. 72, p. 24.
²⁷ Redding's *Memoirs* ii. 347-8. Information following comes from Whitley *Art in England 1821-1837*, pp. 276-80. Chancellor was Lord Althorp, later 3rd Earl Spencer.
²⁸ B's Rembrandts in German museums are the one mentioned in my next paragraph, and his *Christ at the Column* (sold by B. at Christie's, February 1802) now in Hessisches Museum, Darmstadt.
²⁹ Hazlitt (see n.15 for the reference) scornfully includes the Orcagna *Crucifixion*, now in National Gallery (which only has three Orcagna)! B. was pioneer collector of Primitives (which Hazlitt disliked): see my article on B's Taste in *History Today*, October 1960. In this article I omitted a good Beckford picture sold as Van Eyck by Phillips (27th Day, Lot 412) and discussed by W. H. J. Weale in his MS "Notes on Sales of Paintings attributed to the Van Eycks" in V. & A. Library.
³⁰ The nine pictures listed in Seventh Day of Christie's 1822 sale catalogue, ignored by Hazlitt and now owned by the National Gallery (whose attributions I give) are Bellini *Agony in the Garden* and *Doge Loredan*, Perugino *Virgin and Child with St. John*, Cima da Conegliano *St. Jerome*, Mazzolino *Woman taken in adultery*, Garofalo *Holy Family*, follower of van der Weyden *Exhumation of St. Hubert*, Mieris *Lady in Crimson Jacket*, and Dou *Poulterer's Shop*. B. had already sold Gaspar Poussin *Calling of Abraham*, and at some time acquired Elsheimer *Tobias and Angel* (both now in the Gallery).
Whilst in Bath he bought five good pictures now in National Gallery: Raphael *St. Catherine*, Filippino Lippi *Adoration of the Kings*, Velasquez *Philip IV when young*, Mazzolino *Holy Family*, and Dou *Portrait of a Young Woman*. Strete *Edward VI*, bought by Queen Victoria at Hamilton Palace sale, is now at Hampton Court. Lord Harewood has B's Catena *Madonna and Child with St. John Baptist and St. Jerome*.
Some of B's best Bath period pictures may be identified by collating his Inventory with his posthumous Bath sales of November 1845 and July 1848, and with H.P.S., and then with catalogues of subsequent sales, collections and artists (if one can find the modern attribution). For example, Holbein *Portrait of Bishop Gardiner* in B's Inventory was Bath 1848, Third day, Lot 36; it is now called Matsys *Portrait of a Canon* and is No. 928 (illustrated) in Catalogue of the Collection of Prince Liechtenstein, Vienna, 1938, where its pedigree is given.
³¹ Bellini *Madonna and Child* in Metropolitan Museum (Bache Collection), and Gentile Bellini *Doge Vendramin* in Frick Collection. His Bath period pictures now in America include two Fra Angelico panels (*The Virgin*

NOTES

and *Announcing Angel*) owned by Mrs. Edsel Ford; Pesellino *Madonna and Child with Six Saints* in the Metropolitan; Titian *Portrait of Admiral in armour* at Washington (Kress Collection); and Filippo Mazzola *Madonna with Child in lap* at Baltimore (Walters Art Gallery). For B's treasures at Metropolitan see their *Bulletin*, October 1954 (illustrated article by Ten Eyck Gardner).

[32] *Life at Fonthill*, p. 255.

[33] ditto, p. 323, note 3; and Chapter XV here, note 24. Hazlitt mentions it en passant, as a sop.

[34] Christie, 5th Day, Lot 48-9, and H.P.S. 644-5 (illustrated). These cups, perfect of their kind, were made as masterpieces for submission to the Goldsmith's Guild at Nuremberg. The Guild's whole collection was not sold until 1868, so that in B's day they must have been excessively rare (being concentrated in Nuremberg). One is dated 1580, but the catalogues are wrong in thinking that Roemer was the craftsman: he was probably the owner. See also Chapter XV, note 24.

[35] Christie, 3rd Day, Lot 52-3, and H.P.S. 672-3 (illustrated). Franchi's letter in Portuguese from Paris, 6th July 1814, and B's reply in Italian, 14th July, shew that B. was offered them for 600 louis (about £600), whereas in 1882 they fetched £12,075.

[36] I refer to the Reisener bureau at the Wallace Collection (see *Burlington Magazine*, June 1950); and his commode and matching secretaire made for Marie Antoinette, and given by William Vanderbilt to the Metropolitan Museum: see latter's *Bulletin*, mentioned in my note 31. The secretaire is Phillips, 32nd Day, Lot 1579; both pieces are H.P.S. 301-2, where the catalogue says that this suite (including Lot 303, bought by Ferdinand de Rothschild for Waddesdon) is "in all probability . . . the most important and beautiful work of its kind produced in the age of Louis XVI." For B's taste in French furniture, see my article quoted in note 29.

[37] *Life at Fonthill*, p. 279.

[38] That B. criticised West's work is shewn by Farington's *Manuscript*, 1st November 1797: "likes his sketches but not his pictures, and wishes him to make them as much like his sketches as he can"—i.e. freer and more spontaneous. For B's praise of West, see *Life at Fonthill*.

[39] B's undated draft from Paris to West, beginning of 1802. He wrote similarly to Thomas Wildman from Lisbon on 22nd August 1795 about the Calonne auction. For his mockery of the Dutch and Flemings in *Biographical Memoirs of Extraordinary Painters*, see Chapter II. The existence of so many of these pictures at Fonthill (a few are described in P. G. Patmore *British Galleries of Art*, 1824) is partly explained by *pietas:* some of them were his father's (Redding's *Manuscript*, ii. 32). It is sometimes erroneously thought that the Alderman's were sold at Christie's on 23rd January 1789; in fact, this was the sale of the illegitimate W.B. of Somerley, in order to meet his debts.

[40] *Life at Fonthill*, p. 206. For the Claudes, see ditto, pp. 69 and 57.

[41] Edmund English (Junior) from London to B., 2nd April 1844.

[42] Redding *Manuscript* ii. 109-110.

[43] Beckford understandably liked pictures of youths, etc.; for example, Bronzino's fine portrait of a Medici Prince, and a Luini once called Leonardo's *Laughing Boy*, both in *Italian Art and Britain*, Royal Academy, 1960 (No. 91, 27).

[44] *Life at Fonthill*, p. 168.

[45] See p. 233. Inventory, p. 15, calls this picture *A Mother anxiously watching her sleeping Infant*, which makes this association seem all the more likely. Watts *Alaric Watts* (1884), pp. 111-113, gives different and equally valid reason for B's choice. Both could be true; B. would not have told

young Watts, a stranger to him, the private reason for his choice.

[46] Gilchrist *Etty* (1855), ii. 80, 82. Inventory marks it "London", meaning that Duke of Hamilton was going to take it to his London house (or conceivably sell it there instead of in Bath).

[47] Farington's *Manuscript*, 1st November 1797.

[48] Paragraph based on Redding's *Manuscript* ii. 83-4. Edward Young chiefly remembered for his poem *Night Thoughts*. Foscolo's poem published 1807. Quote from Quevedo is taken from Duff's 1926 ed. of his translated *Works*, pp. 186-7; this comes from "Third Vision: Pluto's Lairs" in L'Estrange's 1667 translation *Visions; or Hel's Kingdome*.

[49] MS *Avertisement pour l'edition de Vathek avec les episodes, Janvier 1838* (see Chapman's ed. of *Vathek & the Episodes*, 1929, ii. 162). The 1815 draft is in Chapman and Hodgkin *Bibliography of W.B.*, 1930, pp. 36-7. Speaking of books, B. disapprovingly mentions the atheism of "the atrocious de Sade" in his Italian letter to Franchi, 19th August 1817.

[50] *Life at Fonthill*, p. 318.

[51] Hughes' *Itinerary*, 1822, pp. 214-15. B's comment is on reverse of draft to Rutter which B. sent to Hume, 3rd October 1822.

[52] Redding *Memoirs*, ii. 316.

[53] B's note in his copy of *Rejected Addresses* (1833), now at Brodick Castle. B. refers to footnote on p. 45 reporting remark of Mme de Stael.

[54] *Life at Fonthill*, p. 96.

[55] *Memoirs of 'Buck' Whaley*, pp. 296-7.

[56] Susan's letter in French to Duke of Hamilton, 28th July [1835]—the year *Alcobaça* was published. Rest of paragraph based on Redding's *Manuscript*, ii. 114-115.

[57] Redding *Memoirs* ii. 392.

[58] Meister (Swiss ed. in French—see my note 9), pp. 251-7 (better than English ed., pp. 310-13). B. was on flying visit to Fonthill from Switzerland.

APPENDIX

[1] Senator Angelo Querini to B. in French, Venice, 11th December 1782 (about Countess Rosenberg); it is quoted here.

[2] Lord Archibald Hamilton to B., 20th September 1782.

[3] This room at Splendens is described in Drysdale's undated second letter (see Chapter I, note 21).

NOTE ON ILLUSTRATIONS

1. *Beckford as a boy* was sold by Christie's from Hamilton Palace in November 1919 (Lot 11) for £168. The catalogue, which is full of errors, attributed it to Nathaniel Dance. Prof. Waterhouse is "reasonably sure" that it is by William Hoare (*c.* 1707-92), who painted B's godfather Chatham and did posthumous portraits of earlier Beckfords for the Alderman. It had not yet been painted when Drysdale wrote his undated second letter (between October 1768 and December 1769; see Chapter I, n.21).
2. This is the only known portrait of Beckford's father, apart from a few engravings in books. It is interesting that he is shewn with a builder's line, his hand on building estimates or plans. This alludes to his fondness for building, and may have special reference to the rebuilding of Fonthill House after the fire of 1755. The artist is unknown. It hangs in the House of Commons, and has never been illustrated. *Yale*, No. 1, is a small oil by Laroon of unknown provenance, and bears no resemblance to this one.
3. The caricature of Beckford is on the back of Pedley's letter to him in Paris, dated 1st April 1803 (Melville, pp. 266-7). Above the sketch Beckford, referring to news in the letter, has written "Upwards of £2,000 to be paid in to R[ansom] and M[orland—his bankers] this morn (*1st April*)." This sketch is similar to Behnes' drawing of Beckford (*Life at Fonthill*, pp. 344-5).
4. This is the only known likeness of Lady Margaret Beckford and has never been illustrated. The Harrowbys got it by descent through B's eldest daughter.
5. When sending this self-portrait of the Chevalier Sequeira from Paris on 15th June 1826, Franchi wrote to Beckford in Portuguese: "B. Sequeira . . . today brought me this little memento to send you, thereby showing that if he cannot kiss you in person at least he kisses your name—because of the great pleasure and *saudade* he experiences in recollecting Your Excellency". Beckford may first have met him as a small boy in the circle of the Marquis of Marialva in Paris in 1814. He wrote from there: "Angels large and small abound here . . . A certain object seemed to pass like summer lightning at the Marquis'." (*Life at Fonthill*, p. 160).
7. This is the only known portrait of the dwarf and was identified from the caricature reproduced in *Life at Fonthill*.
8. *The Ruins of Fonthill* was drawn the week after the fall of the Tower.
10. The head and shoulders only of Hoppner's portrait was reproduced in *Life at Fonthill*, where it was discussed in the Appendix; the complete portrait has never been illustrated. Except for this and No. 9 (Beckford's deathbed), a list of portraits of Beckford is given in Chapman and Hodgkin *Bibliography of W. Beckford*, 1930, pp. 115-119.

   This list does not include an alleged sketch of him in old age by C. F. Tayler, reproduced in Brockman *Caliph of Fonthill* (1956). The sitter's identification was made by the last Director of the Victoria Art Gallery, Bath; but I know of no evidence whatever to connect it with Beckford. I examined it in 1954 and felt unable to make use of it as an authentic likeness of him. He would have been more likely to sit to young Willis Maddox of Bath, of whom he was perhaps the earliest patron. Maddox, who painted good portraits, illustrated the interiors of Lansdown Tower under Beckford's supervision, and was commissioned by his daughter to paint her father on his deathbed; he also did portraits of the Hamiltons.

INDEX

Fonthill, Portugal and Switzerland are not indexed because most references are in the relevant chapters.

Ailesbury, Earl of, 51-2, 274
Almeida, ambassador, 128
Amelia, Princess, 18
America:
  American companion, 105; War of Independence, 126-7, 178; prophecy, 149; immigration to, 149-50; projected journey, 277; land purchases, 150-1, 219-20, 282, 292; B's treasures in, 247, 252, 268, 296-7; reading, 150, 151, 281; and see West
Angerstein, Julius, 228, 293
Anglesey, Marquis of, 182, 269, 285
Anspach, Margravine of, 15, 156, 185-6, 285
Arabian Nights, 41, 100
Aranjuez, 18
Arcadia, 179
Argyll, Duke & Duchess, 182
Ariosto, 82, 178
Armida, 173
Arne, 44
Arras, 140
Artaxerxes, opera, 44, 273
Arthur, King, 153, 154
Arveyron River, 105

Bacon, Francis, 241, 295
Bailly, 272
Balliol, 31, 33, 60
Banks, 220
Barclay, Sir Robert, 245
Barnett, 194
Barrier Wall, 157-8
Barry, Sir Charles, 168
Bastille, 142
Batalha, 168
Bath, 226-8, 236, 296
Bath, Marquis of, 185
B.B.C. recording, 15
Bearcroft, Edward, 217, 292

Beaumont, Sir George, 168
Beckett, 28
BECKFORDS:
  Ballard, 201
  Barbara: see Mrs Wake
  Charles, 34
  Francis, 201
  John, 35, 55
  Julines, 201
  Louisa, 10, 80, 82, 264, 265
  Lady Margaret, 15-16, 47, 104, 105-6, 108-10, 119-22, 181, 232, 233, 254, 277, 299
  Maria (mother), 36-8, 46, 55-7, 60, 68, 113, 210, 234, 241, 289
  Nathaniel, 54, 56-7
  Peter (earliest), 29, 271
  Peter, Governor, 29-31, 200, 271
  Peter, Speaker, 30-1, 200, 204, 206, 207, 289
  Peter (uncle), 209, 289
  Peter (cousin), 10, 51, 58-9
  Richard, clothworker, 29, 271
  Richard (uncle), 201
  Richard, bastard, 33, 51-4, 55-9, 272
  Rose, 33, 55
  Susannah, 33
  Thomas, Sir, 29, 271
  Thomas, bastard, 33
  William, Alderman, 31-5, 40-1, 55, 91, 98, 123, 152, 156, 198, 200-203, 204, 206, 209, 241, 254, 271, 272, 289, 290, 297, 299; his Will, 51-2, 272; Bastards' names, 33-4
  William of Somerley (cousin), 151, 186, 201, 213, 282, 297
BECKFORD, WILLIAM:
  Book-collecting, 12-13, 195, 287; devotion to books, 139, 228; library in Paris, 141; at Fonthill, 169; its size, 196-7, 288;

300

INDEX

in Bath, 232-3; sale to Farquhar, 198; books excluded, 196; manuscripts, 114, 147, 227, 268, 281; Inventory, 281
Daughters, 186-7, 234; see Hamilton (Duchess), Orde
Dreams, 47-8, 77, 115-16, 235-6, 241, 275; see Shakespeare
English estates (besides F. A.), 63, 156, 189, 203, 215, 218, 288, 289
Expenditure: on F. A., 196, 223, 224; elections, 215-18; legal, 214, 215, 288; unemployed, 219; marriage settlements, 222, 289, 293; London rent, 233
Finances and money: anxiety over, 59, 151, 195, 202; reliance on, 118, 222, 242, 246-7; debts, 189-91, 197, 211, 224-5, 286; mortgages on F. A., 190, 286; other mortgages, 211, 214-5, 218, 225, 289; income, 203, 205, 219, 286, 289, 292; investments, 150-1, 197, 219, 220, 222-3, 292; assets, 189, 197, 218; annuities given by B, 59, 190, 230, 280-1, 287; accounts, 274, 284, 290, 294; losses at law, 205-6; other losses, 220-1; Wildman's extortions, 212-14, 224-5; see America
Gardening, 18, 172-80, 284
Homosexuality, 10, 76, 95, 102, 137, 241, 278, 299; first affair, 67-8, 275; in Works: see *Al Raoui, Épisodes, Hylas*; guilt assessed, 112-16, 263-5; believers in B's innocence, 108-9, 114, 121; frame-up, 114, 277; and see B's Dreams, Cornaro, Devon (Earl of); sex, 59, 67, 68-9, 187; see Necrophilia
Lawsuits, 214, 274; Executors, 53, 203, 210; Collett, 54, 274; House of Lords, 54, 55; John B., 55; Campbell, 190, 197, 204-5, 286, 290; Quarrell, 206; Wade, 207; Cargill, 207; Sarah Wildman, 212; Henry Wildman, 221, 293; Thomas and James Wildman (junior), 221-2, 293
Parliamentary seats, 107, 211, 215-18; see Hindon, Saltash
Peerage, 107-8, 133, 216, 222, 245-6, 292
Pictures, 25-6, 195-6, 197, 227, 229; Primitives, 25, 169, 229, 253, 254, 296; prices, 196, 253-4, 269, 288; patronage of contemporaries, 249-50, 253, 254-5; by the State, 250; B's in National Gallery, America, Germany, etc., 296-7; B. on restoration, 229; on Taste, 250; Inventory, 249; Hazlitt, 251-2, 296; the Dutch, 253; visits Gallery, 261; other treasures, 247, 252-3, 297; their prices, 288, 297
Plantations, 156, 198, 206; Harbourhead, 55, 212, 293; Stanton Harcourt, 55; Fonthill, 189; Clarendon group, 189, 190-1, 286, 288; Campbell group, 204, 290; Catherine Hall, 206, 282; Quebec, 212-14; Draxhall, 221, 282, 290-1; Esher, 224-5, 293; Lime Hall, 290; Ward's, 290; Gordon's, 291
Radicalism, 132, 141, 143, 144-7, 149, 150, 281; attitude to poor, 141-2, 144-6, 148, 149, 150, 243-4, 294; other Radical novelists, 146
Reading-notes, 241, 248, 259-60, 295; Chinese, 85-7, 276; African, 87-8, 276; Gilles de Rais, 88-9, 276; Siberia, 111; Aeschylus, 112, 278; Louis XI, 122, 279; American, 151, 281; religious, 239, 258-9; contemporary interest in them, 89
Religion, 156, 160, 163, 167, 172, 237, 238-9, 240, 243, 255-9, 279; sense of Fate, 37, 77, 111-12, 115, 130, 248, 264, 266; see St. Anthony, Methodism
Slavery, 151, 218-19
WORKS:
Alcobaça and Batalha, 136-7, 261
Azemia, 36, 144, 145-6, 206
Biographical Memoirs of Extraordinary Painters, 47-9, 272, 273
Diaries: Aranjuez, 18; Green Notebook, 104-7, 277; other diary jottings, 67, 74, 78, 119; now lost, 275; and see here under titles
Dome of Setting Sun, 177-8, 284

Dreams and Waking Thoughts, 75
English Journal, 10, 68, 72-4, 163
Episodes of Vathek, 16, 35, 91, 92-100, 188, 198, 277
L'Esplendente, 11-12, 13, 40-1, 42, 44-6, 248, 273
Excursion to Grande Chartreuse (essay): quoted, 63-4.
Hylas, 68-9, 275
Italy; with Sketches of Spain and Portugal, 18, 75, 131
Journal in Portugal, 17-18, 115, 130-1, 218, 279-80
Journal of 1794, 136; quoted, 20-1, 142
Life at Fonthill (letters), 19, 116, 166, 264
Modern Novel Writing, 144
Opera Score, 15, 268
Poems, 240, 244
Popular Tales of the Germans, 22-3
Vathek:
  16-17, 66, 240; V's eye, 35, 92; sources and inspiration, 80, 84, 89-90, 276; autobiographical nature and parallels in B's life, 91-2, 152, 153, 156, 176, 198, 232, 236, 238, 252, 262, 264; Swinburne on, 242; Prefaces, 256-7; illustrations, 285
Vision, The, 64-7, 275, 276
Zinan, 27, 41, 295
Reviews of B's Works, 23, 49
see also America, Sales
Bellini, 252, 254, 288, 296
Beltz, Sir G., 245
Bennett, John, 288
Berlin museums, 252, 281, 296
Birmingham, 71
Bitham Lake, 176-7
Blake, William, 250, 296
Blonay: castle, 62; de Blonay, 279; woods, 61-2, 106-7
Blundstone, Mr., 126
Bois de Bologne, 78
Bon-Nant River, 104
Bonaparte, Lucien, 227
Bonington, 249
Boringdon, Lord: see Morley
Bossons Glacier, 63
Bourrit, 106, 277
Boys, Shotter, 249
Bridgewater, Duke of, 71
Bright, Edward, 62, 275
Brighton Museum, 272
British Critic, 144, 281

British Museum, 227, 293
Britton, John, 169
Bronzino, 297
Brooks' Club, 107
Brown, factor, 189, 192, 196, 210, 221
Brown Parlour, 162, 284
Bruce, Lord: see Ailesbury
Brunet, 280
Buckingham, Marquis of, 217-18
Buckler, J. C., 168-9
Buller, James, 218
Buller, John, 217
Burt, W. M., 51-2, 274
Byron, 135, 188, 211, 255, 256, 280

Calthorpe, 56
Camoens, 178
Campagna, 226-7
Campbell: see Beckford: Lawsuit
Canada, 235, 294
Canaletto, 25
Canals, 71, 220
Canary Isles, 178
Carracci, A., 228
Carter, Mrs. E., 110
Carter, John, 169
Castlehaven, Earl of, 34
Cat diamonds, 39
Catena, 296
Cattermole, George, 168
Cellini, 252, 288
Chamonix, 104
Chancery suits, 145; see Beckford: lawsuits
Chardin, 140-1, 280-1
Chatham, Earl of, 21, 42
Chatterton, 33
Chilham Castle, 211
China, 45, 84-6, 276; Chinese objects, 227
Christie, 193-4, 196-7, 252-3, 296
Churchill, Charles, 145
Cima da Conegliano, 296
Cimarosa, 234
Clark, Kenneth, 161
Claude, 253, 288
Clennell, Luke, 250
Clive, 202
Cloncurry, Lord, 182
Cobbett, 180
Collett, Capt. Thomas, 126, 274
Collett & Evans, 52-3
Colt Hoare: see Hoare
Columbine cups, 252, 288, 297
Commendatore, the, 241
Coniston, 73

INDEX

Constable, John, 167, 169, 284
Constant, Benjamin, 249
Cope, Charles, 254, 297
Cornaro, 75-6, 114, 275; Marietta, 76
Corvo, Baron, 242
Cosway, 15, 46
Cottington, Lord, 34
Courtenay, Charlotte: see Rosslyn
Courtenay, William: see Devon
Cozens, Alexander, 13, 44-7, 64, 70, 80-3, 99, 153-6, 250, 252, 273
Cozens, J. R., 15, 25, 103, 254
Craven, Lady: see Anspach
Crofts Sale, 12
Crouchback, Edmund, 169
Cumberland, Richard, 33
Cundale, John, 221
Curtis, John, 211, 218, 291, 292

Danby, Francis, 160, 283
Daniell, artist, 249
Dante, 255
Davis, Thomas, 196, 288
Debtors, imprisonment of, 146, 151
Demezey, 235
Derwentwater, 73
Deschamps, 143, 281
Destournelles: see Deschamps
Deverell, Robert, 215, 218
Devisme, Gerard, 135
Devon, Earl of, 69, 70-1, 78, 92-4, 98, 108, 112-13, 114, 264-6, 275
Dies Irae, 240
Disraeli, 235
Dixon, architect, 166, 168
Dodington, Bubb, 33
Dogs, 235-6, 239
Don Juan, poem, 256
Dou, Gerard, 48, 253, 296
Douglas, Marquis of: see Hamilton
Douglas-Hamilton, Anne: see Westenra
Dover, 109
Dreams: see Beckford
Drysdale, 37, 126, 272
Duckett, Sir George, 220, 292
Duckett, Morland & Co., 220, 292
Dujardin, Karel, 253
Dunmore, Earl of, 80
Dunning, John, 146
Duquesnoy, François (Fiammingo), 294
Durazzo, Signor, 167, 284
Durer, 25
Dwarf, 183

East Hatch, 198, 288
East Knoyle, 33, 289
Eastern Transept, 166, 245
Eastlake, Sir Charles, 251, 254
Eaton Bray, 40, 215, 289
Eblis, 84, 99, 101, 242
Eclipse, ship, 221
Effingham, Lord, 213
Eginton, painter, 169, 284
Egmont, Count of, 187
Ehrhart, Dr., 237
Eldon, Lord, 206
Elections, disputed: see Hindon, Saltash
Elsheimer, 296
Emigrés, quarrel with, 186
Enchanted Gardens, 82, 178-9
Etty, 249, 254
Europe, 150
Evans, David, 52, 55
Evans, Robert, 55
Evian, 61
Exhumation of St. Hubert, picture, 169

Falmouth, 18, 119, 125-7
Farquhar, John, 194-5, 198-9
Fawkener, Miss, 268
Fawkenor, 107, 277
Feudalism, 150
Fiammingo: see Duquesnoy
Fielding, Copley, 249
Fir, 196
Fitzroy, Henry, 268
Fonthill Bishop Farm, 189, 286
Ford, Mrs. Edsel, 297
Forreste, 114
Fortunate Isles, 177-8
Foscolo, 255
Fownes, 191, 193, 210, 223, 286-7, 291
Foxhall, 26, 206
Fra Angelico, 296-7
Franchi, Gregorio, 19, 114, 117, 133, 183-4, 187, 192, 193, 195, 197, 230-1, 287, 294
Frankenstein, 19
French Revolution, 137, 141, 142-3, 147-8, 150
Frenguis, 74, 275
Frick Collection, 296
Froissart, 195
Funchal, 18

Galland, 100
Garofalo, 288, 296
Gaunt, John of, 40

Genesee River, 150, 220, 282, 292
Geneva, 60; Lake of, 61-2, 106-7, 182, 197
Genista, 105
George III, 31, 75, 216
George IV, 185, 285
Gibbon, 22, 121, 248, 288
Gibbons, Sir John, 51-3, 274
Gilles de Rais, 88-9, 98
Girtin, 249
Gluck, 275
Goddard, Ambrose, 186, 285
Goldoni, 106
Gomm, Capt., 126-7
Gordon Riots, 35, 74-5
Government Loan, 201
Gower, Lady: see Stafford
Grande Chartreuse, 63-4, 156, 172
Gray, Bishop R., 188, 285
Gray, Thomas, 63
Great Western Avenue, 173-5
Great Western Hall, 198, 245
Greek vases, 227
Grenfield, Mr., 286
Grenville, Lord, 128, 217-18
Greville, Charles, 111

Hafiz, 11
Hafod, 226
Haiti, 151, 208, 282
Hamilton, Hon. Charles, 172, 284
Hamilton, Duchess of, 28, 37, 187, 222, 231, 237-8, 261
Hamilton, 8th Duke, 192, 287
Hamilton, 9th Duke, 26, 265
Hamilton, 10th Duke, 26, 181, 190-2, 210, 215, 222-3, 228, 246, 286, 287, 293
Hamilton, Col. E., 60-1, 274-5
Hamilton, Emma, 162
Hamilton, Lady (first wife of Sir W.), 13, 76
Hamilton, Lady Ann, 165, 283, 287
Hamilton, William (artist), 167, 284
Hamilton, Sir W., 59, 111, 114, 134, 159, 162, 181
Hamilton Palace, 187; Sale Catalogues, 169, 281-2, 296, 297
Hampstead, 233
Hampton Court, 296
Hankey, Plummer & Wilson, 221
Hankey, Thomson, 293
Hankey (Thomson) & Co., 221, **293**
Harewood, Lord, 296
Hartford Bridge, 235, 294
Harvard, 296
Hayter, George, 166, 223

Hazlitt, 170, 228, 244, 246-7, 251-3, 295, 296
Hell, 49, 83-4, 97, 155, 166, 240-1, 255-6, 276
Henderson, John, 15
Henley, Samuel, 14, 16, 80
Henry VIII, 112
Herbelot, D', 92
Hertford, Marquis of, 189, 286
Hesiod quoted, 178, 284
Hesperides, Gardens of, 107
Hindon, 55-8, 175, 189, 211, 215, 216-17, 274, 282, 286, 292
Hoare, bankers, 290
Hoare, Henry, 51-2
Hoare, Richard Colt, 184-5
Hoare, William, 299
Hogarth, 228
Holland, 247
Holland, 3rd Baron, 151
Homosexuality: trials, 34, 88-9, 110, 114; laws, 112; flights abroad, 114, 117, 275; and see Beckford
Hope & Co., 33
Hoppner, 184
Horne, 134, 135, 280
Hours of Master of Mary of Burgundy, 147, 227, 281
House of Commons: Select Committees, 56-7; disputed elections: see Hindon, Saltash
Howard, Sir George, 75
Huber, Jean, 60-1, 106, 112, 275
Huber, Jean-Daniel, 61
Hughes, John, 258
Hugo, Victor, 256
Huitzilopochtli, 142, 281
Hume, Robert, 230-1
Humphrey, Ozias, 186
Huntly, Marquis of, 15, 108-9
Hyde Park, 233

Ibbetson, 249
Ides, Ysbrants, 86, 276
Inchiquin, Earl of, 30
Income Tax, 203, 290
Ironworks, 73-4
Italy, B's attitude to, 21

Jamaica:
 Earliest B.s in, 29-30, 271; Secretaryship of, 55; visit by B. planned, 125, 127, 279; the B. fleet, 125; slave rising, 151; B. property in 18th century, 200-1; B's income from, 203, 205; decline, 207-9, 220-1;

INDEX

absenteeism, 209-10; exchange rate, 225; currency, 225, 290; and see Beckford (Lawsuits, Plantations), Slavery, Sugar, W. India agents and merchants
Jamaica College, 291
Jay, William, 295
Jennings: see Beckford, Charles
Jervoise, Sir S. C., 286
João VI, 128, 132-3
Johnes, Thomas, 226
Jomelli, 240
Josephine, Empress, 254
Joy, 148
Jubilee, Papal, 117
Julius Caesar, ship, 125-6, 221

Kenyon, Lord, 183, 216-17, 285
Ki, Emperor, 84
King Edward's Gallery, 164, 245
Kress Collection, 297

Lafões, Duchess of, 129
Lafões, Duke of, 116, 129, 278
Lakes, the, 73
Landseer, 249
Lane, Josiah, 172
Lansdown, Mr., 288-9
Lansdown Tower, 28, 159, 226-7, 232
La Vallière sale, 13
Lawrence, Sir Thomas, 251
Le Brun, Charles, 253
Lebrun-Tondu, 141
Ledoux, 46
Le Fort, 105
Le Keux, 168-9
Leonardo da Vinci, 254
Lettice, John, 4-5, 36, 42, 60, 70, 103, 118-20, 137-8, 164, 173, 184, 273, 278, 283
Leuk Castle, 25, 269
Leymerie, Dr., 141
Liechtenstein, Prince, 296
Limoges, 252
Lippi, Filippino, 296
Lisbon, 125, 131, 135, 160-1, 240, 280, 283
Listenais, Princess, 242
Liston, Dr., 237, 294
Liston, Sir R., 237
Liverpool, 53, 71
Lloyd's Corporation (Insurance), 228
Lobineau, 88-9
London, 233-4, 294
London Magazine, 244

Long, Edward, 207
Loudon, 148-9, 175, 179, 284
Loughborough, Lord: see Rosslyn
Louis XI, 122-3, 158
Loutherbourg, 46, 80-4, 249
Louvre, 24, 253
Luini, 297
Lumiares, 142
Lussan, Mme. de, 122, 279

Macquin, Abbé, 168, 287
Maddock, Margery, 245
Maddox, Willis, 299
Madeira, 125, 127, 269, 279
Magic, 46, 47, 82, 153
Magna Carta, 245, 246
Malmaison, 254
Marialva, 5th Marquis, 17, 129-34, 231-2, 279
Marialva, 6th Marquis, 129, 222
Marlborough, Duke of, 134, 195
Marnoir, de, 281
Maroons, 151
Martin, John, 66, 253
Mary of Burgundy: see *Hours*
Matsys, 296
Mazzola, 297
Mazzolino, 229, 288, 296
McMahon, Sir John, 245-6, 295
Meissen, 247
Meister, 261-2, 284
Mellon, Harriot, 193
Mérigot, 140, 281
Mervin family, 34
Mesihi, 11
Methodism, 36-7, 151, 240
Metropolitan Museum, 247, 252, 296-7
Mexico, 281
Michelangelo, 228
Mieris, 253, 296
Milan, 117
Milford, 189, 286
Milton, 82-4, 267, 278-9, 255, 283
Mohammed, boy, 115
Moisasour, 64, 276
Monserrate, Quinta of, 135-6, 280
Montagu, Wortley, 100
Montagu, Mrs., 110
Mont Blanc, 63, 104
Montego Bay, 206
Monte Video Estate, 150
Moore, Tom, 167
Morecambe Bay, 71-3
Morgan, Pierpont, 253
Morland, banker: see Ransom
Morley, Earl of, 182, 285

Morocco, Emperor of, 87-8
Morton, Lord, 13, 44
Motassem, 91
Mozart, 234
Mulai Ismail, 87-8, 276
Murphy, J. C., 161
Murray, publisher, 18
Mushrooms, 111

Napoleon, 24, 222-3, 259-60
Narcissus, 241
Nasmyth, Patrick, 250
National Gallery, 169, 227, 228-9, 251, 252, 254, 288, 296; of Ireland, 283
Necker, 141; and see Staël
Necrophilia, 89, 97, 277
Negroes: see Slavery
Nelson, 162
Newspapers, 110, 119, 121-2, 158, 219, 283
Newstead Abbey, 211
New York Historical Society, 282
New York State, 150, 220
Nicholas I, 185
Normanton, Lord, 193
Northcote, James, 229
Nouronihar, 64, 66-7
Nuremberg, 252, 297

Octagon at F. A., 161, 165-6, 171; at Monserrate, 135
Odin, 154
Oldfield, T. H. B., 56
Opera, 11, 15, 44, 78, 110-11, 144, 219, 234, 268
Oratory at F. A., 171-2
Orcagna, 196
Orde, General, 245-6
Orde, Mrs, 26-7, 120, 129, 187, 190, 287
Ouseley, Sir W., 101

Paccard, Dr., 104
Pacchierotti, 11, 15, 39, 78, 80, 276
Paget, Sir Arthur, 181-2, 268; and see Anglesey
Pain's Hill, 172, 284
Palmela, Count, 222
Palmer, Samuel, 249
Pandemonium, Palace of, 83, 166, 167, 283
Paradise, 177, 179
Paris, 139-41, 142-4, 222, 269
Parliament: buildings, 165, 168; debates, 219; grants, 228
Passingham, Col., 114, 278

Patapouf, 116, 278
Pedley, John, 211, 214-15, 218, 225, 291
Penn, John, 44
Penn, William, 281
Pennsylvania, 44, 220
Perregaux, 281
Persian Ambassador, 195
Perugino, 229, 288, 296
Pesellino, 297
Peter the Great, 47
Phelps-Gorham Purchase, 150
Phillips, auctioneer, 25, 194, 198; catalogue, 169
Picture-restoration, 229
Pinto de Sousa Coutinho, 128
Piozzi, Mrs, 147
Pitt, Harriet, 80, 82
Pitt, Thomas, 289
Pitt, William, 21, 144-5, 259
Plessis, 122-3, 158
Plummer, John, 211, 291
Plummer & Wilson, 220-1, 286, 293
Plymouth, 10
Pope quoted, 177, 284
Porden, C. F., 149, 167, 168, 282
Portland, Duke of, 132
Poussin, Gaspar, 296
Poussin, Nicholas, 228
Powderham Castle, 70, 107-8
Prangins, Baron, 277
Praz, 89, 248
Press: see Newspapers
Price, Uvedale, 176
Prince of Brazil, 131-2
Prince Regent: see George IV
Prince Regent of Portugal: see João VI
Prison reform, 281
Public executions, 146
Pugin, A. W., 169
Puppet shows, 44, 273
Pyne, W. H., 83
Privy Council, Judicial Committee, 204, 206
Prout, 249
Provident Life office, 220

Queensberry, 3rd Duke, 15, 268
Quevedo, 255, 298
Quinet, Edgar, 256

Radcliffe, Mrs, 73
Railways, 220
Rambler's Magazine, 85
Ransom, Morland & Co., 206, 286, 292

INDEX

Raphael, 24, 227, 229, 250, 288, 296
Reform Bill, 147
Reisener, 297
Rembrandt, 84, 252, 269, 296
Revelation, book, 160, 260
Rex v. Passingham, 114, 278
Reynolds, Sir J., 229
Rigaud, J. F., 184
Rijksmuseum, 247
River shares, 220
Robert, Hubert, 25, 249
Roberts, David, 250
Robertson, William, 257
Rosenberg, Countess, 115, 263-6
Rosenwald Hours, 268
Rossi, J. C., 162, 283
Rosslyn, Countess of, 108, 113
Rosslyn, Earl of, 108-10, 112-13, 277
Rossmore, Lord, 287
Rousseau, 243
Rowden, 36
Roxburghe, Duke of, 195
Royal Academy, 184, 251, 254, 283, 297
Rubens Vase, 197, 252, 288
Rue de Grenelle, 141
Rundell & Bridge, 286
Russia, 46-7
Rutter's *Fonthill*, 173, 176, 179, 283, 284

Sade, Marquis de, 89, 257, 298
St. Anthony of Padua, 48, 91, **124**, 130, 159, 161, 162-3, 279
St. Bruno, 63-4
S. Caetano, Archbishop, 131
S. Domingo: see Haiti
St. Hugo, 63-4
St. John's Wood, 231
S. José de Ribamare, Quinta, 135
St. Michael's Gallery, 162-4, 171
St. Pancras, 215
St. Petersburg, 47
Sales:
　B's, 25-6, 164, 193-5, 196-7, 249, 268, 294, 296; Crofts, 12; La Vallière, 13, 268; Roxburghe, 195; Marlborough, 195; Farquhar, 196, 198; Angerstein, 228, 293; Seguier, 229; Lawrence, Sir Thomas, 251; Hamilton Palace, 268, 281
Salève, Curé of, 40
Salisbury, Bishop of, 189
Sallanches, 104
Saltash, 215, 216, 217-18, 274, 292
Sand, George, 256

Santerre, 143
Sardinia, 62
Satan, 82-3, 167, 255-6
Saunders, boy, 116, 264
Schöll, Dr., 22, 278
Scott, Jonathan, 101
Sebastiano del Piombo, 25, 228
Secretaryship of Jamaica, 55
Seditious Meetings Act, 144-5
Seguier, 229
Sequeira, Chevalier, 299
Sertorius, 178
Seymour, Georgina, 14
Shakespeare, 119, 155, 255, 278
Siberia, 111
Sill, Joseph, 135
'Sinks', 116
Slavery, 151, 206, 207-8, 212-13, 218-19, 282
Smith, Charlotte, 146
Smith, Gen. Richard, 55-8, **274**
Smith, 'Warwick', 249
Soane Museum, 25
Society of British Artists, 261
Soho Engineering Works, 71
Soho Square, 36
Solomonian literature, 45, 153
Somerset, Duke of, 193, 287
Southampton, Lord, 15, 268
Southey, Dr., 230-1, 294
Speenhamland, 148-9
Spencer, 82, 153, 178
Spencer, 3rd Earl, 251, 296
Staël, Mme. de, 112
Stafford, Marchioness of, 109
Stafford, Marquis of, 120
Stagging, 201
Stained glass, 169, 284
Stewart, Lady Euphemia, 37, 119-20
Stop's Beacon, 152, 157, 158-62
Stothard, 249
Strathavon, Lord: see Huntly
Strete, artist, 296
Sugar prices, 166, 190, 203, 208-9, 219, 221; duties, 207-8, 218
Summerson, John, 168, 171
Surajah Dowlah, 62
Susquehannah River, 220, 292
Swinburne, 242

Talleyrand, 251
Tan-Ki, Empress, 85
Tarascon, 258
Tasso, 82, 178
Theocritus, 68
Thrale, Hester: see Piozzi
Thurlow, Lord, 107-8, 120, 216

Thwaites, Mrs, 33, 272
Tierney, George, 277
Titian, 24, 297
Tom Thumb, 43
Tour de Peilz, 118
Traitorous Correspondence Act, 139
Treasonable Practices Act, 144-5
Tripolitanian Ambassador, 115
Trumbull, John, 150, 219, 292
Turner, 25, 167, 250, 284

Uxbridge, Lord: see Anglesey
Uxbridge House, 268

Vanderbilt, William, 297
Vandyke, 233
Velasquez, 227, 229, 296
Venice, 75, 76, 77-8
Verdeil, Dr., 126, 141, 182, 287
Vernet, Joseph, 25, 250
Vevey, 118, 120; Testimonial, 121, 278-9
Victoria & Albert Museum, 284, 285, 296
Vie des Peintres Flamands, 49, 273
Vies des Pères des Deserts, 273
Vincent, gardener, 236
Vitzlipochtli: see Huitzilopochtli
Voltaire, 243

Waagen, 170, 227
Waddesdon, 297
Wadsworth, James, 149-51, 282
Wadsworth, Jeremiah, 150, 292
Wake, Rev. Charles, 33, 51-4, 57, 272
Wake, Mrs, 33, 54, 57
Wallace Collection, 297
Walpole, Horace, 63, 127, 256, 268
Walpole, Robert, 127-9, 131
Walters Art Gallery, 297
Wansey, Henry, 151
Wardour Castle, 180
Warner, Richard, 34-5
Watt, James, 71
Webber, John, 249
Wellington, Duke of, 193
Wells, 107, 216, 218
West, Benjamin, 113, 160, 164, 184, 219-20, 253, 255, 260, 283, 292, 297

West, Raphael, 219-20
Westall, Richard, 184, 285
West-End, Hampstead, 36, 233-4, 294
Westenra, Mrs, 192, 287
West India agents in Jamaica, 209-10
West India merchants (London): commission-rates, 52; chances of corruption, 53; B's debts to, 190; crashes, 220-1; and see Pedley, Plummer, Wildman (Henry)
Westminster Abbey, 169
Westminster School, 31, 70, 181
Whaley, 'Buck', 121
White, lawyer, 219, 220
Wilberforce, 219
Wild, Charles, 168, 284
Wilde, Oscar, 94
Wildman, Henry, 211, 214, 215, 221, 224-5
Wildman, James, 210-14
Wildman, Sarah, 211, 212, 215
Wildman, Thomas, 112, 125, 210-14, 279, 291
William IV, 147
William V, Stadholder, 247
William Beckford, ship, 221
Williams, Capt. N., 159, 211
Wilson, Richard, 249, 296
Winchester, Bishop of, 189
Witham Abbey, 63, 156
Wolverhampton, 34
Woodburn, Samuel, 251
Woodford, 189, 286
Woodward family, 245
Woodyate, 57
Wortley Montagu: see Montagu
Wyatt, Benjamin, 168, 284
Wyatt, James, 157, 158-9, 161, 165-6, 184, 223-4, 282
Wyatt, Philip, 168
Wyatville, Sir Jeffry, 168, 185, 284

Xavier, Abbé, 130, 278

York Minster, 82, 163
Youkaguirians, 111
Young, Edward, 255, 298
"Young Jacobins", 147-8